1999

Recreation
for
Older Adults

Recreation for Older Adults

Individual and Group Activities

by Judith A. Elliott and Jerold E. Elliott

Venture Publishing, Inc.
State College, Pennsylvania

Production Manager: Richard Yocum
Manuscript Editing, Design, Layout, and Graphics: Diane K. Bierly
Additional Editing: Deborah L. McRann and Richard Yocum
Cover Design and Illustration: © 1999 Sikorski Design

Library of Congress Catalogue Card Number 99-64970
ISBN 1-892132-08-7

Contents

Chapter XI
Theme Events 115

Chapter XII
Working With the Low-Functioning
Client 123

Staff Tips 129

Resources 133

Acknowledgments

We would like to thank the following people for their contributions of ideas and/or time as testers:

Ginny Altenderfer
Samuel Barr
The Bothner Family
Lisa (Sorg) Brunermer
Michele Daly

Nellie Elliott (Jerry's mom who lived at home alone until she was 97)
Sis Eggler
Greta Janssen
Elizabeth Sorg (Judy's mom who has dementia)
Elaine Ritzert, RMT
Stephanie Yocum

Introduction

This book has been written for the recreation professional as well as anyone who works with older adults in the field of recreation. Its purpose is to help the person who is providing recreation programming gain new ideas and revisit old activities that haven't been used recently. It is hoped that it will encourage the recreation staff to examine the entire repertoire of programs and activities in order to determine which are effective and which need to be revised. Our goal is to help provide low-cost, client-intensive, recreation programming for older adults regardless of the level at which they are able to function.

Certified Therapeutic Recreation Specialists, activities leaders, and volunteers may utilize these ideas in an adult day-care facility, personal care home, extended care unit, senior center, or nursing home. Anyone working with people with disabilities may utilize these ideas, but they have been designed and tested for use with older adults.

In this book we refer to "high-level functioning" and "low-level functioning" older adults. High-level functioning older adults are those who have no cognitive impairment in terms of memory, disorientation, or confusion. These people may not be high-level functioning physically, but they are very capable mentally. The low-level functioning persons may or may not be physically frail, but exhibit many signs of confusion, memory loss, and/or disorientation.

The setting is important in defining higher and lower functioning individuals. A person who exhibits some signs of disorientation in a senior center program may be considered a lower level client, but the same person would be labeled at a much higher functioning level in a nursing home. We look at the functioning level as a continuum that varies with the setting, so you will need to determine which activities are the most appropriate for your clientele and even consider modifying some of them to suit your setting.

A majority of the activities that we have included are designed for use with those clients who must have individual attention from a staff member in order to participate. We use the "1:1" designation to identify these activities. The designation "Sm Grp" identifies the activities that are usually used with groups of three to ten clients. Activities that are useful with groups of 10 to 24 clients have the designation "Md Grp" and those that can be successfully used with groups of 25 or more are labeled "Lg Grp." In addition, we use "First Comer" to identify activities that can be used with medium to larger groups as the clients are arriving for a scheduled program. You will find one further designation; "Ind" is used for such activities as solitaire and paper games that higher level individuals could enjoy with little or no supervision.

Many of the activities are what we call "old favorites revisited." You may recognize some of them as adaptations of children's games. There is a great deal of debate over the use of such games with older adults. Should we use puppets? Can we use crayons? This book does not answer these questions for your agency, although in our work we have adapted so-called "children's activities" and used them with great success. We encourage the usage of lifelike animal puppets and large-size crayons because they can elicit the response we are looking for in the lower functioning client. The agency staff should discuss their personal philosophies and be encouraged to explore the many possibilities to determine if these activities may be made age-suitable for their clients.

It is our philosophy that everything we do with the client under "recreation" should have a purpose or a goal. Therefore, a discussion of program schedules, quality programming, goal development and evaluation has been included, although not in as great a detail as in our earlier book, *Recreation Programming and Activities for Older Adults.*

Much to our dismay the word *diversionary* is being utilized extensively in the field today to describe many of the activities for older adults. The term implies that pursuing a recreational activity such as a holiday party, bingo, or even a movie is something scheduled only to fill in the time. Our philosophy holds that any recreational activity can and should be of benefit to the client, and even those programs that are designed simply to provide a fun afternoon or evening, should have a goal and carry equal weight

in the overall programming schedule. We hope you find the suggestions in this book helpful in providing a more challenging program for your clients.

Judith A. Elliott, M.S.
Assistant Professor
Department of Recreation
Lock Haven University
Lock Haven, Pennsylvania

Jerold E. Elliott, Re.D.
Associate Professor (Retired)
Department of Leisure Studies
Pennsylvania State University
University Park, Pennsylvania

Chapter I

Reality Check

No book of programming and activity ideas would be complete without looking at the overall recreation schedule in terms of daily events, special events and the number of one-on-one (1:1) offerings. This becomes a bit of a chicken and egg problem in terms of what comes first. Do we schedule the programs and then set up the goals or the reverse? When do the clients' needs and interests enter into the equation? If you are working in a nursing home setting, there are many guidelines to follow in terms of the minimum amount of programming that must be scheduled for the clientele. In some ways, this is very helpful because it gives us a framework on which to build the program. In other facilities such as adult day-care, senior centers, and personal-care facilities there may or may not be guidelines in terms of the amount of programming that is to be scheduled. In most cases, where there are guidelines, they are stated as *minimum* programming rather than *optimum* programming recommendations. These guidelines tend to become the standard followed by many agencies (sort of like having to work for minimum wage, isn't it?).

For example, at one facility the weekly games event became indoor bowling every week. "Games" is a good activity category for the weekly schedule because the clientele will be familiar with the day of the week because of the event. However, playing the same game of indoor bowling week after week, year after year is not good programming. Why not try boccie ball one week, bowling another, indoor Wiffle ball and koosh ball on another occasion? None of these takes much effort to set up. Each involves a team effort and emphasizes coordination and motor skills as well as providing a bit of exercise for the clients. Consider using a couple of different games within one session such as wheelchair soccer and

balloon volleyball. This would allow the clients to utilize their upper and lower extremities. If physical activities are scheduled several times a week, it may be possible to specify one as sports and one as games.

A Look at Schedule Development

It's time to take a good look at schedule development in terms of the needs of our clients and the goals that we have set, based upon those needs. The first step is to determine the needs of the clients based on their ability levels. The next step is to analyze our present program to see how well it meets those needs. Only then can we adjust the program offerings and schedule activities that are truly client-oriented.

What is the present procedure for program scheduling in your agency? Is the first step to determine the number of programs to be held, or what special events you already have booked for the month? If the department is required to offer so many types of programs, that is probably the first thing the staff looks at each month. Many agencies just use the previous month's schedule and make minimal changes based on the events that were used in that season the previous year. This way, unless the regulations have changed, they know they have an acceptable program, because it is based on what was required in the past.

We suggest that it is not only important, but imperative, to start from the beginning with a blank schedule at least four times a year. This ensures a review of the program offerings to make certain that the activities are client-oriented rather than staff-oriented. It must be remembered that the client base changes frequently. Some of the clients become more frail and additional very frail and confused people are admitted to the agency on a regular basis.

In the past a larger percentage of the clients may have been very independent and attended a lot of outings and special programming. This may no longer be true and it may have taken only a few months for this dramatic change in the client base to occur. For years, we have heard how the people who are admitted into nursing homes are much older and frailer than in the past. Part of this is certainly due to the increasing numbers of personal care homes and adult daycare programs. But, we also hear the same statement about more lower level clientele living in personal care facilities and attending day programming.

Look at the Client First

We do not want you to label your clients such that they cannot change levels; we recognize the importance of having to determine how many of the clients need one-on-one attention and how many will be able to participate in group programming. It is also important to determine the percentage of clients who need one-on-one attention due to their physical and/or mental functioning capacity, and those who are uninterested, embarrassed or unwilling to participate in a group and require one-on-one visitation to encourage participation. It is imperative to remember this categorization is to optimize programming and not to limit client opportunities. Clients who have been ill or who have recently left the hospital may be functioning at a lower level than usual. The staff must be encouraged to evaluate the percentage of clients in each of the functioning levels on a regular basis to determine the amount of quality time that should be allocated for one-on-one visitations and activity.

Recreation professionals who work with the older population are often looked upon as the "fun and games" people. Without facts to refute the assumptions that have been made regarding the recreation program, we cannot hope to provide the optimal recreation programming activities for therapeutic growth. To get the facts, we must take a careful look at the needs of our clientele and their functioning levels. We have found that, with little difficulty, the clients can be placed in one of five functioning levels. If you do not feel this system will work in your facility, consider what is best for your clientele and create your own. You may wish to have three, or maybe four categories, rather than the five that we utilize.

Begin to evaluate the level at which the clients are functioning as a group, physically and mentally, by assigning a functioning level to each of the clients based upon staff observation and the assessment tool utilized by the agency. Remember, this is to enable you to evaluate the overall program needs in terms of the amount of time to spend on individual, in comparison to group, programming. Do not get too worried that someone is between levels. Assign the person to the functioning level that appears most often.

The five functioning levels or categories that we use are:

- Level 1—Unable to attend group activities (due to a medical condition such as advanced dementia).
- Level 2—Able to attend, but disruptive to group (due to repetitive unacceptable actions).
- Level 3—Capable of attending but refuses (motivated not to attend group events).
- Level 4—Selective, attends a few events such as church or bingo (limited attendance).
- Level 5—Motivated, ready to attend any program and/or activity.

Notice that levels 3 and 4 do not take into account the person's capability to participate in programming, but categorize by the client's motivation or attitude toward attending recreation events. We have to remember that we are still working with a population that worked throughout life and had very little time for, or inclination toward, recreational activities, play, or travel.

After classifying the clients' functioning levels, have a staff member or a volunteer calculate the number and the percentage of people who fall into each category. For example, if there are 100 residents in the facility and 35 are level 1, that means 35 percent of the population is not physically capable of leaving their rooms to attend activities. Notice, too, that the first three categories are clients who need the most individualized recreation programming. Therefore, if over 50 percent of the clients are in categories 1, 2 or 3 then approximately 50 percent of the programming should be geared toward one-on-one, or in-room small group activities, until such time that the clients in level 3 who are motivated not to attend, move into category 4. The people who are motivated to be in the selective category will benefit from an occasional in-room visit. Let's face it, we all enjoy visitors to our home, but time usually does not permit one-on-one visits for the more motivated clients. Knowing what percentage of your clients fall into each category will make it much easier for the staff members to utilize their time effectively. It will also provide support for requests for any additional staffing necessary to meet the needs of the clients.

When time has been taken to evaluate the clients' functioning level via this method, most agencies find that they offer far too many activities which not only require the clients to leave their rooms, but also their units, and often the floor where their rooms are located. In other words, a major amount of staff time is utilized in transporting clients that may or may not benefit from the program being offered! This does not mean that we should eliminate every large group activity or special event, but it does mean that we should make certain that we are not running 90 percent of our programs for the benefit of less than 10 percent of our clients.

We are big proponents of special events and outings because they are so different and a break from the routine. They are something special to look forward to. The experiences can be shared with friends and relatives when they visit, as well as with other staff members. We also believe in small group activities which are regularly scheduled, such as the every Monday morning news group or Tuesday's game activities. The clients need and like routine. It does help them to keep oriented to time and place. However, we want to encourage more recreation professionals to spend quality time running small group activities and one-on-one events in clients' rooms. In order to provide adequate stimulation of all five of a client's senses, it is important to do more than just chat on a one-on-one visit. It is also helpful to the Therapeutic Recreation Department's image for the unit staff members to see the recreation professional in action.

Goal Planning and Development

The Mission

If the staff never looks at the overall program, it is difficult to determine if the program is meeting the mission and goals of the department, let alone the agency. It is vital to decide what we want to accomplish and make sure everyone has the same mission. If one person thinks we are here to entertain the clients while another thinks therapy should be the focus of all of our efforts, one will be providing many large group activities and the other will be conducting only individual sessions.

Although this seems like just one more task to complete, determining your mission and goals actually gives the department a focus and a starting point. If everyone agrees to work toward the same end, it will be much easier to get there as a team.

Playing the Numbers Game

If the team never evaluates or reviews the programs, neither staff nor program effectiveness can be determined. It is tempting to fall into the numbers trap and call it evaluation. Listing the number of events and how many people attended each one is not the measure of successful programming. If numbers were all that counted, we would push everyone into a multipurpose room and show movies all day long. It is vital to utilize the numbers effectively by looking at the entire range of programs and numbers of clients served in each participatory level. Maintaining attendance records is an important part of evaluation, but it is only one step in the process.

Everyone working in long-term care knows about developing individual goals for each client. Some day-care programs, senior centers and personal care homes also develop individualized goal plans for their clients. A few agencies develop goals for each event and program. Agencies that operate under a Quality Assurance or a Continuous Quality Assurance plan often have extensive policy and procedure manuals that have prescribed program goals.

Programming goals save time in the scheme of things. For example, when you want to try a new activity, listing all of the information you need to run the program helps to keep you organized as you go about gaining the necessary support and equipment. A clear set of goals provides the basis for evaluating the effectiveness of the program. Start by developing goals for the new activities and then prepare goal statements for ongoing programs such as the discussion, exercise, and cooking groups. Establishing program goals lets the programmer select the important facets of the activity on which to focus, such as group interaction or using short-term memory skills.

Program goals help the staff to determine whether too many activities share the same focus and/or goal. They also will indicate if there are any gaps in the programming based upon the physical, social, emotional, or psychological needs of the clients. Activity analysis forms are available and helpful in developing program goals. A simple activity analysis form is found on page 14 of our earlier book *Recreation Programming and Activities for Older Adults*.

Program Goals

Program goals (like client goals) should include:

- what is to be accomplished (i.e., the goal is to stimulate client interaction);
- by what time frame (i.e., to be reviewed in six weeks); and
- how will it be evaluated (i.e., by the number of clients that initiate conversations).

Don't forget fun can and should often be included in program goals. The number of smiles observed during the activity easily demonstrates the amount of enjoyment. Since programming goals are client-based, they will look similar to individual goal plans. The different programming goals are based on the group rather than the individual client. The number one reason to develop group goals is to evaluate the activity and determine its effectiveness from the clients' point of view.

Finding the Time

At this point, you may feel that it is difficult to find time for completing all of the required paperwork, let alone adding more. Actually these reviews generate very little in terms of additional paperwork, and do not take a great amount of time, yet give you a much clearer view of your programming needs. Work on these reviews first thing in the morning or during the time before or after lunch when the clients are not available for recreation activities. In most agencies there is "down time" that can be utilized for planning and evaluation.

For a week, keep track of the actual time each staff member spends with clients, including the time necessary to transport them to and from the activi-

ties. We did staff time studies in several long-term care facilities and determined that the recreation staff averaged only four to five hours of direct client contact per day. It certainly cannot take all of the rest of the workday to do the required paperwork. We propose that some of the time when the staff is not with clients be utilized for program review and updating program goals to meet client needs.

Have you ever added up the amount of staff time spent transporting clients to and from activities? Even with the help of the nursing staff and volunteers, almost all recreation professionals spend an inordinate amount of time transporting. To document this, have the staff make a "tick" mark on their daily schedule for every five minutes spent in transporting. Do this for a week and calculate the daily average. It is often between one and two hours a day per staff member, depending on the events and size of the facility. Consider running the same activity on each of your units for a shorter time period, with smaller groups, instead of transporting the clients from one or more floors to one central location.

Another way to make more client program time is to cut down on the amount of staff time involved with making door, bulletin boards, and seasonal event decorations. Use purchased decorations, ask volunteer groups to assist, and organize materials and decorations so they can be stored and reused for the same event next year. Have the clients make the decorations. It is good use of a staff member's time to work with small groups on such a project. Consider cutting down on the amount of decorating. If the decorations take longer to make than the rest of the planning and the special event itself, they are too elaborate. It must be remembered that the professional staff is hired to work with the clients, not to be artists in residence!

Older adults in senior center programs enjoy making decorations for others and can help make them for the nursing home program. Young children also enjoy working on art projects. Work with a local children's day-care or after-school care program, or an elementary school for party decorations. Students from art schools or the higher level art classes might be able to complete murals or drawings such as portholes and palm trees for special events. Instead of generating the weekly and monthly calendar by hand, use a computer and then enlarge the calendar for easier viewing on a copy machine. Have local flower clubs rearrange the funeral flowers and have clients help.

One agency makes use of the time the clients wait for lunch to be served by holding a sing-along three days a week. Since many of the clients begin arriving for a meal an hour ahead of schedule, they effectively utilize this time to provide a lively, yet relaxing activity which people can easily join as they come into the dining area.

It is important that staff time and tasks be analyzed if an optimum level of programming is to be achieved. It is difficult, if not impossible, to convince the administrative staff that more help is needed if the recreation staff spends less than 65 percent of its time with the clients.

Reviewing the Program

In order to determine the overall effectiveness of the recreation program, the staff must review it from all angles, looking for variety and balance. The entire schedule of events should be looked at as well as each individual event and activity. Even one-on-one programming needs to be included in this process. Wouldn't it be wonderful to have an outside consultant, with lots of experience in this area complete this process for your agency? Forget that idea! Aside from the expense, no one knows the clients as well as the staff that works with them on a regular basis. Now that the staff has determined the functioning levels of the clients, it is time to review the factors which affect the total recreation program.

The following statements relate particularly to programs for clients in resident facilities; however, many of the statements are applicable to activity programming in day-care facilities. The statements are based on observation of optimum- rather than minimum-based programs, therapeutic recreation literature, and from workshops for recreation leaders. Have your staff review them before continuing with a more formal review of your agency's recreation program.

Program Time and Length

- Programs are scheduled throughout the day at times convenient to the clients.
- Evening and weekend programs, in addition to worship service, are regularly scheduled with professional staff leadership.

- Activities of varying lengths (15 minutes up to extended periods) are scheduled on a regular basis.
- Classes are planned for various periods of duration (some for as little as two sessions and others for up to four weeks).

Activity Location

- Lounges, patios, and clients' rooms, as well as the craft and multipurpose rooms, are regularly utilized for programming.
- All available space is scheduled for optimum activity use with minimal transportation.

Group Size and Balance

- 15 minute one-on-one activities are scheduled at least three times per week for each client who cannot attend group programs.
- Each client who is able to attend is encouraged to participate in at least one small group activity on a daily basis.
- Activities for groups of 15 to 25 clients are available on a daily basis.
- Special events for larger groups are scheduled at least twice a month.

Program Variety

- The range of regularly scheduled activities includes music, drama, art, crafts, exercise, sports, games, nature, horticulture, and intergenerational programming.
- Events range from quiet activities to physically active pursuits.
- There is a variety of programming for all clients regardless of abilities.
- Client participation is just as important as entertainment.
- There are noncompetitive, drop-in, and competitive activities and programs.
- Classes on a variety of topics are offered regularly.
- When planning activities, the staff takes into consideration the use and limitations of the clients' sight, hearing, smell and taste.

Putting It All Together

Many people do not realize the program has become stale until they seriously review the present program. Perhaps the program has become staff-oriented because the staff tends to schedule activities they like and which take limited preparation time, instead of scheduling the activities that are best for the clients. Of course, there should be regularly scheduled activities like exercise and current events, but within the overall program there should be variety and balance.

To determine the status of your agency's therapeutic recreation program, we suggest that the following tool be used to provide the basis for a staff in-service. Prior to the in-service meeting, a team of two staff members, or one staff member and an intern or volunteer should use these tools to provide the initial review. We recommend two people for the initial review to give the benefit of a second perspective. Discussing the review findings will provide the basis for some exciting program revisions.

Program Variety

Does your program have innovative variety, or do you tend to replicate an old schedule on a new calendar? Use the accompanying check sheet with a typical month program calendar. Each time a program was offered, place a slash (/) in the proper square for the type and format that was used. When you have finished, you will be able to see at a glance the breadth of your program offerings:

- Classes—Sessions that last from two to three activity periods such as baking, stenciling, or crafts, to those meeting regularly for three to four weeks such as drama and exercise.
- Clubs—Interest groups that meet on a somewhat regular basis such as a hometown club, bowling club, or major league club.
- Competitive—Events for the clients who love competition, such as checkers tournaments, Wiffle ball, badminton, and horseshoes (even if the activity is modified).
- Special Events—Outings and theme events in which the clients participate. Events in which the clients perform as individuals or in groups, or exhibits such as craft fairs.

- Open—Times of the day when clients can drop in to utilize an area such as a game room, library or craft room.
- Additional Categories—Create additional categories that may be unique to your operation for the activities that don't fit into any of those in the accompanying chart.

Group Size Considerations

Programming should be for all of your clients and should give each person an opportunity to participate in activities that are presented for groups of varying sizes. To check for balance in group size offerings, use the accompanying form and that same month-long program that you used to determine the variety of programs. We hope that you will discover that your program offerings are distributed across the chart, reflecting the needs of the clients.

Length of Programs

There should be a variety in the lengths of your program offerings to meet the needs of your clients. Many participants can only be expected to respond to very short activity sessions, while a few will have the stamina and need the stimulation of longer sessions. Are you providing the variety necessary to meet these needs? Use the chart (see page 8) to check a one-month program schedule to help analyze the scope of your offerings.

Program Locations

Are you taking advantage of all the possible locations for holding activities? Sometimes we end up using valuable time transporting clients to a program when it would be much easier to take the program to the clients. We should be making maximum use of all of our activity site possibilities. Chart your present programs as to where they are being held and perhaps discover some possibilities for saving time for you and the clients, while offering more interesting and challenging activities (see page 8).

Program Variety

Program Formats					
Types	Classes	Clubs	Competitive	Special Events	Open
Games					
Sports					
Music					
Crafts					
Exercise					
Nature					
Gardening					
Dance					
Drama					
Animals					
Children					
Religious					
Verbal					

Group Size Considerations

Program Formats by Group Size					
Group Sizes	Classes	Clubs	Competitive	Special Events	Open
1:1					
Small Group (under 10)					
Medium Group (10–24)					
Large Group (25-plus)					

Programming and the Senses

When we used this next chart (see page 9) to analyze several nursing home programs we found that a majority of the programs were heavily dependant upon the two senses that were the clients' weakest—eyesight and hearing. Use this tool to find out if you have adequate programming that utilizes all of the senses.

Day-By-Day Programming

In a residential setting, the people are there seven days a week. There should be an opportunity for them to participate in activities on a daily basis. By using this chart (see page 9) to view your present program, you can tell if (and where) there are gaps in the programming for your agency. It can also prove useful when you ask for additional staff to fill the vacancies in the schedule. In a day program, there should still be opportunities for group, as well as individual events.

Length of Programs

Program Length by Format					
Length	Classes	Clubs	Competitive	Special Events	Open
15–20 minutes					
30–40 minutes					
45 minutes to 1 hour					
1–1½ hours					
Over 2 hours					

Program Locations

Program Sites and Formats					
Sites	Classes	Clubs	Competitive	Special Events	Open
In Room					
Dayroom or Lounge					
Craft Room					
Dining Area					
Multipurpose Room					
Patio or Deck					
Off Site					

Evaluation

At some point we need to look at everything together. For example:

- Are outings scheduled for all clients not bedridden and at various times of the day?
- Do competitive events involve other activities as well as sports?
- Do some of the competitive events, other than sports, provide an opportunity for multiple play-offs?
- Is there a variety of therapeutic-oriented activities scheduled for different session and program lengths, or are they all the same length in the same time period, week after week?

- Are special events activities scheduled periodically?
- Are one-to-one visits viable activities or are they just "chats" with the clients in their rooms?
- Are there a variety of activities involving all of the senses, as well as sight and hearing?
- Do special events include participation in the activities, or are the clients spectators with the only participation activity being a snack?
- Do intergenerational programs involve small group participation, or are they always scheduled as large group special events?
- Are there opportunities for the clients to form clubs where they are taking on part of the leadership (i.e., the neighborhood group, the card club,

Programming and the Senses

Activities and the Senses					
Senses	Classes	Clubs	Competitive	Special Events	Open
Touch					
Taste					
Smell					
Hearing					
Eyesight					

Day-By-Day Programming

Activities and Time of Day/Week					
Times	Classes	Clubs	Competitive	Special Events	Open
Morning					
Early Afternoon					
Late Afternoon					
Evening					
Mealtime					
Weekends					

men's and women's clubs, the boccie ball team, resident council)?

- Are there programs and areas where the clients can drop in and/or leave at their convenience (i.e., must the client stay through the entire coffee hour, tailgate party)?
- Are there therapeutic-oriented programs such as the exercise group which have a leader and set programming goals?

Ask the staff to create their own questions which are to be answered while searching out the answer to the question of "Does your recreation program provide a wide range of programming offerings which are client-oriented and include variety and balance?"

Evaluate Your Program

Many agencies have adopted the philosophy and principles behind such methods as Quality Assurance and Continuous Quality Management. The framework is in place for an in-depth look at the therapeutic recreation offerings. Rather than making sure we have every square on the calendar filled, we will be making sure the activities are appropriate, offer a wide range of opportunities for the clients and include time for one-on-one programming. The goal planning and programming results used in combination with the rating system shown on page 10 should give the staff an all-around look at their total program. Use the rating scale to provide a profile of your program.

Program Rating Scale

Rating Scale: 0 = Never, 1 = Occasionally, 2 = Regularly, 3 = Frequently, 4 = Always

Classes

Do you offer any	0	1	2	3	4
One to three sessions	0	1	2	3	4
One session per week for several weeks	0	1	2	3	4
Two or more times per week for all season	0	1	2	3	4
One or more times per week all year	0	1	2	3	4

Clubs

One or more meet weekly	0	1	2	3	4
One or more meet twice a month	0	1	2	3	4
One or more meet monthly	0	1	2	3	4
One or more meet sporadically	0	1	2	3	4

Competition

Team sporting events	0	1	2	3	4
Individual sporting events	0	1	2	3	4
Team nonsporting events	0	1	2	3	4
Individual nonsporting events	0	1	2	3	4

Special Events

Clients are spectators only, i.e., movies	0	1	2	3	4
Clients are active participants, i.e., carnivals	0	1	2	3	4
Clients help plan events	0	1	2	3	4
Clients prepare materials: decorations, snacks	0	1	2	3	4

Open

One or more per week	0	1	2	3	4
One or more twice a month	0	1	2	3	4
One or more seasonally	0	1	2	3	4

Making Program Decisions

If you find that you need to add more individualized programming to the schedule, you will be faced with the question of what should you drop. And that always raises the question of should you base the drop decision on expense, number of attendees, amount of staff time it takes to prepare, or what. Another answer may be to have some of the events run by a volunteer.

If we based all programming decisions on cost and efficiency in terms of staffing, we would simply pipe movies into the clients' rooms or lounge areas. They are very low cost to rent, and the staff wouldn't have to transport. We could always run bingo all day, everyday; there are lots of ways to play the game, most of the clients like it, and it takes very few staff members to run. On the other hand, if these were the only types of programming the clients receive, there would be a problem.

Probably the most expensive and staff-intensive events are outings, but should they be eliminated because of the expense? Remember these are often the clients' favorite activity because they feel they are part of the community once again. Although you cannot eliminate the staffing and budgeting concerns, provide a balance of activities that are cost-effective, meaning that the clients receive the most benefits for the cost of the programming.

We hope the activity ideas presented in the following chapters will assist you in the development of a cost-effective therapeutic recreation program for your clients.

Chapter II

Alive and Active

It is about time we get into some suggestions for things to do with the clients. The word "activities" implies being active. Becoming "active" will frighten many of the clients, because they think the activity will be too physically challenging for them. On the other hand the term *games,* for many staff members, suggests that the activity can't possibly be age-appropriate. Whatever the choice of the words that are used, it is up to the leader to get the group moving and having fun without realizing the benefits that accrue in terms of eye-hand and eye-foot coordination, concentration and socialization. For this to occur, the leader must be prepared and exhibit a great deal of enthusiasm.

Many of the following activities are useful as part of a carnival or other theme event, as well as for one-on-one or small group use.

Tossing Things

Bandanna Ball   1:1, Sm Grp

Materials:
    Men's bandanna handkerchiefs
    Tennis balls (tennis clubs usually will donate "dead" balls)

Directions:
Tie a tennis ball in one corner of a 24-by-24-inch brightly colored bandanna. Tie a knot in the opposite corner. The bright color and the knot in the corner make it easier to catch when tossed to a client. The ball kind of "floats" through the air giving the re-

ceiver time to focus on its flight and be ready to catch it, even though the reflexes may be a little slow.

In our earlier book, we tied the ball in the toe of a sock. This works well when the clients are a little more advanced, for the ball moves a little faster when thrown.

Start by calling the name of the person to whom you are going to toss the ball so that he or she will be prepared to receive it. Have the person toss it back to you. Call the name of the next person and toss the ball to him or her. When the clients know the names of each other, toss the ball to the first person and have him or her call the name of the person to whom he or she is going to toss it.

Variation:
For the highest level clients, have a person in the middle trying to catch the ball as it is thrown from one person to someone across the circle. If the person in the middle catches the ball, he or she trades places with the person who threw it.

Beanbag Toss   1:1, Sm Grp

Materials:
    Three rings, 2, $2\frac{1}{2}$ and 3 feet in diameter
    A lightweight color-coded beanbag for each player

Directions:
The rings may be made from old garden hose held together with a short length of dowel. To make them, insert a 3-inch length of dowel in the end of the hose and shove the other end of the hose over the other end of the dowel. Use short nails to hold the ends in place.

Beanbag Toss

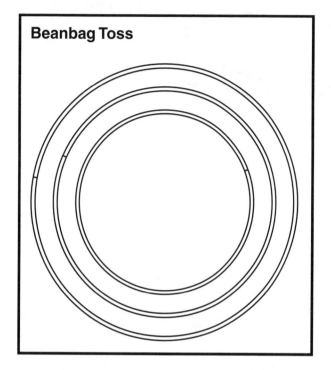

A 6¼-foot length of hose makes a ring 2 feet in diameter. Use a 7¾-foot length for a 2½-foot ring. For a 3-foot ring use 9½ feet of hose.

Place the rings inside each other on a carpeted floor as shown in the illustration and have the players toss their beanbags from an equal distance to the rings. Score 25 points for small ring, 15 points for middle ring and 10 points for large ring. The player that gets 100 points first is the winner. Bags touching a ring are given the score of the larger ring.

Variations:

- Use different sized boxes instead of the rings, or you may want to place a series of boxes at different distances and see how many tosses it takes to get the beanbag into each successive box.
- Another variation would be like Quoit Golf described on page 118 of our book, *Recreation Programming and Activities for Older Adults,* using beanbags only instead of rope quoits.
- Toss some of the beanbag figures such as Beanie Babies that are currently on the market.

Bucket Catch   1:1, Sm Grp

Materials:

>   Three or four lightweight plastic buckets or baskets, 6 to 8 inches in diameter
>   A belt on which to fasten them
>   Duct tape
>   Five or six 3-inch Nerf or Wiffle balls

Directions:

Fasten one lightweight bucket to the belt with duct tape. Fasten the belt around the leader's waist with the bucket in front, to start. Have clients toss the balls, which the leader tries to catch in the bucket. As the skill of clients (and the leader) improves, add buckets to the belt, up to a total of four (one on each hip, one in back and the other in front). This is a lot of fun for participants to watch as well as to take their turn at tossing a ball for the leader to try to catch in one of the buckets.

Variation:

- Have two leaders doing it. Divide the participants into two groups and have a relay race.
- Modify it for Easter by using plastic Easter eggs.
- If older children are visiting, have this as a relay race of four groups with the children wearing the buckets.

Bucket Catch

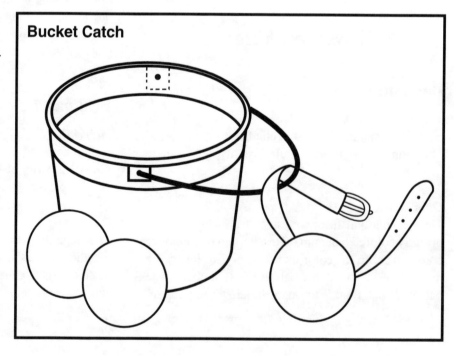

Catch Ball 1:1

Materials:
Commercial Velcro Catch Ball Set (It consists of a set of two flat "mitts" covered with Velcro and a ball that will stick to them when tossed and is available at most toy and discount department stores.)

Directions:
Have the player toss the ball for the leader to catch on his or her "mitt." After a few trials, the leader has the client hold up a "mitt," and try to catch the ball tossed by the leader. After a few tries, they should be able to toss it back and forth, each person catching it on his or her "mitt."

Koosh Balls 1:1, Sm Grp

Koosh balls are made of a rubberized string material and come in a variety of colors and sizes. They are fairly easy to catch and a soft bat can be purchased to use with them.

Jug Ball 1:1, Sm Grp

Materials:
Two to four 2-quart and 1-gallon round plastic jugs with handles
Several tennis balls and 2- or 3-inch Nerf balls

Directions:
Cut off the jug bottoms at an angle, as shown in the illustration, to make "scoops" for catching the balls. Start the activity by having the clients hold the larger scoops by the handles. Toss a ball to someone who

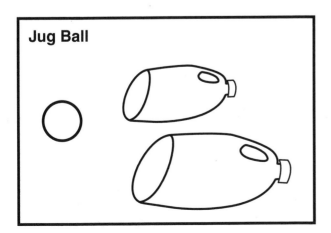

Jug Ball

tries to catch it with the scoop. Have the client toss the ball back and you try to catch it in your scoop. As the skills of the group improve, switch to the smaller scoops. Some of the clients may have enough skill to be able to toss the balls to each other (it might be desirable to have a volunteer available to chase the balls that are missed).

Variations:
- For lower level clients and as a 1:1 activity, you may want to have the clients hold the larger scoop in an upright position with two hands. You can then toss different size balls into their scoops, and if they are capable, have them toss them back.
- One-gallon plastic buckets may be used instead of the jugs.

Nerf Basketball 1:1, 2:1

Materials:
Nerf basketball
Wastebasket or cardboard box of similar size

Directions:
Use tape or twine to fasten the wastebasket to the seat of a chair. From a distance of 4 or 5 feet, toss the Nerf basketball into the basket while seated in another chair. For more of a challenge, put the chair holding the basket on a table. If you want to make it competitive, have two players taking turns, or set up two baskets with each player having a ball. You will need to have someone available to toss the balls back to the players and to retrieve the balls that miss the baskets.
Note: This is a good game to include in a carnival or similar special event.

Velcro Darts 1:1, 2:1

Materials:
Commercial Velcro dart game (available from many toy stores)

Directions:
This is an inexpensive game that uses 4-inch foam darts with Velcro ends. The darts are tossed from a distance of 4 or 5 feet and adhere to the dartboard. They can be tossed overhand or underhand. This is a good game for hand-eye coordination. If you want to

keep score, each circle on the board has a value printed on it.

Note: This is another excellent activity that can be used as a carnival game.

Ooff Ball   1:1, Sm Grp

Materials:
Several balls of different sizes and weights such as a 6-inch foam ball, an 8-inch play ball, a 10-inch soccer ball and a 12-inch beachball

Directions:
Toss one of the lighter balls to a client and have him or her toss it back. If you are working with a group, toss the same ball to each person in turn, then switch to a different ball. The different sizes and weights of the balls gives the clients an opportunity to adapt to the changing conditions.

Variations:
- Stretch a piece of brightly colored flagging tape (available at hardware stores) between the backs of two chairs to use as a "tennis net." Toss the ball over the net to the clients and have them toss it back the same way.
- Another variation for higher level clients is to have two or three clients on each side of the net and have them toss the different balls back and forth over the net to each other.

Hula-Hoop Horseshoes   1:1, Sm Grp

Materials:
Two Hula-Hoops or similar rings made from garden hose
Four tennis balls
Two old pairs of men's socks with different colors or patterns

Directions:
Tie one of the balls in the toe of each sock leaving the rest of the sock as a "tail." This will make it easier to toss and it won't roll far when it lands. Place the two hoops 15 to 20 feet apart if used outside and a little closer for inside use.

Play as regular horseshoes. Each of the two players has a pair of matching "sock-balls." The players take turns tossing their two balls from beside one of

the rings, trying to hit the other ring. After the balls have been tossed, the players move up to the ring where the balls landed and score as follows: 5 points if the sock is completely within the hoop, 4 points if the sock touches the hoop, and 2 points if it hits in the hoop but rolls out. Whoever gets a total of 21 points first wins the game.

Note: This is another good game for your next carnival.

Variations:
- Use one hoop and let each person throw all four balls from a distance of 8 or 10 feet and total up the score as an individual activity.
- Use balls tied in bandannas (as described for Bandanna Ball).

Plastic Ring Polo   1:1, Sm Grp

Materials:
Several small safety rings from gallon milk jugs (those rings that separate when you unscrew the lids for the first time)
One large margarine tub or eight small tubs in a shallow cardboard box

Directions:
For the less skilled client, place the large tub on the floor a foot or two away from the person and have the client toss or drop the rings into the tub one at a time. With higher level clients, use the cardboard box with the smaller tubs in it. Use a felt-tip pen to label each cup with a value of 5, 10, 15, or 20. Place the box with the tubs on the floor and with clients seated

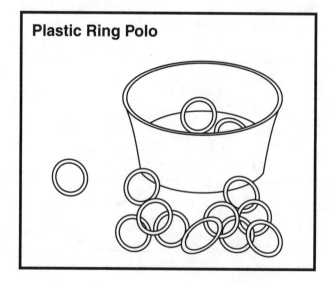

Plastic Ring Polo

a couple of feet away, have them toss five rings into the cups. Add up the total score of the cups in which the rings land.

Note: This is a great game for a carnival.

Variations:

- We often use double-sided tape to fasten a smaller container (like the top from a spray paint can) inside a large margarine tub. Toss rings from a couple of feet away. Score 10 points if the ring lands in the inner cup and 5 points if it is in the outer bowl.
- For lower level clients, use the same type of rings but toss them into a large margarine bowl placed on the table.
- Drop the rings into a 1-pound coffee can.

Pitching Checkers   1:1, Sm Grp

Materials:

> Eight checkers or poker chips
> One large margarine tub
> 12-by-12-inch piece of carpet
> 24-by-24-inch pressed wood or cardboard

Directions:
Use double-sided carpet tape to fasten the carpet to the center of the large square and the cup to center of the carpet as shown in the illustration.

From a distance of 4 or 5 feet and in a seated position, toss the checkers or poker chips into the cup. Score 5 points for each one in the cup, 3 points if on the carpet, and 1 point for the playing pieces that land on the square.

Note: This is a good game for your carnivals.

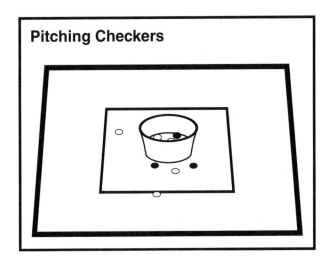

Pitching Checkers

Pendulum Swing   1:1, Sm Grp

Materials:

> 1-liter plastic bottle
> 3-inch Wiffle ball

Directions:
Fasten a string to the ball and attach it to the top of an arch or doorway so that the ball clears the floor by about 3 inches. If there is no available door or arch, you may be able to rig up a support arm and clamp it to a portable chalkboard. Stand the bottle on the floor beside the ball while it is at rest.

The player sits about 4 feet from the bottle and holds the suspended ball with the string taut. He or she releases the ball so that it swings past the bottle and hits it on the return swing. Each person gets five tries and receives 10 points for each successful swing.

Note: Try either of these versions at your next carnival.

Variation:
Have lower level clients try to hit the bottle on the forward swing.

Rolling, Kicking and Hitting Activities

Tossing things is important to eye-hand coordination. Now we want to look at some activities that feature rolling a ball using hand, foot, and lung power. There are several suggestions for activities that require returning a ball or moving it in a desired direction by hitting it with a paddle or bat. We'll start with a miniature bowling game. Since most clients have had experience with regulation-size equipment, this activity should be familiar and easy to use.

Miniature Bowling   1:1, Sm Grp

Materials:

> 10 toilet paper tubes or small plastic bottles
> 3-inch Nerf or Wiffle ball
> Cardboard box to fit end of table (cut box as shown in illustration to keep "pins" from falling off table)

Directions:
Set the "pins" as in bowling. Roll the ball from the opposite end of table. Score as in regular bowling.

Note: This is another good game for a carnival.

Fanball   Sm Grp

Materials:
   Table tennis ball
   Newspaper or cardboard fans
   Long table

Directions:
Teams of two or three people sit on opposite sides of the table. Each person has a fan or a newspaper folded into a fan. Drop the ball in the middle of the table. Players use fans to try to move the ball off the opposite side. Warn them that the fans are not allowed to touch the ball. We usually play until one side gets 5 points.

Warning: This is more difficult than it sounds, so try it with your highest level clients

Straw Ball   1:1, Sm Grp

Materials:
   Table tennis balls
   Large drinking straw for each player
   Long table

Directions:
This is like Fanball except the players blow through their straws to move the ball. The players must sit close to the table but may not touch the ball with their straws. A point is awarded the team that successfully maneuvers the ball off the opponents' side of the table. Three points is about the limit for this game. It is a good activity to exercise lungs and chest muscles, but don't play it too long or there will be sore chest muscles.

Warning: This activity is best used with highest level clients.

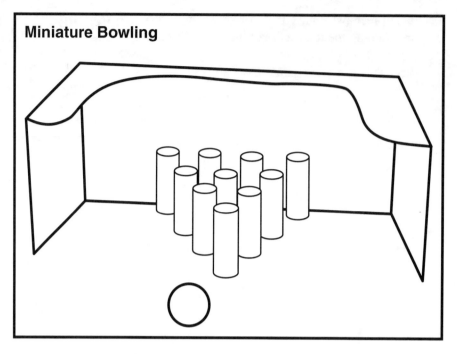

Miniature Bowling

Variation:
When using it as a 1:1 activity, see how far the client can move the ball with one puff.

Kick It   1:1, Sm Grp

Materials:
   Soccer-size Nerf ball
   Cardboard box approximately 18 by 18 inches

Directions:
Lay the box on its side about 10 feet in front of the players with the opening facing them. Each player takes a turn at kicking the ball toward the box. Players may be seated or standing beside their chair and holding the back of it for support. It can be a non-competitive game or played for points, such as 5 points if it goes in the box and stays there, or 2 points if it hits the box but does not stay in.

Note: This one can be used in a carnival, too.

Variations:
• For lower level clients, have them kick it towards a wall. Give them encouragement for any effort and if they hit the wall, move back further from the wall for the next try.
• Have the higher level clients seated in a circle and kick the ball to another person.
• If there is enough space, lay a broomstick or a length of $\frac{1}{2}$-inch plastic pipe across the seats of

two chairs to make a temporary "goal post" and have the clients try to kick a "field goal" from a few feet away.

Badminton
1:1, Sm Grp

Materials:
Large-size badminton rackets or lightweight paddles
Large-size badminton shuttlecocks
Net (optional)

Directions:
The materials are usually found in the children's game or sporting goods section of a discount department store such as Wal-Mart or Kmart. The paddle area is larger and the handles are shorter, making them easier for the players to control. The larger shuttlecocks are easier to see and float more slowly when hit. Start without a net and toss or hit the shuttlecock to the client and have him or her try to return it. When the person can successfully hit and return the shuttlecock, have two clients serve and return to each other. A low net can be added for the more advanced players.

Golf
1:1, Sm Grp

Materials:
Set of young golfer's clubs
Regular and practice golf balls
Indoor golf putting "hole"

Directions:
A golf set for young golfers is available for around $20 (at larger Sears stores). The clubs are lightweight and shorter metal clubs (not plastic!), good for golfing from a wheelchair. These are great because they look and feel like real golf clubs and don't look like a child's toy.

Have the clients hit the practice balls indoors or outside. Set up a driving range. You will probably need to have volunteers to retrieve the balls. An indoor practice "hole" can be used, or you might even sink a shallow tuna can in the ground and use a fiberglass or dowel wand with a flag on it for a putting green. Old golfers will love to play again.

Variations:
- Set up a driving or putting course on the grounds of the agency.
- Use small cans with both ends removed, sunk in the lawn and make a "par 3" course.
- Obtain enough sets of the clubs that a "foursome" can play.

Fun Sticks
1:1, Sm Grp

Materials:
Two foam plastic wands
Two $^3/_4$-inch diameter dowels

Directions:
Fun Sticks are inexpensive and easily modified for use with a variety of activities. You will need to look in the toy section of a large discount department store for the colorful 5-foot long, 3-inch diameter, foam plastic wands with a $^5/_8$-inch hole through the middle. The ones that we purchased are called "Fun Noodles" and cost less than $2 for each one. You should buy at least two of them, to start. Use a sharp knife to cut each of them into thirds. You will now have six pieces almost 20 inches in length.

Purchase two $^3/_4$-inch dowel rods from a hardware store. They will be 3 feet in length and you will have to use a saw to cut each one into four 9-inch pieces. Insert one of the short dowels into an end of each noodle until only 4 inches of the dowel sticks out to serve as a handle (believe us, the $^3/_4$-inch dowel will fit in the $^5/_8$-inch hole because the foam stretches) as shown in the illustration.

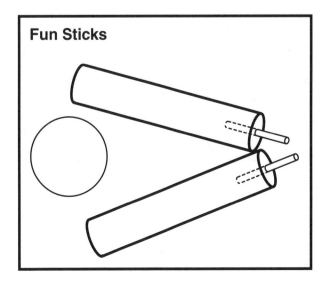

Fun Sticks

You now have six lightweight Fun Sticks that will be safe for your clients to use, and are ready to use for the activities that follow.

Box Hockey   1:1, Sm Grp

Materials:

Two large boxes for goals
One 6-inch Nerf ball
A Fun Stick for each player

Directions:

Seat players so they are facing their goal (the boxes are placed on edge with the open side toward the group) as shown in the illustration. Make certain that the clients have use of their arm closest to the line of play to make it easier for them to swing the Fun Stick. The two lines of players should be close enough for them to touch the legs (or wheels) of the chair across from them with their Fun Sticks.

Drop the ball in the middle and the play begins. The clients try to hit the ball toward their goal. If the ball is knocked out of the line of play, drop it back in by the clients where it went "out of bounds." Score one point for each goal.

You will want to have breaks after each goal, or after a couple of minutes of play, to give the clients time to rest. You can also have the people change positions after each goal to make certain that everyone gets in on the action. It is usually best to have no more than four people on each team.

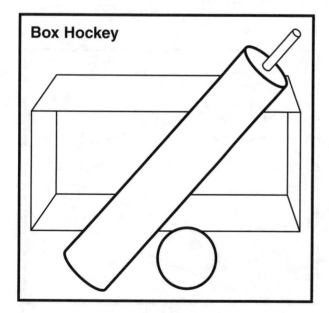

Box Hockey

Variations:

- Practice hitting the ball into a box from various distances.
- If there is enough room, set up the goals at each end of the playing area and have two players using wheelchairs move about, trying to hit the ball into the opponent's goal.

Baseball   1:1, Sm Grp

Materials:

One 3-inch Nerf ball or Wiffle ball
One Fun Stick

Directions:

This is more of a "see if you can hit the ball" activity. Toss the ball to the client holding the bat. He or she tries to hit it. Give each client several tries. Depending on how each person does, he or she may have a "strike," a "base hit," a "double," a "triple," or a "home run" ("umpire" makes the decision). Keep track of the "statistics" on a chalkboard and make a "big deal" about how well they hit the ball.

Variations:

- Why not follow up with a real ball game on the lawn? Use a plastic bat and a Wiffle ball. The clients may need help "running" the bases that are set closer than regulation.
- This is a good 1:1 activity, but to make it easier on the leader, use several balls that can be retrieved after all have been tossed to the client.

Fun Stick Golf   1:1, Sm Grp

Materials:

A Fun Stick for each player
A 3-inch color-coded Nerf ball for each player
Four or five 2-foot Hula-Hoops or rings made
    from garden hose

Directions:

This game is best played on the patio or on the lawn, but may be played inside if space is available. Place the rings around the area, spacing them at varying distances from one another (they are the "holes" for your golf course). Clients can play in twosomes, threesomes, or foursomes, just like in real golf. Each person "tees off" from the same spot and uses the

Fun Stick as a golf club to hit his or her Nerf ball toward the next "hole." The players move to where their balls lie, and again take turns to move their balls toward the next ring. Each person keeps track of the number of strokes it takes to get his or her ball in the ring. After every one in the group has "holed out," the group plays the next "hole." The person with the lowest score after playing around the course is the winner.

Variation:
For lower level clients, just being able to hit the ball with the club would be notable.

Swordplay   1:1

Materials:
    Two Fun Sticks

Directions:
Residents will remember swordplay as children. In this version, the leader and the client just hit each other's Fun Stick. It's a good way for the client to take out frustrations. This activity should only be used with the leader and one client. Two clients should not be permitted to use them with each other.

Other Uses for Fun Sticks

- Fun Sticks can be used to keep time to music.
- Residents can tap them on their knees or on their hands or even on the table or floor.
- Another use is to lay the Fun Sticks on the floor, and while sitting on chairs with shoes removed, the clients roll the Fun Sticks under the soles of their feet. It gives a comforting massage.

Fine Motor Skills

Beans in a Bowl   1:1, Sm Grp

Materials:
    10 dried beans for each person
    A plastic spoon and knife for each person
    A small margarine tub for each person

Directions:
Players are seated at a table. In front of each is a plastic margarine tub, 10 beans on the table and a knife and spoon. The players hold the spoon in one hand and use the knife to push the beans onto the spoon. The object is to see how quickly each person can get the beans in the tub. When using the activity with lower level clients, use dried lima beans or unshelled peanuts.

Variations:
- Use a toothpick and a spoon to move the beans or peanuts.
- Use unshelled peanuts and two toothpicks for the activity. Remember that many of the clients shouldn't eat them. We sprayed our peanuts with clear lacquer so they would last longer, and when told that they were sprayed, the clients didn't want to eat them.

Pass the Clothespin   1:1, Sm Grp

Materials:
    Six or more spring-type clothespins

Directions:
Seat the group in a circle. Clamp a clothespin to the sleeve of the first person. The player must release it and clamp it to the sleeve of the next person. See how quickly it can go around the circle. More challenging is to pass several around, one after the other.

Variations:
- Use as a relay by having each team pass the clothespins down the line, one after the other. The first team to have all of the clothespins attached to the last person in the line is the winner.
- When passing a single clothespin around the circle, each player says "Thank you for the clothespin, _____" (saying the name of the person).
- To make it even more of a name game, the person can say, "I'm giving you a gift, Mary," (stating the receiver's name) before passing it to the next person.
- For a 1:1 activity, attach a clothespin to the client's sleeve and have the client take it off and attach it to your sleeve, or just have the client pass it back.

- With the more confused client, have him or her clip several clothespins to your sleeve and after they all are attached, have the client count them.

Pass the Lifesaver   Sm Grp

Materials:
    A pack of Lifesavers mints
    A box of large round toothpicks

Directions:
Adapt the old game! Instead of holding the toothpick in his or her mouth, each player holds a toothpick in his or her hand. Put a Lifesaver on the first player's toothpick. The next player removes it with his or her toothpick and passes it to the next. It's best to do this seated at a table in case the Lifesaver is dropped.

Variation:
For lower level clients, or as a new game, use sucker sticks or drinking straws and the safety rings from gallon milk jugs.

Penny Pass   Sm Grp

Materials:
    Small paper or plastic cup for each person
    Several pennies

Directions:
Give each person in the circle a small paper cup. Put a penny in the first person's cup and have him or her "pour" it into the next person's cup. As soon as the first person has passed the penny, start another one. See how quickly all of the pennies can be passed around the circle without any being dropped.

Variation:
- Make it a relay by having two or more lines and passing the pennies from person to person.
- Use other items instead of, or along with, the pennies (i.e., nickels, beans, buttons and poker chips).

Find the Ring   Sm Grp

Materials:
    Ball of string
    Small "finger-size" ring

Directions:
Seat the group in a tight circle. Give the end of the string to one player and pass the ball of string around having each person hold onto the string as the ball is passed. Have everyone hold the string with both hands while you slip the ring on the string and tie the ends. Now there is a circle of string around which the players can pass the ring freely.

Have one person in the center of the circle that is going to try to find the ring as it is being passed around. To make it more difficult to find, the players keep moving their hands back and forth on the string, pretending they have the ring and are passing it to the next person, whether they really have it or not. When the person in the center points to a player's hand, the player must open it. If caught with the ring, the player must trade places with the person in the center.

Variations:
- The person in the middle must call a player by name, before that player has to open his or her hands.
- Have the leader in the center all of the time with a lower functioning group.

Land a Fish   1:1, Sm Grp

Materials:
    3-by-10-inch piece of poster board (or cereal box
        cardboard) for each person
    10-foot string for each fish
    Paper punch
    Colored pencils, crayons or Magic Markers
    Pattern like the illustration

Directions:
Each person is to draw or make a tracing of a fish on his or her cardboard as shown in the illustration. We often use cereal boxes for the cardboard. Make certain that the tail is the full 3-inch width or the fish will be harder for the player to "land." After tracing the pattern, each person draws in the details and colors his or her cardboard fish before cutting it out. Use a paper punch to make a hole in the center of the head as shown. To make it easier for the clients, the leader should prepare several patterns for them to trace.

To play the game, tie a small loop in one end of the string. Anchor the loop under a chair leg. Pass the other end of the string through the decorated side of the fish and pull it taut, leaving the fish with its tail about 10 inches from the chair. The player sits on another chair holding the other end of the string. The game, which should be played on a carpeted floor, is to see if the players can land their fish. If the leader lines the chairs up so the players are beside each other with the fish moving in the same direction, the game is more exciting.

The fish should be in line with the string heading toward the player. The leader should make sure the end of the string the person is holding comes out on the underside of the fish. Each "fisherperson" holds his or her string taut with his or her hand about 6 inches from the floor. By moving the string up and down, the players can "walk" the fish toward them. See who "lands" a fish first.

Note: This is a good activity for an intergenerational program.

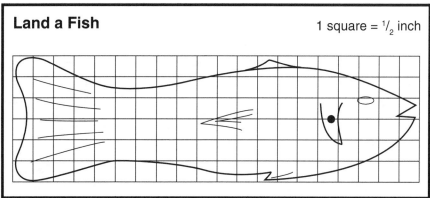

Land a Fish   1 square = $\frac{1}{2}$ inch

bottom of a chair leg. Hold the other end of the string, as in Land a Fish.

Start the race with the turtles a foot away from the players' end of the string and an equal distance from the anchor, which is the finish line. The turtles should be on the floor facing the chairs where the strings are fastened. Players move the string up and down to move the turtle toward the finish line that should be about a foot from the chair. This is a little easier to do than in the fish game. Line up several

Turtle Race   1:1, Sm Grp

Materials:
 8-by-8-inch piece of poster board (or cereal box cardboard) for each player
 10-foot string for each turtle
 Cardboard pattern similar to illustration
 Colored pencils, crayons or Magic Markers
 Paper punch

Directions:
Each person should draw or trace the turtle on the cardboard, cut it out and color it. Make sure that the feet extend at least as far back as the end of the shell, or it will be difficult to make the turtle move correctly. Punch a hole in the shell near the back of the head and pass the string through the hole. Using the end of the string coming from the bottom of the turtle, fasten it near the

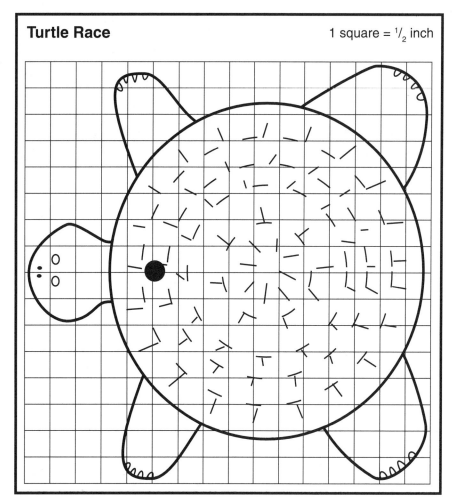

Turtle Race   1 square = $\frac{1}{2}$ inch

racers and see which turtle wins the race. The turtles are easier to move if the activity is being done on a carpeted surface.

Note: This is a good activity for when children visit the clients.

Dustpan Relay   1:1, Sm Grp

Materials:

Two small clean plastic dustpan and brush sets
About a cup full of dried beans or Styrofoam "peanuts" used for packing
Large margarine tubs

Directions:

Form two teams and place a dustpan and brush set on a table in front of each group. Give the first person in each line a large margarine tub half filled with the dried beans or "peanuts." On the word *go* they rush to their tables and dump the tubs. They then use the brush and dustpan to gather them up and dump them back in their tub without touching any of the beans with their hands. As soon as all of the beans are collected they take the tub back to the next person in their line, who repeats the same actions. The first team to complete the routine is the winner.

Note: This makes a good event for an "Olympics" week program.

Variation:

• As a 1:1 activity, dump several beans on the table and have the client brush them onto a dustpan.
• Use with a mixture of children and clients for an intergenerational program.

Wading   1:1, Sm Grp

Materials:

Small plastic wading pool
Towels for drying feet
Chairs

Directions:

This activity should take place outdoors on the patio. Fill the pool with 2 inches of water and allow time for the sun to warm it to a comfortable temperature. Make sure that the clients have the proper sunscreen protection and are wearing hats if the pool will be in a sunny area when you run the activity. Have the par-

ticipants remove their shoes and stockings, sit in the chairs around the pool, roll up their pant legs and place their feet in the water. It is best not to let anyone stand in the water, for he or she might slip and fall, but wiggling toes and flexing ankles is a good small muscle activity and on a warm day the water feels so-o-o good.

Play some of the "talk" games like I Spy or I'm Going or reminisce about when the clients went swimming in their childhood. You might even have a beachball to toss around.

Variation:

Use aqua-shoes and take the higher level clients wading in a shallow stream or place a lawn chair in the stream and have them dangle their feet (Judy did this with her nursing home clients in a nearby lake and they loved it).

Bubble Fun

Most older adults never take a real deep breath or use even a fraction of their lung power. Blowing bubbles requires them to take a deep breath and to control their exhaling which provides excellent exercise for their chest muscles. These activities are fun for the clients and provide a great intergenerational activity when there are young visitors. You can purchase the bubble mix or have the clients make their own. They can even make the bubble devices. Directions for making and using the materials follow.

Bubble Soap   1:1, Sm Grp

Materials:

Joy or Dawn liquid dish detergent
Vegetable oil
Water
Food coloring (optional)
1- or 2-quart container

Directions:

Add about $1/8$ cup of detergent and a tablespoon of vegetable oil to a quart of water. These are just approximate measurements and we just guess at the amount, often making less than a cup of liquid at a time. Try it out and if your bubbles "explode" when you try to blow them, add a little more detergent (the oil is added to make a little more surface tension so the bubble lasts longer). If you wish, add a little food coloring, but, if you are going to have the activity indoors, the food coloring may make a stain where the bubble lands.

Bubble Cups   1:1, Sm Grp

Materials:
    Bubble soap
    Disposable 8- or 10-ounce plastic (not foam) cups
    Waxed paper or cheese cloth
    Small rubber bands
    Scissors, round toothpicks
    Ice pick or similar sharp punch
    Shallow margarine tubs

Directions:
Use the sharp punch to make a $^3/_{16}$-inch hole (approximate size) in the bottom of each plastic cup. Stretch a piece of waxed paper over the top of the cup and hold it in place with a rubber band. Use a toothpick to punch 10 or 12 holes in the waxed paper. An alternate method for covering the top is to use cheesecloth or a piece of nylon stocking. The mesh makes it unnecessary to use the toothpicks, but you will have smaller bubbles. Why not try both methods? Anyway, you are ready to blow bubbles.

    Give each of the participants a margarine tub with about a half-inch of bubble soap in it. Have them touch the top of their bubble cup to the surface of the soap, then lift it up. If they hold the cup so they can gently blow through the hole in the bottom, bubbles will form on the covered top. By gently shaking the cup the bubbles will dislodge from the surface. They should be able to make several sets of bubbles before having to "recharge" the cup.

    Note: When using with lower level clients, have the bubble maker constructed in advance and let the clients blow the bubbles. Have them inhale before putting the bottom of the cup to their mouth, or they may inhale the soapsuds.

Wire Bubble Makers   1:1, Sm Grp

Materials:
    Bubble soap
    20-gauge wire
    Small cookie cutters

    Plastic 35mm film cans
    Pliers or wire cutters
    Plastic margarine tubs

Directions:
Rolls of 20-gauge wire are available from hardware stores. Cut two or three 12-inch lengths for each person. Make a round bubble maker by wrapping the middle of a length of wire around a film canister once and twisting the ends of the wire together to make a handle. A star-shaped cookie cutter makes an interesting form to shape another wire in the same manner. Some of the clients may want to make one in a free-form shape.

    After making each bubble maker, try it out by dipping it into a margarine tub filled with about a half-inch of bubble soap. Remember to blow gently. See who can blow the biggest and the most unusual bubble with the devices they have made.

Giant Bubble Wands   Sm Grp

Materials for each wand:
    One 24-inch piece of $^1/_4$- or $^5/_{16}$-inch dowel
    One $^1/_2$-inch diameter plastic ring
    $3^1/_2$ feet of heavy acrylic yarn
    Two small rubber bands

Directions:
Slip the ring on the yarn and bring both ends of the yarn together. Run the dowel through the ring and use a rubber band to fasten both ends of the yarn to the end of the dowel as shown in the illustration. Wrap the remaining rubber band around the other end of the dowel to help prevent the ring from slipping off. You should now be able to slide the ring along the dowel to change the size of the loop made by the yarn.

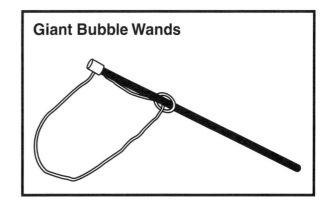

Giant Bubble Wands

To prepare the wand for making bubbles, hold it by the handle and let the ring slide down toward the end where the yarn is tied. Let the doubled yarn hang down and dip it into the soap solution until it is wetted throughout. Now lift the wand to a horizontal position and slowly move the ring until the yarn makes a loop encircling a soapy film. Move the wand slowly to inflate the bubble or, if there is a gentle breeze, it will inflate on its own. Now slide the ring to close the bubble. After the bubble has departed, close the loop and it should recharge without having to dip it in the solution. You should be able to make several large bubbles before having to recharge the wand.

Bubble Blowing Contest   Sm Grp

Materials:
> Bubble soap
> Margarine tubs
> Homemade bubble devices
> Hula-Hoop or ring of similar size

Directions:
Suspend the hoop waist high in a vertical position. Each person takes a turn blowing a bubble and maneuvering it through the hoop. See who does it from the greatest distance. You need to make sure the hoop is hung at a location where there is a gentle breeze flowing toward the hoop. You can help a little by using hand-held fans or folded newspaper to move the bubble in the chosen direction.

Somewhat Active

Auto Race   Sm Grp, Lg Grp

Materials:
> Two 10- or 12-inch plastic cars of different colors
> A large pair of dice, each one a different color
> 50-foot piece of flagging tape marked at 6-inch intervals with felt-tip marker
> Masking tape

Directions:
Stretch the flagging tape across the room and tape it to the floor. Mark the tape at 6-inch intervals with a felt-tip pen. Seat half of the group on each side of the tape, far enough from it that everyone can see the two cars. Place the cars at the starting line and explain that each of the dice represents a car and when the dice are thrown, the cars move the number of spaces (designated by the markings on the tape) shown faceup on each car's die. A player is selected from each race team to roll the die for that team's car. One of the clients can be assigned to move the cars with a shuffleboard stick. After the cars are moved, another team member throws the die for the next move. The first car to cross the finish line wins.

Variations:
- When the car gets near the finish line the exact number to match the number of spaces left must come up in order to cross the finish line.
- Substitute toy horses for the cars and call it a horse race. You might want to have several horses in the race and roll a die for each horse.
- Some facilities have even printed up play money and let each person bet on the outcome of the races.
- Use as a part of a theme event with related activities.

Treasure Hunt   Sm Grp

Materials:
> 5-by-7-inch cards
> Medium point felt-tip pen
> Small "treasure chest" (cardboard or plastic box with a lid)
> Gold foil covered chocolate "coins"

Directions:
This takes a little planning ahead of time, which can easily be done by a couple of volunteers. The game consists of consecutive clues being written on the cards, with the last clue giving the location of the treasure chest. The difficulty of the clue depends on the level of the participants. A group of three or four is given the first card which will reveal the location of the next clue (for instance, "Where the nurse

stays"). When the treasure hunters get to the first location (the nurse's station in our example), they should look for the next clue which is within plain sight. This card gives the location of the next clue (maybe, "Let us sing hymns" which could lead them to the chapel). After a number of clues, the last one could be, "The treasure is buried 3 feet under crafty water." They will discover the treasure chest, filled with "pieces of eight," beneath a blanket under the sink in the craft room. If you collect the cards after the group has found the treasure, you can use them again for another group. If your outdoor area is large enough, it is fun to have the treasure hunt start on the patio.

Chapter III

On the Quiet Side

Paper and Pencil Challenges

Paper and pencil games have many uses, but they are pretty much limited to those clients who still function on a fairly high level mentally. They can be used as an introductory activity while the rest of the group is gathering, as a break during a more strenuous activity, or they may be given as an individual challenge. A pencil and paper challenge can be explained at the end of a program session. Give some examples and work sheets (if needed) to the people before they go back to their rooms. Suggest that they get together in groups of two or three to work on the task. When everyone gets together again after a few days, each of the work groups can share its findings.

Backward/Forward   Ind, Sm Grp

Materials:
    Paper and pencil for each person

Directions:
Hand out the paper and pencils and tell the group members that they have so many minutes (usually four or five) to make a list of as many words as possible that when spelled backwards will also form a word. Give a couple of examples like "pot/top," "saw/was," "toot/toot," "ban/nab," "dad/dad" and "mom/mom."

    Make a master list of the words they discover on a chalkboard or large sheet of newsprint. When they see the large list, maybe they can suggest others.

Variations:
- If you want a competition, give 1 point for each pair, 2 points if the words are spelled the same forward and backwards and 5 points for each pair with five or more letters.
- Another method is to go around the group having each person give the first pair of words on his or her list. Anyone having the same word should cross it off. If no one else has that word, the person gets 5 points; if only one other person has it, they each get 2 points. Keep going around the group, each giving a word that hasn't been used until all lists are complete, and then add up the scores to determine the winners.
- You can use it as a first-comer activity by having the group members call out the words as they think of them.

Weird Words   Ind, Sm Grp

Materials:
    Paper and pencil for each participant

Directions:
This activity is a high-level challenge.

    Explain that the English language is full of weird words and that sometimes the words that describe them are even more weird. For instance, if two words are spelled and pronounced alike, but have different meanings (iron/iron), they are called homonyms. On the other hand, if two words are pronounced alike, but have different spellings and meanings (air/heir), they are called homophones. Now if two or more words are spelled alike, but are pronounced differently and have different meanings (read/read), they are called homographs. Don't bother trying to remember what they are called, just see how many weird word combinations your group can remember. This is a good take-home assignment for individuals or partners.

Explain to the group that the object is to make as long a list as possible, of words that sound alike, or are spelled alike, but have different meanings. Give some examples such as air/heir, bridal/bridle, cent/scent/sent, aloud/allowed, or cereal/serial, to get them started.

Here are some more in case you get stuck:

Alter/Altar
Bale/Bail
Break/Brake
Capitol/Capital
Coarse/Course
Cord/Chord
Deer/Dear
Do/Dew/Due
Dough/Doe
Flee/Flea
Flour/Flower
Great/Grate
Him/Hymn
Hire/Higher
Hole/Whole
Know/No
Lean/Lien
Lie/Lye
Loan/Lone
Maid/Made
Main/Mane
Male/Mail
Naval/Navel
Not/Knot
Pain/Pane
Pare/Pair
Peace/Piece
Red/Read
Rite/Right/Write
Roll/Role
See/Sea
Sheer/Shear
Sore/Soar
Taut/Taught
Through/Threw
To/Two/Too
Wait/Weight

Weak/Week
Wood/Would

Is it any wonder people from other countries have trouble learning English?

Famous Couples   Ind, Sm or Lg Grp

Materials:
Pen or pencil for each participant
Duplicated copies of the following list with a blank for the second name

Directions:
Write the name in each blank space to complete the list of famous couples:

George Burns and _____ (Gracie Allen)
Hansel and _____ (Gretel)
Lewis and _____ (Clark)
Cain and _____ (Abel)
Samson and _____ (Delilah)
Laverne and _____ (Shirley)
Dr. Jekyll and _____ (Mr. Hyde)
Sonny and _____ (Cher)
John Alden and _____ (Priscilla)
Laurel and _____ (Hardy)
Napoleon and _____ (Josephine)
Amos and _____ (Andy)
Gilbert and _____ (Sullivan)
Jack and _____ (Jill)
Cleopatra and _____ (Mark Antony)
Romeo and _____ (Juliet)
Clark Kent and _____ (Lois Lane)
Barnum and _____ (Bailey)
Archie Bunker and _____ (Edith)
Batman and _____ (Robin)
Roy Rogers and _____ (Dale Evans)
Porgy and _____ (Bess)
Dagwood and _____ (Blondie)
Punch and _____ (Judy)
Fibber McGee and _____ (Molly)
Abbott and _____ (Costello)
Fred Flintstone and _____ (Wilma)
Maggie and _____ (Jiggs)

Variations:
• Use as a first-comer activity by calling out the first name and having the group members call out the matching name.

- It also works well as a competitive game.
- This is an excellent take-home challenge.

Common Sayings   Sm Grp, First Comer

Materials:
> Duplicated sheet of sayings for each person with a blank for the answer
> Pencil for each person

Directions:
Give each person a sheet of sayings to complete. See if the group can come up with any others. Discuss sayings the clients, or their parents, used.

Here are some common sayings from which to make your list:

> As thin as a _____ (rail)
> As pretty as a _____ (picture)
> As neat as a _____ (pin)
> As smart as a _____ (whip)
> As stiff as a _____ (board)
> As right as _____ (rain)
> As fresh as a _____ (daisy)
> As light as a _____ (feather)
> As green as _____ (grass)
> As pale as a _____ (ghost)
> As limp as a _____ (rag)
> As slow as _____ (molasses)
> As sly as a _____ (fox)
> As warm as _____ (toast)
> As white as a _____ (sheet)
> As happy as a _____ (lark)
> As easy as _____ (pie)
> As cool as a _____ (cucumber)
> As good as _____ (gold)
> As blind as a _____ (bat)
> As hungry as a _____ (bear)
> As clean as a _____ (whistle)
> As busy as a _____ (bee)
> As pleased as _____ (punch)
> As ugly as _____ (sin)
> As sober as a _____ (judge)
> As dead as a _____ (doornail)
> As stubborn as a _____ (mule)

Variation:
As a first-comer activity, give the first part of the saying and have the group call out the rest of it.

Threesomes   Sm Grp, First Comer

Materials:
> Prepared sheet with the first two names of each threesome and a blank for the third name with duplicated copies to hand to the group
> Pencils or pens

Directions:
Give the participants about 10 minutes to see how many of the threesomes they can complete. You might suggest that they work in pairs for this task. Have the group members see if they can come up with other threesome groups.

Here is a list to get you started:

> Tom, Dick and _____ (Harry)
> Lock, Stock and _____ (Barrel)
> Kukla, Fran and _____ (Ollie)
> Hook, Line and _____ (Sinker)
> Stop, Look and _____ (Listen)
> Niña, Pinta and _____ (Santa Maria)
> Tall, Dark and _____ (Handsome)
> Friends, Romans, _____ (Countrymen)
> Healthy, Wealthy and _____ (Wise)
> Bell, Book and _____ (Candle)
> Animal, Vegetable and _____ (Mineral)
> Baubles, Bangles and _____ (Beads)
> Butcher, Baker and _____ (Candlestick Maker)
> Flopsy, Mopsy and _____ (Cottontail)

Variations:
- When used as a first-comer activity, read the first two names on the list and let members of the group call out the third.
- Use as a handout for individuals to complete for the next session.

Card Games

We get so used to thinking of activities for the lower level client that we sometimes forget we have clients who are mentally capable, but physically frail or totally uninterested in interacting with groups. Card games may be a good way to keep this type of client mentally challenged. Card games are not for everyone, but the following are either done in small groups or by an individual. Even a client who does not like cards may be interested in playing some of these games.

SkipBo   1:1, Sm Grp (3 or 4 players)

Materials:
Set of SkipBo cards (available at many discount department stores)

Directions:
The directions included with the cards are easily followed. It is a number game that is simple to play and score. Play with two to four players individually or as partners.

Variations:
- Simplify the game for lower level clients by removing all of the cards numbered 6 and above.
- Use the numbered cards with lower mental ability clients for matching numbers and colors and for sorting numerically or by color.
- Use for playing card bingo, a game that is explained next.

Card Bingo   Md Grp

Materials:
Two decks of playing cards

Directions:
Each of the players is dealt eight cards, which are displayed faceup on the table, in two rows of four. The "caller" shuffles the second deck and calls out the suit and number of each card, in the order it is drawn. When a player has the card that is called, he or she turns it over. When the last of a player's eight cards are turned over, the player calls, "Winner."

Variation:
When playing with lower level clients, use a deck of SkipBo cards. They have colored numbers from 1 to 12 and there are four sets of each number. Separate one set out for the caller and play the game with up to three players, giving only four cards to each player.

Memory Numbers   1:1

Materials:
Deck of SkipBo cards

Directions:
Sort the deck so that there are two piles of cards with numbers 1 through 12. The rest of the deck is not used for this activity. Shuffle the two piles and lay them both facedown on the table. Have the client turn up the top card in each pile. If the cards match, the client gets to "keep" them. If they are not a match, the client places the cards into faceup discard piles beside their respective starting piles. Once the decks are exhausted, reshuffle and have the client continue to draw the top two cards for matches.

Variations:
- The staff member can take a turn or have two lower level clients playing with the staff member.
- Only use cards numbered from 1 to 5 for the lowest level players.

Solitaire Card Games

Many of the clients will know some solitaire card games. We are including several here that are found on many computers. If the clients are capable of playing on a computer, they will have a new challenge. However the directions have been included so that they can be played with a regular deck of playing cards. The mentally alert clients can play all of these games. A good activity is to have a deck of cards for each person and teach the same game to all of the individuals in the group, letting them play individually, but being available to answer any question they may have while they are learning. Don't confuse them by teaching more than one game at the same session. The following games are easier than traditional solitaire, and we have included some suggestions that would make them even easier. Be sure to use cards with large numbers.

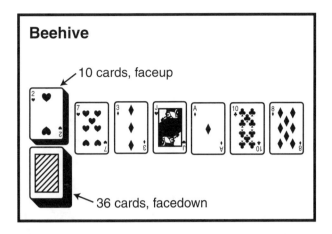

Beehive

Ind, Sm Grp

Materials:
    Deck of cards

Directions:
Shuffle the deck and deal 10 cards faceup in a pile on the left upper side of the area. This is the "beehive." Deal the next six cards faceup in a line, to be the "garden," as shown in the illustration. Place the remaining 36 cards, facedown, below the beehive as the stockpile. The object of the game is to build foursomes of like cards in the garden and then discard the pile. You win if you can get the whole deck into foursomes and discard them.

Begin play by putting any cards that match in the garden together. The top card from the beehive can be used if there is a match in the garden. Fill each empty garden space with the top card from the beehive. If there are no more matches in the garden or from the top beehive card, use the stockpile by flipping the first card faceup. When there are four-of-a-kind in the garden, discard them.

Continue the game, filling in the empty garden spaces from the beehive and flipping the stockpile cards one at a time. After going through the stockpile, turn it facedown and continue flipping the cards and making matches. Play continues until all four-of-a-kind matches have been made (a winning game) or until no more matches can be made.

Variations:
- A more challenging way to play the game is to go through the pile only one time. Or another variation is to flip three cards over at a time utilizing the top card to make matches. You can go through the deck flipping three cards at a time until no more matches can be made.

- Eliminate the beehive and do all of the work from the stockpile.
- Instead of six spaces in the garden, play with three or four spaces.
- Remove in pairs of two instead of having to find all four.

Elevens

Ind, Sm Grp

Materials:
    Deck of cards

Directions:
This is a fun game and encourages math skills. Although this is a solitaire game it could be used as an intergenerational activity with an older adult and a young person working together to practice skills of addition. Place nine cards in three lines faceup, with three cards per row, as shown in the illustration. The remaining 43 cards are placed faceup in a stockpile to one side.

The object of the game is to match two cards whose value adds up to 11. Each card is worth its face value, with the ace equal to 1. When two cards that are faceup have a combined value of 11, they are removed from play and discarded facedown. The empty spaces are then filled from the top of the reserve pile. The jack, queen and king can only be removed as a trio, before they are added to the discard

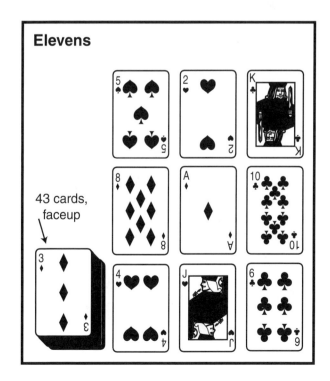

pile. Color and suit do not matter. So, if you have an ace on the table, you need a 10 in order to total 11, a 6 and 5 equals 11, and so on. Remember that jacks, kings and queens are removed as a trio. Keep filling the spaces from the reserve until you are stuck, or you win.

Variation:
Use six cards instead of nine and in two lines instead of three.

Tens   Ind, Sm Grp

Materials:
Deck of cards

Directions:
Although this game has more cards, it is quick, easy to play and very easy to adapt for the clients. Place five cards faceup in a line across the table. Place five more cards faceup in a line below the first five. Now place three cards faceup in a third line below the other two. The other 39 cards are placed facedown in a stockpile (as shown in the illustration). Aces have a numeric value of 1 and numbered cards are equal to their face value. Any two cards with a total value of 10 are removed and the spaces are filled from the stockpile. In order to remove 10s (i.e., 10 of hearts, 10 of spades, 10 of diamonds, 10 of clubs), all four must appear on the table at the same time. The same rule applies to the jacks, queens and kings. Go through

the pile of cards only one time. When no more matches can be made, the game is finished.

Variations:
- Instead of waiting to get all four of the 10s, jacks, queens or kings on the board before removing, remove them when two of a kind are present.
- Remove the 10s, jacks, queens and kings from the deck and play the game as before.
- Go through the stockpile of cards until all are used, instead of just one time.
- Instead of three rows that equal 13 cards, play with fewer cards on the table.

Thirteens   Ind, Sm Grp

Materials:
Deck of cards

Directions:
This is another matching game and in some ways the easiest. Place five cards faceup in the first line, and five cards faceup in a line below (as shown in the illustration). The numbers are equal to their face value, the ace is equal to 1, a jack is 11, queen is 12, and a king is 13. Remove cards by matching two cards to add to 13. The king is removed by itself. Fill openings with cards from the stockpile. Play is complete when all of the possible matches have been made. Go through the stockpile once.

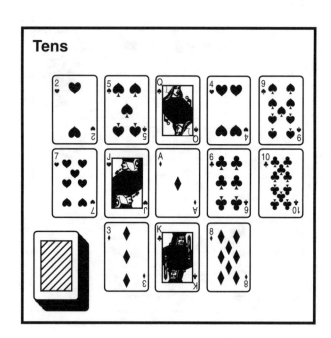

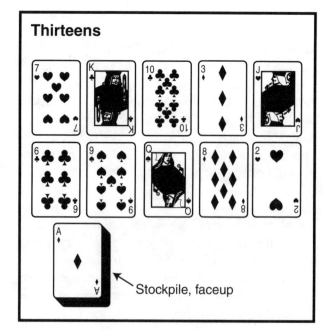

Variation:
Work with one row of five cards instead of two rows of 10 and keep going through the pile making matches that add up to 13. Remember, each king is discarded separately.

At a Table

Find It in the Paper   Sm Grp

Materials:
One old magazine or newspaper, with lots of ads and pictures, for each person
List of items for participants to find

Directions:
The staff should go through the magazines and papers to make up a suitable list of items prior to beginning the activity. Print the list in large letters on a chalkboard or large sheet of newsprint. When a player finds one of the items on the list, he or she calls out the name of the item. The leader then writes the player's name beside the name of the item on the list. The winner is the first person to find all of the items, or the person who finds the most items in the allotted time.

Variation:
The leader calls the name of an item from the list and sees how many can find the item in their papers, or who is the first to find it.

Dice Bingo   Sm or Md Grp

Materials:
Pair of dice
Paper and pencil for each player

Directions:
Have each client write the numbers 2 through 12 on a card or sheet of paper (have cards prepared for lower level clients). The player rolls the dice and crosses out any number on his or her card that corresponds to the total number he or she rolled. The dice are then passed to the next person. Whenever the person rolls a number that has already been crossed out on his or her sheet, the dice must be passed on to the next

player. The first person to roll all of the numbers is the winner.

Bingo-Type Activities   Sm Grp

Many older adults love to play bingo. Some will only settle for the real thing with prizes for each winner, but most just like the competition associated with this type of activity. For these people, we suggest you use your imagination (and the clients' as well) to make up your own bingo-like game.

Let's make up a simple one to show you how. We'll use birds as an example and we can call it "Birds-Ho." Let each player make his or her own card. To prepare for the activity you will need to use your computer or pen and ruler to make a master card template. For this example we'll make a nine-square playing card, but if you wanted to, it could be 16 or 25 squares. Remember you will need an extra row of squares across the top for the names of the columns, as shown in the illustration.

Duplicate enough of these cards so that each player can have several (one for each time you play the game with the group).

Birds-Ho		
Robin	Crow	Eagle

Now you need to make a set of small squares for the caller. Use some index card stock or similar heavy scrap paper and cut it into 1-inch squares. You will need to make 10 squares for each column (30 squares for Birds-Ho, for there are three columns). Let the group members pick three birds—our mythical group picked "robin," "crow" and "eagle," and we happen to have 10 people in the group. Give 10 of the caller's squares to three of the people who arrive early. Have the first person write "R 1" on one square, "R 2" on the next, and so on, up to "R 10" on the last square (the *R* is for robin). The second person uses *C* (for crow) and makes cards from "C 11" through "C 20." The third helper uses the letter *E* (for eagle, of course) and the numbers from "E 21" to "E 30."

By this time everyone has arrived, so give each person three or four card templates depending on how many games you want to play. In the spaces above the columns they are to draw caricatures of the three birds with a robin in the first column, a crow in the second, and an eagle in the third. Instruct them to put a capital *R, C,* and *E* in the spaces also, so they will remember what they drew.

Now it is time for the players to fill in the columns with their own numbers. Have each person write any three numbers from 1 to 10 in the three spaces under the robin. Then fill in three numbers from 11 to 20 under the crow and three numbers from 21 to 30 under the eagle.

The leader places all of the caller's squares in a box and shakes them up. Then he or she draws one out at a time as in regular bingo. The players cover that number on their card. Three in a line, horizontal, vertical, or diagonal and the player calls out "Birds-Ho" and wins that game. Players can make up several cards with different sets of numbers, and play the game again.

It really takes less time to have the clients make up the game than it takes for us to explain how to do it. However, having the clients make the game is an enjoyable part of the activity and if you use corn or beans to cover the squares (rather than felt-tip bingo pens), you can collect the cards and use them again. Games with 16 and 25 squares can be made using the same procedure. It just takes more time, so try the nine-square version first.

Variations:
- Try various themes, like leaves, colors, seashore items, nature, vegetables, sports, kitchen items,

boating, and cartoon characters using the same procedures.
- Have a volunteer make up the cards on his or her computer for some of the bingo games (high-school age volunteers probably know how).
- Instead of numbers use a theme and fill each space with a name of a flower, color, or bird to give a few examples. A flower card might have a daisy, impatiens, rose, violet, and black-eyed Susan as the names.

Tabletop Shuffleboard   Sm Grp

Materials:

　　Sheet of 6-mil plastic the width and length of a
　　　　6- or 8-foot table
　　Picnic table clips or masking tape
　　Permanent felt-tip marker
　　Eight large checkers, mason jar rings, or similar
　　　　disks (two sets of four in two different col-
　　　　ors)

Directions:

Mark a shuffleboard pattern as shown in the illustration on each end of the plastic. Use clips or masking tape to fasten the plastic to the table. Use the checkers or similar disks to play shuffleboard. Players stand at the end of the table and use their hands to propel the disks.

　　Adjust the distance from the players to the scoring area according to the skill level of the clients. If

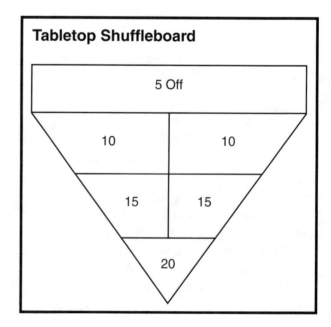

Tabletop Shuffleboard

5 Off
10　　10
15　　15
20

they play from a seated position, they should be beside the table in order to facilitate hand movement.

Variation:

If you use a 4- or 5-foot round table, draw concentric circles in the center of the plastic you use to cover it. Players are seated around the table and each player uses his or her hand to propel a disk toward the center circle that should have the highest score. As in shuffleboard, the disc must be completely inside the circle to score.

Pyramid Puzzle Ind

You see this old game in many restaurants. It usually can be purchased there or you can order it from any number of catalogs. Most of the game boards have 10 holes in a 4-inch triangle made of $\frac{3}{4}$-inch wood. There are nine golf tees with one hole left open. The game is played to remove the tees, one at a time, by jumping them with another tee to any available open space. When a tee is jumped, remove it. The object is to end with only one tee left on the board. We made our boards like those in the illustration and only had to purchase the golf tees. This is a good project for a volunteer who has a wood shop. Have him or her make up several of the games to use with the more alert clients.

Note: Any time that players end up with less than four tees on the board, they are doing very well.

Jumbo Checkers and
Tick-Tack-Toe Two Players

This is a commercial version of a regular checker game with an oversize checkerboard printed on a thick woven material that folds for storage. The checkers are 3 inches in diameter but are made of a lightweight plastic. A tick-tack-toe grid is printed on the reverse side of the material. Ours was a gift from a friend but we have seen them on sale for about $10. Check the resource section of this book to find the address of a source for these and other games.

T, E, and *H* Puzzles Ind

Materials:

Poster board or index card stock to make puzzles

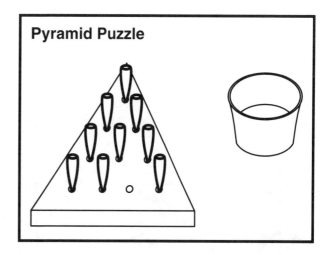

Pyramid Puzzle

Directions:

Many clients will remember this fairly high-level puzzle from their childhood.

Very carefully cut out each piece from poster board or index card stock with the dimensions shown in the illustrations. Make sure that the material used is the same color on both sides. This adds to the difficulty of fitting the pieces together to make the letter. Place all of the pieces for each letter in an envelope and label it with "*T* Puzzle," "*E* Puzzle," or "*H* Puzzle" being careful not to get any of the pieces in the wrong one. The challenge is to use the pieces to make the letter named on the envelope. Make sure that the pieces are returned to the proper envelopes. To make it easier, draw an outline of each of the pieces on the outside of the envelope.

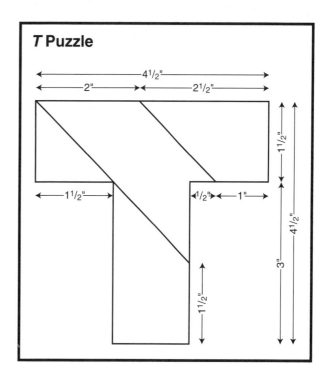

***T* Puzzle**

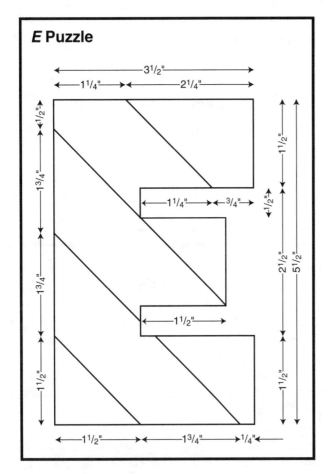

E Puzzle

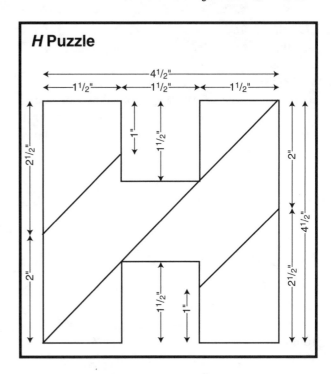

H Puzzle

Note: Make certain that staff members try this out before using it with clients. It may be desirable to make larger circles or even squares and adjust their spacing to fit the clients' abilities.

Variations:
- Another method would be to print the commands on 3-by-5-inch cards, one set for the right hand and one for the left. Shuffle the two piles of cards separately and draw one from each pile for the player to attempt the action.
- Instead of circles on the playing surface, use small colored carpet squares cemented to the poster board base to add texture.
- The playing surface could be made from squares of colored material sewn together.

Tabletop Twister   Sm Grp

Have a group of higher level clients make an adaptation of the Twister game to be played on a table using just hands and arms. Cut 4-inch circles from different colors of art paper and arrange on a piece of poster board in a random order. When making the board, experiment with the spacing because only wrists, hands, fingers and elbows may be used. Instead of a spinner, as used in the commercial version, make two large dice out of wooden blocks and print the challenges on each side. The dice are rolled and the player has to try to follow the directions that are on top of the dice. One of the dice is for the left hand to follow and the other for the right.

Here are some examples of commands that might be used. Both dice have the same directions:

    Thumb on green
    Elbow on red
    Index finger on white
    Little finger on orange
    Wrist on yellow
    Middle finger on black

Tabletop Twister

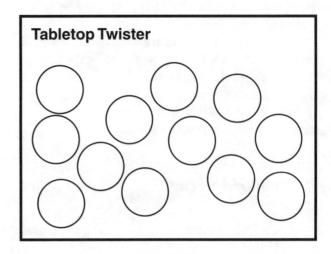

Chapter IV

Something to Talk About

Activities that get the clients talking with one another are often listed as discussion groups, current events, life experiences, travel, or reminiscence. They all have a common goal of encouraging the participants to utilize their mental abilities and to respond in a verbal manner. Sometimes we forget how much effort it may take for an older person to hear the question or information, analyze this material, retrieve the appropriate information, decide on the correct response and to articulate an answer. The process is completed very quickly in a person with no memory impairment, and very slowly for those who have lost some of their mental capacity.

It is important to keep in mind that the more disabled the person's memory, the more difficult it will be for that person to make an adequate verbal response. Also, if more than one sense is being stimulated at the same time, any response will be more difficult for the person with memory impairment. For example, if you hold up a photograph of someone kneading bread while passing a loaf of homemade bread and talking about how to make bread all at the same time, the person with an impaired memory may not be able to verbalize due to the number and variety of stimuli. It is extremely important to know your clients' level of functioning before presenting more than one type of stimuli at a time. It is also important to remember that a visual cue is easier for a mentally impaired person to understand.

Verbal messages are often difficult for these clients to decode. So, for some individuals and/or groups it would be better to simply pass around the loaf of bread without any verbal command or comments and see what happens.

There is usually no problem to recognize quickly the physical limitations of clients with physical dis-

abilities. Too often, however, we equate a lower mental ability with a low physical ability. Many clients who are physically frail are still very active mentally. If people are physically normal for their age, it is sometimes more difficult to easily recognize the level at which they function mentally. For these reasons we suggest that the activities presented in this chapter be utilized with one client at a time (1:1) or with small groups of four to six clients (Sm Grp).

Verbalization Approaches

We often look for new approaches or names for our activities. You may have utilized such titles as Let's Talk, Discussion Group, Current Events, Reminiscence or Remotivation Therapy. Although to some professionals, each activity would focus on a different aspect of verbalization, the main goal would be to have the clients communicate with the staff and other clients. Each of these verbalization activities usually has the same format. The leader introduces the topic and keeps the activity moving along, remembering to have everyone participate and keeping the more talkative one or two people from monopolizing the conversation. The following are some ideas to encourage verbalization. Although it is possible to use some of the activities as competitive events, be careful not to make everything a competition.

Most of the ideas we have included can be used on a one-on-one basis or with a group of six or fewer clients. If used with a group that is too large, individual responses are severely limited. It is better to conduct the same activity twice, for a shorter time period, than trying to have everyone participate in a larger group.

Older people usually love to see their names in print, so write down a few of their answers or stories to post on a bulletin board or publish in the facility's newsletter. Make sure you obtain permission and include the person's name with the quote. This is also a great way to use more clients' names in your publication. Many agencies have the clients' pictures displayed. Try posting one of their quotes by their picture as a way to liven up the display.

Good places to obtain ideas for discussions include *Idea* magazine, *Good Old Days* magazine, *Creative Forecasting, Discussion Topics for Oldsters,* and *Chase's Annual Events.*

Conversation Starters

Favorite Things   1:1, Sm Grp

When the group or an individual is comfortably situated, share some of your favorite things. It even helps to bring a personal object to show to the group members. The following types of questions will help to stimulate their responses about favorite things:

> What is your favorite flavor of ice cream?
> What is your favorite place to travel to?
> What is your favorite season?
> What is your favorite animal?
> What is your favorite fruit?
> What is your favorite dessert?
> What is your favorite holiday?
> What is your favorite color?
> What is the best present you ever received?
> What was your favorite vacation?

Variations:
- Play in categories so that all of the questions relate to the same topic. For example, you could have all of the questions relate to nature, food, travel, holidays, dessert, or family.
- To help the confused clients, show pictures or pass around an object relating to the topic to be discussed. Once the object has been returned to the leader, begin the discussion.
- Utilize a different format than question and answer. For example, you could turn it into a team

competition and the most creative answer from each side receives a point.
- Make it into a board game, in which the person moves a marker around the board answering questions. The spaces are marked with topics, and the player picks a card with a question relating to the topic.

Emotions   1:1, Sm Grp

Emotions encourage the clients to verbalize as well as analyze their feelings. Using photographs, magazine pictures, or a set of cards with characters depicting emotions drawn on them, have the group select which emotion they want to discuss. Ask how many have experienced that emotion and under what circumstances. There are small poster-size photographs available, or you can make your own set of cards with emotions depicted in circles such as a smile, frown, tears or laughter. Have the group make up a story involving one or more emotions. The story can be posted on a bulletin board or placed in the newsletter. Always remember that the clients need recognition for their efforts.

There are now picture books available at bookstores, like the baby pictures by Anne Geddes, which express a variety of emotions. We have found that some confused clients who haven't talked for a time will be able to verbalize when seeing these pictures. The leader should select one picture at a time to use with a confused patient.

Don't forget to follow up even the simple comments with probing questions such as "Why," "When did you do that," "Can you tell us more about it," and "Who was with you at the time?" These are all good follow-up questions which encourage the person to explore the topic more thoroughly. Comments like "That must have been fun," or "I bet you felt good about it," also helps to stimulate further conversation.

What If . . .   Sm Grp

This one requires some thought before answering and often stimulates lively conversation, if the leader exhibits a great amount of interest and enthusiasm. Hopefully, there will be some people who will volunteer an answer, before the leader has to call on those who haven't yet responded. When there are as many as eight or ten in the group, the leader should not attempt to have everyone answer every question. Here are some starter questions for the session:

If you were president, what would you do?

If you were in charge of adding new sports to the Olympics, what would you add?

What sport would you drop if you were in charge of the Olympics?

If you were an inventor, what would you like to invent?

If you could be an animal for a day, what would you be?

If you could blink and be any place in the world for a day, where would you be?

If you were in any place in the world, who would be there with you?

Remember, as leader you should not forget to ask, "Why?" after each response.

Variation:
Use this activity with a higher level group while they are on a walk or exercising to add to the aerobic action.

Have You Ever . . .   Sm Grp

This activity can be serious or silly depending upon the mood of the group. Some participants may even want to make up questions for the rest of the group. Be sure to follow up with the where, when and why questions to stimulate further discussion.

Have you ever . . .

Baked a cake?
Rode a horse?
Planted a garden?
Picked corn?
Picked blueberries?
Made jelly?
Milked a cow?
Shot a deer?
Swam in the ocean?
Walked on stilts?
Cleaned a fish?
Been really scared?

Ridden a motorcycle?
Ridden a bicycle?
Gone on a hayride?
Been to a cornhusking bee?
Ridden a roller coaster at an amusement park?
Flown in an airplane?
Piloted a plane?
Gone up in a balloon?
Lived outside of the United States?

Variation:
This may be used as a competition by giving points to those who have done the activity. Give 10 points if only one person has done the activity, 5 points if two have done it, 2 points if three or more have done the activity.

I'm Glad I . . . or I Wish I'd . . .   Sm Grp

This is similar to the previous activity in that the questions can be outlandish or more fantasy-based. Instead of the leader asking a specific question the leader leaves the question open-ended and asks the clients what they are glad they had done or wished they had done. If the group members are having difficulty getting started, give them categories such as travel, careers, adventures and start them out with a statement of your own such as "I'm glad I've gotten to know you," "I wish I could take a vacation in Hawaii," or "I'm a glad my family lives close enough to visit."

Quickies

One of the hallmarks of successful programming is that there is something for everyone to do from the time they arrive for an activity session until they leave the area where the activity is being held. To make this happen, the leader must have a repertoire of activities that can have a growing number of participants, or that can be used as the number of participants dwindles as people are being transported back to their rooms. The following first-comer activities require no preparation or materials and work with a couple of people or a busload of travelers.

Alphabet Lists   Any Number, First Comer

This is a good activity to use on a bus or while you are waiting for the rest of the group to be transported to an event. It can be used several different ways. Start with the letter *A* and have the group members give as many words as they can beginning with that letter, then move on to *B*. Another version is just to call out a letter. You can also use categories, like trees, flowers, fruit, colors, cities, and rivers. See how many things they can name in a category beginning with each letter of the alphabet.

Unusual Words   Any Number, First Comer

Ask the participants to name the most unusual word they can think of that begins with the letter of the alphabet they have been given at random. With a lower level group start with *A* and go through the alphabet.

Word List   Any Number

This is a good activity for a special day or event as well as a small group activity. Choose a word or phrase that is appropriate for the day or event. Give each player some paper and a pencil. Write the word or phrase on a chalkboard or a large piece of newsprint, in large enough letters that all can see. The object is to see who can make the longest list of words from the letters in the master word or phrase.

Variation:
Instead of having the clients write the words, we often have the people call out the words for us to write on the chalkboard.

Describe Your Favorite   1:1, Sm Grp

Use this one while waiting for group members to gather. Use it on a bus outing or even as a one-on-one activity. Ask the clients to describe their favorite television show, ice cream, animal from the zoo, pet, time of year, holiday, movie, food, dessert, state, child's toy, or restaurant. Any of these can lead to a general discussion. The answers often make interesting items for the facility's newsletter.

Go-Together
Words   1:1, Sm Grp, First Comer

This activity may work well for some of your lower level, but not the lowest level clients. As the leader, you ask them to say a word that goes with the one you give. Use an example like "shoes and stockings."

Here are some suggestions to get you started:

> Ball/Bat
> Pick/Shovel
> Bread/Butter
> Knife/Fork
> Black/White (or Blue)
> Pots/Pans
> Ham/Eggs
> Come/Go
> Pencil/Paper
> Hat/Coat
> Shirt/Tie
> Shoes/Stockings

Opposites   Any Number, First Comer

Give the first word of a pair of opposite words and let the group call out the word that is its opposite. After using a few that you have presented, see if the group members can come up with some pairs.

To get you started, here are some examples:

> Here/There
> Up/Down
> Right/Left
> North/South
> East/West
> Go/Come
> Pitch/Catch
> Far/Near
> Now/Then
> Love/Hate
> Friend/Enemy
> Off/On

Nursery Rhymes, Songs and Poems

Any Number, First Comer

Recite the first line of a song, poem or nursery rhyme and leave off the last word. See if the group can supply the word. After doing a few, ask the group to think of some.

Jack and Jill went up the _____ (hill)
. . . To fetch a pail of _____ (water)
Row, row, row your _____ (boat) . . .
    Gently down the _____ (stream)
Little Miss Muffet sat on her _____
    (tuffet) . . . Eating her curds and
    _____ (whey)
Ring-around-the- _____ (Rosey) . . .
    Pocket full of _____ (posies)
Little Boy Blue come blow your _____
    (horn) . . . The sheep are in the
    _____ (meadow)
Little Bo Peep has lost her _____
    (sheep) . . . And doesn't know
    _____ (where to find them)
Over hill, over dale, we have hit the dusty
    _____ (trail)
Way down upon the _____ (Swanee
    River)
Oh beautiful for spacious _____ (skies)
I think that I shall never see a poem as
    lovely as a _____ (tree)

Animal Quizzes

Any Number, First Comer

This can be done verbally with the leader giving what the female is called and the group calling out what the male is called. It can also be used as a paper and pencil game by duplicating a list of one gender with a blank to be filled in for the other.

Try it out either, or both ways.

What are the male animals called?
    Goose (Gander)
    Doe (Buck)
    Cow (Bull)
    Hen (Rooster, Cock)
    Duck (Drake)
    Sow (Boar)

What are the females called?
    Tiger (Tigress)
    Ram (Ewe)
    Stallion (Mare)
    Fox (Vixen)

What are the babies called?
    Bear (Cub)
    Cat (Kitten)
    Sheep (Lamb)
    Oyster (Set)
    Duck (Duckling)
    Seal (Calf)
    Frog (Tadpole, Pollywog)
    Lion (Cub)
    Swan (Cygnet)
    Goose (Gosling)
    Chicken (Chick)
    Bull (Bullock)
    Hen (Pullet)
    Cow (Heifer)
    Horse (Colt, Foal)
    Cod (Codling)
    Mare (Filly)
    Deer (Fawn)
    Elephant (Calf)

Nicknames

Sm Grp

Have each client think of two words which start with the initials of his or her first and last names which fits his or her personality. If the person cannot think of suitable words, have the group help by asking questions about the person's favorite activities. Have the people try to think of nicknames to describe the staff or their children. This is a simple activity which helps the clients utilize their creative thinking skills. This is one of Judy's father's favorite activities and although she hates to admit it, the nicknames do suit the people. Here are a few of his favorites:

Jerry Elliott—Junk Exotic (He hates to
    throw anything away)
Judy A. Elliott—Just an Exaggeration
    (She tends to enhance her stories)
Michael Brunermer—Mosquito Bite (He
    always has at least one)
Stephanie Brunermer—Seasonal Boo-
    boo (Always gets a bump or a
    scratch)

State Game   Any Number

This is actually a song that we used to sing in summer camp. Some of the clients may remember it. If they don't you can still use it as a quickie game. Give the group the idea of how it is played by asking the question, "What did Dela-ware (wear)?" The answer, of course is another state, "She wore her New Jersey." Here are some more, along with the correct response. They have to be used verbally, or they may not make sense.

> What did Ida hoe? (She hoed her merry land.)
>
> What did Tenny See? (He saw what Arkan saw.)
>
> How did Wiscon sin? (He stole a new brass key.)
>
> How did Flora die? (She died of missery.)
>
> What did Ioe weigh? (She weighed a washing ton.)
>
> What did Mrs. Sip? (She sipped her minni soda.)
>
> Where has Orie gone? (He's gone where Michi's gone.)

There may be more, but these are all we remember.

"I'm in" Stories and Games

This type of activity is for higher level clients. It makes a great first-comer activity, too. As the leader, you explain that you are going to do something that the group is to watch closely. The audience is then invited to replicate the action, one person at a time. If they repeat the words and action correctly, and do it twice in the same manner as the leader, they are then "in." When they are "in," they are cautioned not to divulge the "secret" of the action, but they can repeat it for others and can check new members "in." The clients will enjoy stumping the volunteers and visitors with these.

Johnny, Johnny   Sm Grp, First Comer

The leader demonstrates while saying the words in this order, "Johnny, Johnny, Johnny, Johnny, whoops,

Johnny—Johnny, whoops, Johnny, Johnny, Johnny, Johnny." Make sure that the audience watches every movement closely. To do the action correctly, the person must hold the fingers of one hand extended, with the palm up. Use the forefinger of the other hand to touch the extended little finger, then the ring finger, the middle and then the index finger, saying "Johnny" at each tip. On "whoops" slide the pointing finger down the extended index finger and up to the tip of the thumb where "Johnny" is said again. Now using the same pointing finger and the same extended fingers, reverse the procedure as the "Johnny, whoops . . ." is repeated in reverse. When finished the hands are folded at the waist (this is the "I'm in" part of the game). Many will be able to complete the first part of the action correctly, but will not realize they are to fold their hands at the end. When someone does the action correctly and folds his or her hands at the end, he or she is asked to do it one more time and if he or she does it correctly the second time he or she is told that he or she is "in."

Pass the Pencils   Sm Grp

This is best done with a small group seated in a circle. It is an adaptation of the old parlor game, Pass the Scissors. Instead of scissors we suggest you use two pens or unsharpened pencils. The leader tells the group that the pencils may be passed either crossed (demonstrated by holding them in an X), or uncrossed (hold them side by side). The leader then passes the pencils to the next person, holding them in one of the two positions (at the same time either crossing or uncrossing his or her legs to match the pencils, which is really the action to be watched). As the leader passes the pencils, he or she says, "I pass these pencils crossed" (or "uncrossed") and keeps his or her legs in the correct position while doing so. The person who receives the pencils says, "I received the pencils crossed (or uncrossed, if that is the case) and I pass them uncrossed" (or crossed) and keeps his or her legs in the correct position as the pencils are passed to the next person. The person receiving the pencils may pass them either "crossed" or "uncrossed" and only has to have his or her legs in the correct position when he or she passes them on. If the group members say the phrase correctly and have their legs in the correct position when they pass the pencils, they are "in."

I Know Club　　　　　　　　　　　Sm Grp

The leader starts the game by saying, "If you belong to the club you know about cars, but not about trains." The secret is that if you are in the club you only know about those subjects that *do not* have the letter *I* in them. To become a member the person must say the sentence with two correct words, that have not yet been used.

Examples which meet the criteria for club membership:

> You know about *beavers* but not about *fish.*
> You know about *guns* but not about *shooting.*
> You know about *forks* but not about *knives.*
> You know about *doctors* but not about *clinics.*

Tillie Williams Club　　　　　　　　Sm Grp

The leader says, "Tillie Williams is a friend of mine, she's odd but not peculiar. She likes 'kittens' but she doesn't like 'cats.'" The prospective member must say the sentence correctly using two different things for what she likes and what she doesn't like. Each has to realize without being told that the secret to becoming a member is that Tillie only likes things with double letters (you noticed that both her first and last names have double letters). If each does it twice with different words that no one has used, he or she becomes a member of the club and can test other prospective members.

Some other examples of Tillie's likes and dislikes:

> She likes carrots but doesn't like peas.
> She likes burros but not horses.
> She likes slippers but not shoes

I'm Going . . .　　　　　　　　　　Sm Grp

You start the game by telling the group that you are going on a make-believe trip and would like to take everyone who can figure out what they should take. Then you say the following, "My name is _____ (state your first name). I'm going on a trip and I'm going to take a _____" (something that starts with the first letter of your name).

Each member in the group has an opportunity to say the same sentence using his or her own name and naming an item to take. The item must have the same first letter as the person's name in order for him or her to go with you. Keep going around the group to see how many will learn the secret of the game.

Variations:
- Another version of the game has to do with shopping. The leader says, "I'm going shopping and I'm going to buy _____," naming something that begins with the same letter as the first letter of the leader's name. For highest level clients this is played as an "I'm in" game, and they may or may not be able to "go along."
- A similar activity for lower level clients is to tell them that they can "go" with you, if they can name something that would be appropriate to take along. You can take them "on a picnic," "to the beach," "to the zoo," or "on a boat ride."
- Another version, which is a little more difficult, has the participant having to take something that starts with the same letter as the destination.

The Minister's Cat　　　　　　　　Sm Grp

Like many similar games this one utilizes each letter of the alphabet. The first person says, "The minister's cat is an active cat." The second person changes the word *active* to a word which starts with the letter *B* and the next person uses *C* and you continue until the group has been through the alphabet. If a player can't think of a descriptive word that begins with the letter he or she is to have, let him or her go to the next letter.

Rhyme-Bo　　　　　Any Number, First Comer

The leader starts the game by choosing two words which rhyme such as *boat* and *goat.* The leader says, "I am thinking of a word that rhymes with 'boat.'" The player who guesses goat gets to select the next rhyming pair and lead the game. You can't play this game very long because the group usually runs out of ideas. However, it is a good first-comer activity or a filler between more active games.

Masterminding   Sm Grp

The leader starts by thinking of something which is nearby and visible to the group. The leader indicates whether it is animal, vegetable or mineral. Players then ask questions that can be answered yes or no. The player to guess correctly is the next "it." This is the high-level version of I Spy.

I Spy   1:1, Sm Grp

This is a lower level version of Masterminding. The leader thinks of something in the room that is visible to all of the participants and says "I am thinking of something in this room that begins with the letter _____." The participants try to guess what it is. The leader can tell them they are "warm," "cold," or "hot," indicating how close they are. Where the clients are more mentally alert, the leader should encourage the person who guesses the object to be the next leader.

Variation:
Use "I am thinking of something that is _____" (use a color).

Pig   Sm Grp

We heard a couple of disk jockeys use this with call-in contestants on our local radio station. A participant is given a category such as rivers, states, cities, counties, countries, oceans, baseball teams, football teams, movies, or books. An amount of time is given, say, 20 seconds, for the person to name five names in that category. To play the game, start with the first person in the circle and give him or her a category. After that person has tried to complete the number of names in the allotted time, the next person tries with a new category. The first time a person fails, he or she gets a *P,* and for successive failures, an *I* and then a *G*. The object is to win enough of the time that you don't become a *PIG*. Perhaps you should start by having your "contestants" name only three names in the 20 or 30 seconds you give them to answer.

Variation:
For a lower level group, name one or more items in the category without the time limit.

UBI   Sm Grp, First Comer

Useful or Useless Bits of Information (UBI) are a part of all of our lives and can be a lot of fun. For a higher level group have the clients think of trivia-type questions that not everyone can answer. Questions about local history, places of interest, or sports trivia work well. To get it started, have some UBI questions of your own to ask, or you can announce beforehand that people are to think of a UBI to bring to the group (of course, you will have to explain the term and give a couple of examples). The object of the game is to have one that stumps the group.

Variation:
For a slightly lower level group, the leader should have a list of trivia questions, such as questions about local history or geography.

Magic Tricks   Sm Grp

Some of the higher level clients probably know a few simple tricks they can share with the others. Secure a book on simple tricks from the library and teach some to the clients, so they can share them with the group or with children who might visit.

A Little Preparation

The following activities take a little time for the leader to prepare the materials prior to meeting with the group. We have included some that are useful with lower level clients individually, and others which will only work with small groups of clients that are still very active mentally. Selecting the right activity for the appropriate group is very important.

Modified Charades   Sm Grp

Each person is given a slip of paper which has a topic or a question on it. The topics or questions can relate to food, home remedies, travel, jobs, hobbies, or any other topic listed under other activities in this chapter. Each person takes a turn at either acting out or discussing the topic on his or her slip.

For a higher functioning group, have the participants write a topic on a slip of paper, place the slips in a hat and have each person pick a slip. If they pick their own slip, they have to put it back in the hat and select another. Each person then acts out or discusses the topic he or she picked out of the hat.

Variation:
A variation for this group is to have the participants write on a piece of paper something about themselves that no one else would know (do not sign the slips). Gather the slips of paper and pass them out to other members of the group who then ask leading questions until they match the person with the tidbit of information. We met a person who played a piano in the theater during silent pictures, a professor who wanted to be an undertaker, and the inventor of the York Peppermint Patty while doing this activity.

Weather   Sm Grp

Check the temperature and discuss the forecast. Talk about the differences in weather from the group members' childhood. Have them tell about the worst weather they remember and memories of weather-related incidents, like severe storms, deep snows, and dry summers. See Chapter X, All Natural, for more ideas.

What's Wrong With This Picture?   1:1, Sm Grp

Draw pictures, make paste-ups by cutting out an item that doesn't belong in a scene and pasting it in a picture, or obtain pictures from an educational supply house. Each picture or drawing should include something that doesn't fit with the rest of the scene. Many of the simple ones you can use with lower level clients such as a picture with two or three items that are similar and one that is different. This activity works well as part of an intergenerational program involving older adults and young children.

Life   Sm Grp

There is a commercial board game called Life Stories and another known as Life. Both are fun to play, but they can take more time than your group's attention span will permit. There are also other board games available which encourage a person to explore his or her leisure interests and values. We suggest

that you borrow some of these games from some of the facility's staff and volunteer corps to try with your clients before purchasing any of them for your agency.

When you study these games and have an idea of how they work, create your own board game which will be more suitable for your clientele. Use heavy cardboard and markers to create a road marked off in squares, make large dice or even a spinner to determine how many spaces to move. Cover the board with clear contact paper to make it more durable. Make a number of small cards with a trivia question on each.

After each move the player picks a card and answers the question. If the answer is correct the player moves an extra space. A few cards might say "move an additional square," "move back one," and "free turn." With different sets of cards, the game board can be used for several similar activities.

Password, Trivial Pursuit or Jeopardy   Sm Grp

All of these commercial games can be modified to encourage clients to verbalize. The focus may be on creative thinking, reminiscing or being able to respond to a current event. Each can be used with any of the topic ideas listed previously.

50 States   1:1, Sm Grp

Find a copy of an atlas or dictionary that has information about each state. You will also need a large puzzle map of the United States where each of the states is a piece of the puzzle. Players should take turns identifying the states and placing them in the proper place on the puzzle board. See who can identify the capital, any states which border it, rivers that may run through it, and any major points of interest in the state. See how many can name the countries and bodies of water that adjoin the United States. Find out what the major crop or industry is for each state and maybe the state tree, bird and flower. To make it easier give them a couple of choices on the last three items and see if they can guess the correct answer. The higher the level, the more you can do.

This could be worked into a theme day or it would be possible to study one state for each week. If you can find large print books with the information, have the clients each take a state and share the information with the study group. This activity can become a part of a larger theme program like "Travel the United States." The expense of purchasing an atlas is justified by the number of activities that can be developed with the information available in it.

Adverteasing   Sm Grp, First Comer

There is a commercial game called Adverteasing that has a set of cards which ask the player to identify slogans. If one is available, you will find many uses for it with your group. To make the idea more usable with your people, say, as a first-comer activity, make a list of the slogans to read to the group and see how many of the products they can identify.

Another related activity would be to make a matching game. Make a list of old slogans in one column and a list of products in a second column and give each person a duplicated copy to see how many they can match correctly. Here is a starter list:

"Hasn't scratched yet" (Bon Ami cleanser)
"Chases dirt" (Old Dutch cleanser)
"It floats" (Ivory soap)
"Mm-Mm good" (Campbell's soup)
"Good to the last drop" (Maxwell House coffee)
"Mountain grown" (Folger's coffee)
"Squeezably soft" (Charmin toilet paper)
"It takes a licking, but keeps on ticking" (Timex watches)
"Ask the man who owns one" (Packard automobile)
"When better cars are built" (Buick automobile)
"Reach out and touch someone" (AT&T)
"From contented cows" (Carnation milk)
"Breakfast of champions" (Wheaties)
"When it rains, it pours" (Morton's salt)
"How do you spell relief?" (Rolaids)
"When you care enough to send the very best" (Hallmark cards)
"Double the flavor, double the fun" (Doublemint gum)
"Covers the Earth" (Sherwin Williams paint)
"57 varieties" (Heinz)
"The pause that refreshes" (Coca-Cola)
"The Un-Cola" (7-Up)

"You can hear a pin drop" (Sprint)
"You deserve a break today" (McDonald's)

Variations:
• A similar activity would be to have some of the higher level clients cut familiar trademarks from magazines and newspapers and mount them on cards. Write the name of the product on the back of each card. Hold the cards up and see how many products the group can identify. Whenever possible, use the help of the clients and volunteers to make up cards such as these. Again we remind you, professional staff time should be spent leading activities, not using precious time cutting out pictures or making decorations.
• An advanced group of clients might enjoy developing slogans for various products. Slogans could even be developed for nonexistent products or services.

101 Uses   Sm Grp

This is definitely an activity for people who function fairly high mentally. Once they get the idea, they will have fun using their imaginations. Pass a common item like a paper plate and ask each person to name a use for it, different than the original purpose. The answers can be practical or silly, such as a mask, a hat, a Frisbee, a fan, a wheel cover, a bird feeder—anything is possible. We use such things as a sweeper hose, a golf ball holder, a toilet bowl float, a pair of kitchen tongs and an ice cream scoop to see what ideas for uses the clients can create. This activity can be used fairly often if the items are changed each time.

License Plate Game   Sm Grp, First Comer

This is a good activity to use on a bus trip or an outing, but it is also a good armchair activity. It can either be a pencil and paper activity or you can make up large cards with a vanity license plate message on each one, or you can use a chalkboard. The object is to have the group guess the meanings. Have easy ones first, and then the harder ones. Then have the group make up new ones. The idea is also useful for theme events or as a first-comer activity. Here are some examples of vanity plates that we have seen:

NEQT4ME (Any Cutie for Me)
UCANOE2 (You Canoe Too)
US GRLS (Us Girls)
SUZIEQ (Suzie Q)
TRBLX2 (Double Trouble)
IAM4WI (I Am for Wisconsin)
ARTIST2 (Artist Too)
NO1 DOG (Number One Dog)
JDGMNT (Judgment)
10SNE1 (Tennis, Anyone?)
LZY DZ (Lazy Days)
CANUIST (Canoeist)
ERIE RR (Erie Railroad)
X CUSE (Excuse)
2 NICE 4U (Too Nice for You)
BMPYTK (Bumpy Truck)
IMSOBR (I Am Sober)
BIZ E BE (Busy Bee)
FN WGN (Fun Wagon)

YOU/JUST/ME (Just between you and me)
TIME TIME (Time after time or double time)
M CE, M CE, M CE (Three blind mice)
ME/QUIT (Quit following me)
YE ALONG ARS (Along in years)
JAN 1 JAN 1 (Double date)
/R/E/A/D/I/N/G/ (Reading between the lines)
BAL-LOT (Split ballot)
XQQME! (Excuse me!)
YOU LOOK (Look behind you)
S E A S O N (Open season)
TI STITCH ME (A stitch in time)
HA HAND ND (Hand in hand)
M.D. Ph.D. (Paradox)
DICE DICE (Paradise)
NOON LAZY (Lazy afternoon)
GESG (Scrambled eggs)

Worbles

Sm Grp

We have used this with larger groups at senior centers as a first-comer activity by placing the Worbles on tables for individuals or small groups to "decipher" as they arrive. After everyone is seated, we then hold each card up and let them call out the answers. To prepare for the activity, use a felt-tip pen and put each Worble on a 12-by-16-inch sheet of poster board. Here are some examples and their meanings:

HE'S / HIMSELF (He's beside himself)
SIDE SIDE (Side by side)

To Use or Modify

Don't hesitate to try these ideas with your clients. Some work best on a one-to-one basis, while others work best with a group. Some of your clients will be functioning at too low a level to be able to participate, while others will be functioning on such a high level that the activities would not be appropriate. The leader must determine any modifications necessary to make a given activity appropriate to meet the needs of a client or group of clients being served.

Chapter V

Remember When

Many times the clients remember the past as being a happier time in their lives. A number of them remember the distant past and cannot remember the immediate past. The following reminiscence activities have been found useful in helping to stimulate the clients' memories. We have discovered that while most of the older adults enjoy the reminiscence activities, many are not able to verbalize their thoughts. As a leader you must look for nonverbal signs such as smiles, nods, and hand or even foot movements, that indicate the person has some understanding of what is being shown, discussed, or demonstrated.

Older adults need encouragement to make use of all of their skills, including verbalization and mental acuity. Reminiscence activities provide an excellent approach to stimulating the use of these skills in a nonthreatening manner.

How Do You . . .   Sm Grp

Many people have knowledge of "how to" that can be shared. It usually takes very little prompting to get them started. Sometimes you will get more detail than time will permit, if others are to be given time to participate. You may have to suggest that they continue the description the next time you meet.

So, start with "How do you . . ."

> Can tomatoes?
> Blanch vegetables?
> Make ketchup?
> Butcher a pig?
> Know when to plant peas?
> Plant by the phases of the moon?
> Make shoo-fly pie?

> Start plants in a greenhouse or cold frame?

The questions can be country-based, as the ones are above, or changed to fit the age and home environment of the clientele. For example, "How do you hail a cab?" or "How did you get to work?" would be more appropriate questions for a group based in an urban area.

Home Remedies   Sm Grp

Every family has favorite remedies. When you couldn't get to a store easily, or even if you could, there were always home remedies. Have the group members tell you about the "cures" that were used when they were growing up. Here are some starter questions:

> "What did you do for a stomachache when you were growing up?"
> "What was sassafras tea good for?"
> "Why did so many people take cod-liver oil?"
> "What is a mustard plaster and how is it used?"
> "What was a cure for an earache?"
> "What did you have to take for a physic?"

Although it is best for the leader to know most of the answers before asking these types of questions, be open to their teaching you. Older adults really enjoy feeling useful and pulling one over on the "young" people, so give them a chance to surprise you.

Early Chores   1:1, Sm Grp

Common chore items are shown one at a time and as a person recognizes the chore, for which the item is used, have him or her demonstrate how the item was used and discuss the chore. Choose items suitable to the chores that might have been done by the clients in their young adult years. These are some of the things we have used for this activity:

> Dustpan
> Feather duster
> Shoe polish
> Curling iron
> Washboard
> Curry comb
> Sheep shears
> Nest egg
> Hedge clippers
> Garden hoe
> Hose nozzle
> Oil can

Follow up with such questions as, "What chores did you have to do?" "When did you do them?" "How long did it take to do them?" "What chores did your children have to do?" and/or "Have chores changed since you were young?"

Familiar Places   1:1, Sm Grp

Use pictures of local landmarks such as natural scenes, buildings and monuments that should be familiar. National and international pictures may be used with some clients. Short videos are useful, if available. Care must be taken not to overstimulate the confused client. Ask the client to name the place being shown. Ask if he or she ever visited the place. What was the fartherest place that was ever visited by the client? What other trips were taken? Where did the family like to go the best? What was the favorite vacation spot?

Familiar Tools   1:1, Sm Grp

Show the items one at a time and encourage the client to show how they are used. Even though the lower functioning clients may not be able to speak, they can often demonstrate the motion necessary to the operation. Here are some suggestions of items that we have found useful:

> Carpenter—Hammer, screwdriver, screws, nails, rule, square.
> Homemaker—Measuring spoons, egg beater, scrubber, pancake turner.
> Tailor/Seamstress—Needle, thread, scissors, seam ripper, thimble.
> Mechanic—Wrenches, pliers, drill bits, tire gauge, tire patch kit.

It is important to have the clients hold, or at least touch, the items. If they are able, let them demonstrate and tell how they were used. Such questions as "What was your favorite task?" "How often did you have to do it?" and "What was the most difficult task or the one you liked least?" are examples of ones a leader might ask.

Familiar Sounds   1:1, Sm Grp

You will need a tape player and/or a record player along with tapes or records of familiar sounds. You may purchase recordings or record your own tapes of sounds heard locally. Play one sound at a time to see if the person can identify it. Ask what memories are triggered by the sound. Sounds such as train whistles, truck horns, dogs barking, cows mooing, roosters crowing, birds singing, children playing, and water running over rocks are all good choices.

Many clients have hearing deficits, so mix this activity with others that do not rely so heavily on one's ability to hear these types of sounds.

Thinking Back   1:1, Sm Grp

Start a collection of small antiques or collectible items for this reminiscence activity. Some may be given or loaned by family members or brought in by the staff and volunteers. These items may be used in small group sessions or with individuals. Try to have items that might be familiar to both men and women. The following items are suggested as starters:

> Pressing iron
> Meat grinder
> Apple peeler
> Washboard

Curling iron
Kerosene lamp
Lantern
Bed warmer
Ice tongs
Shoe last
Horseshoe
Hog scraper
Fencing pliers
Smoothing plane
Small car jack

There are several ways to use the items. They may be used as in the Familiar Tools activity described earlier. We like to use them with small groups and pretend that we don't have any idea of what they are or how they were used. By asking simple questions about the item, we soon receive all kinds of information from the group. Questions for the curling iron could be, "How did you heat it?" (over a gas flame, on the cook stove, or over a kerosene lamp), "How did you tell when it was the right temperature?" (wet your forefinger in your mouth and touched the iron; if it "sizzled" it was a little too hot).

Variations:

- For larger groups, the items might be displayed on tables and the participants could go around in twos or threes and look at them. A volunteer could be at each table to ask or answer questions.
- Another use is to display a few of the items in a suitable glass case with a question such as "Do you know what these tools are?" When a family visits, the display might help to stimulate interaction (an answer sheet should be available).
- We've had people at senior centers bring in some obscure attic "treasure" that most people would not be able to identify. Place the items on tables and give each item a number. Give each person a sheet of paper that has lines numbered from one through the number of items on display. Participants go around the tables and write the name of the item by the corresponding number. The same idea would be applicable to a family visitation program in a resident facility.

Pets   1:1, Sm Grp

Pictures of pets, lifelike animal puppets, and toy animals are needed for this activity. Encourage each person to hold the items. Show them how to make the puppets move. Discuss childhood pets. Were they "inside" or "outside" pets? Use questions like "Where did you live?" "What pets did you have?" "What were your pets' names?" "Who took care of them?" "Did any of them have babies?" and/or "What pets did your children have?"

Live animals may frighten the confused client so it is best to start with pictures or stuffed animals with these clients. At first, you may even have to be careful with the lifelike puppets. Later, live animals may be introduced. Having a staff member bring in a well-behaved pet for one day at a time can be a valuable asset to a pet activity.

Many facilities have live-in pets. A well-trained dog, or cat, offers many opportunities for interaction with the residents. The number of pets in a facility should be limited. We have visited several facilities where there were so many pets that they interfered with the daily activities. Rotate the responsibility for feeding the pets among the residents. One word of caution: the staff has to take extra special care, or the residents will overfeed the pets.

School   1:1, Sm Grp

To prepare for this activity you will need to have some of the items that the clients might have used when they attended school. A tablet, eraser, ruler, pencil, hand-held pencil sharpener, chalk, a small chalkboard (like an old-time slate) and some old textbooks will prove useful. Let the clients handle the items and identify them, if they are able. Talk with them about school, where they went to school, how far away they lived, the highest grade that they completed, favorite teachers, best subjects, best friends and the number of students in the class or school. Here are some other questions we have used:

Remember the sound of chalk on blackboard?
How far were you from school and how long did it take you to get there?
How did you carry your lunch and what did you eat?
What did you do after school?

Toys and Games   1:1, Sm Grp

Collect a sample of toys and games from the period when the clients were young. This may be a rather difficult task since many of these items are now collectibles and quite expensive to purchase. You may be able to obtain some on loan from a local historical society, from the staff, or from the clients' families. Such things as dolls, a toy sewing machine, marbles, baseball and bat, toy iron, jump rope, jacks set, large spinning top, a hopscotch layout sketch, and any other early children's game items that can be obtained, are helpful with this activity.

Let the people handle the items, being careful with confused clients handling small items like the jacks. Discuss favorite toys and when they were received. Ask what toys their children had and what friends they played with. Help someone spin the top and have a couple of others turn the jump rope. Ask them the usual questions: "Did you play any of these games?" "What was your favorite game?" "What were some of the rhymes for jump rope?" and/or "What games did boys play that were different from those played by the girls?"

Work Sites   1:1, Sm Grp

Find out what kind of work the clients did and take a small group who had similar jobs to a setting where they can see the tools and machines that were used. Encourage them to tell what is the same and what has changed. Find out what were the hours and the days that they worked. If feasible, have each person do a simple task in the area or watch the workers perform the task. It may be possible to have a local craftsman such as a blacksmith, a woodcarver, or a weaver visit the facility and demonstrate the craft and show some of the items that have been made. Help the confused client on a one-on-one basis to understand what is being demonstrated.

Another possibility is to hold an old-time crafts festival at the your agency.

Hometown   Sm Grp

So many of the clients come from different sections of the town, city or the county that there are many interesting tidbits the clients should remember from growing up in their areas. Ask the families, local historical society, university, or local citizens' groups to help provide additional information. Exhibit any clothing from the time of the clients' youth that families can lend for a display. Have individuals who are capable write stories about growing up, to be shared with the group or in the facility's newsletter. If possible, schedule a "hometown club" to meet and reminisce once a month. It may even be possible to schedule a trip for some of the clubs to take them back to their area and visit with some of the old neighbors, shops, streets, churches and parks. A snack at the local park would also be in order.

Traditional Stories   Sm Grp

Have each person think of a story told in his or her family. As the leader, you should tell a story first and then encourage others to tell a story. The story could be a traditional one or one of an experience of the clients or of someone they knew. Ask the client's family members to recommend stories for you to suggest to the client to get the session started.

Memorable Moments   Sm Grp

Ask the group members to think about some fond memories of earlier years. Start with when they were children. Follow-up sessions could focus on their youthful years, young adult life, or the middle years. Don't try to cover it all in one session!

For the childhood years, ask them to tell about an extremely happy event, or about a time when they were really scared, or a funny thing that happened. The object is to ask in such a way that they will be encouraged to give more than a single sentence response. When working with higher functioning clients, we give them a 5-by-7-inch lined card and ask them to write a short paragraph about a "scary thing" that happened or a "favorite memory" from when they were a child. They are then asked to read their stories to the group at the next session. The best ones could be published in the facility's next newsletter.

Chapter VI

Move It or Lose It

Exercise and the Older Adult

Exercise is one of the most dreaded words in the vocabulary for some people, and a way of life for others. For many older adults, exercise falls into the dread category. The clients' excuses for not exercising can become very inventive. A couple of our favorites are "My doctor told me not to exercise" and "Honey, I am too old to do that young stuff."

The American College of Sports Medicine (ACSM) (they are the experts who decide what is enough exercise) has concluded for "light" exercising, every adult should accumulate 30 minutes of moderate-intensity physical activity every day of the week. That is the minimum amount of exercise a person should obtain through walking, taking stairs, gardening, house cleaning and other daily activities. Although it sounds like a relatively small amount of movement, most of the clients receive the largest percentage of their exercise getting to the eating area and lifting their forks.

If 30 minutes of accumulated movement a day is the minimum, what is better? At least 20–30 minutes of aerobic activity and 10–15 minutes of stretching three times per week is considered to be desirable for the older adult. Unlike other movements, such as bending, stretching, carrying, and reaching throughout the day as done in their earlier years, activities of daily living such as dressing, eating and walking around the room are not demanding enough to constitute "movement." Gardening, walking, dancing, and using the stairs (instead of the elevator) are examples of accumulating movement.

Older adults should engage in strength training exercises, from one to three times a week. Aerobic and strength training exercise sessions must begin with warmup and stretching components and end with a stretching component.

Components of the Exercise Program

Although everyone has heard of the words *flexibility, strength training, aerobics* and *balance,* there may be some confusion over what each of them actually means in relation to the older adult. They can be described as the four components of an exercise program which, if used, will help older adults complete their activities of daily living with less fatigue. Even physically frail older adults have shown improvement in their ability to complete activities of daily living through such an exercise regime. Each component will be discussed in more detail regarding tips, ideas, and safety.

To better understand the meaning of the terms as they relate to exercise for the older adult, we'll examine them individually. To begin with, flexibility is the maximum pain-free range of movement a joint or a series of joints is capable of performing. We improve flexibility by doing stretches for each series of joints and muscles. Stretching is extremely important for the person who has arthritis or limited movement in the joints.

The second component, aerobic activity, aids the cardiovascular systems. Aerobic activity increases the body's ability to efficiently utilize oxygen. This means that the heart and lungs will be strong enough for the older adult to be able to participate in more daily activities without becoming fatigued.

When strength training is mentioned, many people think of the bodybuilder type and cannot imagine this activity for the older person. Strength training is conditioning the muscles to be toned and stronger. Stronger, toned muscles make it easier to maintain balance, and help the person complete daily tasks with less muscular fatigue. Stronger muscles are obtained through either resistance or lifting. That is why this component is often referred to as *resistance training*. Even using light objects such as cans of soup or pint bottles of water helps create the strength a person needs. Elastic tubing can also be used to strengthen the muscles through pulling on the tubing instead of lifting and lowering a weighted object. Stronger muscles are important for the older adult because he or she will be able to complete everyday tasks such as dressing, reaching, sitting, standing and walking with less fatigue of the muscular system.

The final component, balance, has recently been added to the list of important factors for the older adult. Being able to stand without falling to one side and being able to shift weight so the person can walk is a part of balance. Many older people do not realize that practicing shifting their weight from foot to foot in various directions will aid in walking.

Developing an exercise program that includes all four components of flexibility, aerobic, strength training and balance activities is important to help the older person "make it through the day" (complete the activities of daily living) with less fatigue. The stronger the person is physically, the easier it is to recover from a fall or an illness. The following are some of the specific benefits of exercise.

Benefits of Exercise

The exciting news is that more research is being done with older adults, particularly in the area of strength training (generally known as lifting some type of weight). The studies have found that by increasing muscle strength it is much easier for the clients to make it through their Activities of Daily Living (ADLs) with less fatigue, thereby increasing the quality of their lives. Flexibility and balance are other areas researchers are exploring with older adults. The number one goal of an exercise program with older adults is to increase the client's functional capacity. This may not sound like much, but if each step is painful, or raising the arm above shoulder height is

difficult, the person soon begins to do less and less. The less a person moves within a day, the harder it is to move the next day and soon the person becomes fatigued trying to stand up from the chair or walking a few steps to the bathroom. Research has shown that many of the factors we associate with aging, such as weak muscles, stooped shoulders, and increased weight are actually a result of being less active. They have found that prolonged periods of bed rest or long periods of sitting can lead to severe deconditioning. Current thinking is that it will take four to six weeks of activity to restore a person to the level of conditioning prior to one week of prolonged rest. It is also thought that the recovery period after an illness or surgery is shorter for a person who is in better shape, than one who is not. Researchers have found the following benefits of exercise to be true at any age; therefore, when an older person begins to exercise on a regular basis, that person will benefit immediately.

A few of the benefits of maintaining a regular exercise program which includes an aerobic component, a strength training element, and stretching follow:

- increased muscle tone and strength;
- increased blood flow to the organs;
- increased range of motion (ROM);
- improved balance and mobility;
- increased aerobic capacity for the heart and lungs;
- a sense of accomplishment;
- reduction in stress, anxiety and depression;
- less focus on the negative and an improved positive mood; and
- improved functional capacity in activities of daily living.

The Exercise Leader

Recreation professionals are sometimes hesitant to lead exercise sessions because they do not feel qualified. However, in most facilities caring for older adults, if the recreation professional does not lead the exercise sessions, the clients will get no exercise.

Programs often rely on the physical therapists (PTs) to provide clients' exercise. In actuality, the physical therapist has such a heavy schedule of individual therapy that there is no time to supervise 30 minutes of accumulated activity for each client on a daily basis. Therefore, recreation departments must schedule leaders to hold one-on-one and group exercise sessions in order to meet the physical needs of the clients.

Many therapeutic recreation professionals have the education, experience, and a strong interest in exercise science, and are comfortable leading such programs. This chapter may help you by reinforcing the concepts you have learned and the methods you are using.

If you are not now comfortable leading exercise sessions, utilize the material in this chapter to help you get comfortable. Use the resources of your physical therapist or an exercise specialist to help you plan your program to be certain that it is safe and effective.

There are many videos on the market relating to exercise and older adults. Some focus on specific conditions such as arthritis while others emphasize exercise position and technique. Videos are a great source of how to complete a movement and can be an essential teaching tool for the staff. However, a word of caution. Some videos contain exercises that should not be done by older adults such as neck circles, or any exercise that tilts the head back. *Videos should be utilized as a teaching tool for the staff, not to show for the clients to follow.* A video might work well for a person who is exercising at home, but most of the clients we are talking about will be exercising with trained personnel. No matter what anyone tells you, the clients will watch the video instead of exercising. They may make a few token movements, but that does not last long. Even with the staff encouraging participation, it's difficult for the clients to watch a video and complete the movement. It is much better to have a leader who knows the movements, and can slow them down to the clients' level, actually lead the exercise session.

The exercise leader plays an extremely important role in motivating the clients to participate. If the leader is unenthusiastic and/or not confident, then the clients are less likely to participate. The clients must feel like they are an integral part of the group before they will fully participate. An enthusiastic leader who seats everyone in a circle, addresses clients by name and keeps the session interesting by offering a variety of movements is more likely to hold the clients' interest than one who plays a videotape. We have observed video "exercise sessions" where the only activity was on the screen since most of the clients had fallen asleep. Those who weren't dozing got up and left the room. The daily schedules should have shown this as a "rest period" instead of an "exercise period." On the other hand, we have been to facilities where the clients start to arrive for an exercise session 30 minutes early because they enjoy the program and its variety.

It is great to use props such as broomsticks, exercise bands, scarves and various size balls for exercise sessions, but remember, everyone must be able to be involved at all times. If the leader spends time tossing a ball back and forth to each individual client, the others lose interest. It is best to have enough balls so everyone can work the hand muscles, such as squeeze and release, or the arm muscles by lifting a ball overhead and lowering it as far as possible. The key to a successful exercise program is an enthusiastic, highly motivated, knowledgeable leader who uses a variety of exercise activities to help the clients reach their potential.

Tips for the Exercise Leader

- Review exercise videos for appropriate exercises.
- Don't expect the clients to follow an exercise video.
- Seat everyone in a circle or semicircle to facilitate an inclusive environment.
- Encourage socialization before and after the sessions; nametags may be helpful.
- Exhibit enthusiasm and exaggerate the movements.
- Make sure all wheelchair locks are engaged.
- Increase the work load within the exercise session in small increments.
- When using props, have enough so everyone can participate at the same time.
- Avoid individual ball toss and catch, as others get tired waiting their turn. Ball toss and catch is a good activity, if there are enough volunteers to have several balls being tossed and caught at once. If there isn't enough help, use ball toss during a games session versus an exercise session.
- Clients like and need repetition to their movements; however, watch that it doesn't become boring.
- Avoid using "right" and "left"; this is one more thing for the client to figure out.
- Have them follow your movements; don't worry about them learning the movements.

- Avoid exercises that might cause injury.
- Continue a movement for a minimum of 16 counts (32 counts if working with confused clients).

Motivation

Every day on television or radio or in a magazine or newspaper there is some encouragement to exercise, yet Americans are more sedentary than ever. Children are at an all-time high in terms of obesity rates. If this is the case with the general public, how can one expect to get an older person who has not exercised in years to begin moving? How often have you said or heard someone say, "I am going to start exercising tomorrow?"

The first step is to realize that not everyone is motivated in the same way and not everyone likes to exercise in the same manner. For example, Jerry loves to bike, hike, canoe, cross-country ski, and work in his workshop, but don't ask him to go for a fitness walk or lift a weight. Yet, daily he practices the same movements of bending, twisting, and lifting with his activities that Judy does lifting her weights and going on her walks. Judy looks at canoeing as a way to get exercise, Jerry looks at it as a way to enjoy nature.

Many older adults think that exercise can be harmful. Fear of falling is often the number one excuse for not exercising. Clients need to learn that exercising can increase balance and mobility, helping to prevent falls. People who exercise are less likely to be injured if they do fall. One approach to involving clients in exercise is to have the doctor encourage participation or tell them they are part of a research study and helping someone else. In many cases, the staff will be able to involve a variety of clients within the regular exercise session simply by calling the program something other than an "exercise class."

If *exercise* is a deadly word, try making the activity sound like a recreational pursuit such as enjoying nature on a walk. There are still many clients with an extremely strong work ethic. This may mean creating an environment in which the activity appears more like work. One agency combines trivia with exercise. The agency's clients love trivia and hate to exercise. They have to complete two exercises then they get to answer a trivia question. Other leaders find that interspersing activities like those in Chapter IV, Something to Talk About, with the exercise activities makes the session more enjoyable.

Very few older people are motivated by the sheer joy of movement. Once the individuals begin feeling the increased mobility that is a result of exercise, they will become motivated because they feel so much better. Get them moving today instead of waiting until they feel like moving, which may or may not be tomorrow.

Overall Tips for Conducting an Exercise Program

Before beginning any exercise activity with an older adult, the client's physician must give written permission for the client to participate in the activity.

Older adults:

- Often take medications which can cause side effects such as dizziness when exercising. Check with the physician regarding medications and side effects.
- Often have high blood pressure; therefore, blood pressure should be taken before and possibly during the exercise session. This is especially true of a person with irregular blood pressure.
- Cannot tolerate heat as well as younger people because the sweat glands decrease production as a person ages. Keep the room at a comfortable temperature.
- Should utilize the rest room before beginning the exercise session, because having to urinate while exercising can raise the blood pressure.
- Have less total body water and are prone to dehydration. Make sure there is plenty of water to drink. Encourage the participants to drink before, during, and after the exercise program.
- Should wait at least one hour after eating before exercising.
- Worry about losing their balance. Conduct the session seated unless the clients are functioning at a high enough level to stand; even then, keep a chair close by for comfort and balance.
- Should use hardback chairs for support while exercising instead of sitting on sofas or overstuffed lounging chairs.

- Should limit the amount of time their arms are overhead, or higher than their shoulders, especially if they have any heart or lung diseases and/ or conditions.
- Should keep their arms moving when overhead, versus in a stationary position.
- Have difficulty coordinating body parts. Work arms and legs separately, except for activities such as running in place (they can simulate running in place while seated by moving their feet and arms as if jogging).
- Have a tendency to fatigue easily. Allow for longer rest periods between individual exercises.
- Need more time to warmup and cool down.
- Prefer the leader to face the group.
- Are more likely to participate through the entire session when the group is arranged in a circle or semicircle formation.
- Like to do exercises to music with a strong beat.

Flexibility, Aerobic, Strength Training and Balance

Flexibility

Most exercise research has focused on the aerobic component. In the past few years, the benefits of strength training have been added. Only recently have studies been done to examine the role of flexibility. Flexibility is the maximum range (pain free) of movement a joint or a series of joints is capable of performing. This movement is dependent on how well the tendons and ligaments function as well as the ability of the muscles to reach a fully stretched position. The overall amount of a person's joint mobility determines how comfortably the person will be able to complete an exercise movement. Maintaining a high level of flexibility also helps to reduce the potential of injury from falls during everyday life. For example, a person with a higher degree of flexibility is able to absorb the unusual body movements during a fall more than a person with limited flexibility. Flexibility can be improved through consistent range of motion and stretching exercises.

Range of motion exercises allow a person to move a joint through its fullest movement possible. Ex-

amples of range of motion exercises are non-weight-bearing ankle and arm circles, waist bends and shoulder rolls. A person can improve flexibility at any age. It is essential for a person with arthritis to complete these movements in order to keep the joints moving. Stretching exercises are done to keep the muscle fibers pliable and to help the person exercise without strain. Stretching is best done after a warmup activity such as walking and/or marching in place while moving the arms for a minimum of five minutes.

Any activity that takes the joints through an appropriate range of motion will stretch the surrounding muscles. A good flexibility program allows you to accomplish your everyday activities with ease. Examples of common stretching exercises are turning the head from side to side, tilting the head slowly from side to side, and shoulder shrugs. Traditionally we have thought of stretching before we begin any aerobic activity; however, current research has determined that a brief period of walking should precede the stretching. To avoid muscle strains and pulls, warmup briefly before doing stretching exercises, then do the aerobic activity, remembering to finish the session with additional stretching movements.

Tips for Stretching

- Stretch after the muscles are warmed up by walking.
- Stretch every major joint area (chest, arms, legs, shoulder, neck, etc.).
- Hold a stretch for up to 30 seconds.
- Perform each stretch three to five times.
- When stretching, the muscle should feel slight tension, but no pain.
- Avoid any bouncing, swinging or fast rotating movements.
- Stretch after completing the other exercises to prevent muscle stiffness after the workout.

Aerobic Activity

Aerobic activity increases the body's ability to utilize oxygen. Any activity that raises the heart rate for an extended period of time is considered aerobic. The activities that come to mind most frequently are swimming, running, walking briskly, cross-country skiing and aerobic dance. In order for the heart and lungs to benefit from aerobic exercise, the older person should be exercising within his or her target heart rate.

It is difficult for most older adults to reach and sustain an elevated heart rate for 20–30 minutes. Although an aerobic component is desired, a 10–15 minute period is a more realistic goal for this population group. Activities that will raise the heart rate in older adults include walking, marching, jogging motions while seated, simulating the conducting of an orchestra, or punching an imaginary punching bag. To increase the amount of aerobic activity, have the clients sing while completing the movements. Have the client sit in a chair and walk, run, and/or march in place if there is a problem with balance.

To determine if the older adult is exercising within the proper target heart zone, his or her pulse should be taken at the wrist. This is often difficult because the pulse of an older person is often hard to find. There is a tendency to want to take the pulse at the carotid artery in the neck. *Taking the pulse at the neck is dangerous and should be avoided!*

Instead of using the pulse rate to determine whether or not the clients are working within their target heart rate zone, it is recommended that the Borg Rate of Perceived Exertion Scale be utilized. At each exercise session have the clients rate themselves on how intensely they feel they are exercising. This is called their rate of perceived exertion (RPE) and is measured on a scale of 1 to 10.

The Borg RPE scale measures exercise intensity on a scale of 1 to 10, with 1 equal to very weak and 10 equal to very, very strong. Research has shown that if the clients report a perceived rate of exertion of between 4 (somewhat strong) and 6 (strong), they are exercising within their target heart zone (Rimmer, 1994, p. 11). The client should be able to talk comfortably while continuing to exercise. Several times during the session the client should be reassessed to determine if an optimum level of exertion is being maintained.

Tips for Aerobics

- Never take a client's heart rate at the carotid artery as this can restrict the blood supply to the brain and cause dizziness.
- Use the "talk test" to determine if they are exercising at too high a level. They should be able to converse easily with the leader during the exercise program.

- The aerobic portion of the program should be completed after a warmup period and prior to a cool down period.
- Teach the clients how to use the rate of perceived exertion (Borg RPE) scale.
- Ask the participants their RPE several times during the exercise session.

Balance Exercises

Balance is an area that exercise professionals are just beginning to explore. There appears to be a connection between balance, flexibility and strength. The older adult is usually afraid of falling and so begins to limit his or her amount of movement by taking smaller steps and walking slower as a preventative measure. Within a short period of time the person's balance, flexibility and strength are reduced, making a fall more likely. The reduction in strength makes it more difficult to get up after a fall. Medications and medical conditions can also affect a person's balance. Motor skill and coordination as well as balance are affected when a person begins to limit movement. Because the body is not flexible and strong enough to absorb the shock when a fall occurs, the person is more likely to be injured. Balance appears to play an important role in this cycle. A person with better balance is able to compensate when his or her body weight is shifted due to an uneven surface such as a pebble or some other factor. With practice a person can improve both his or her standing and walking balance. It is important to practice a wide variety of movements that relate to balance.

Tips for Balance Exercises

- Start balance exercises utilizing both hands on a chair for support and then practice with using one hand on a chair or wall before trying the exercises without any means of support.
- Use a volunteer or staff member to watch that the older adult does not lose balance when beginning balance exercises.
- Make sure the clients have warmed up before working on balance activities; they are best completed after an aerobic portion of the program.
- Complete each movement at least three to five times to reinforce the action.

- Practice with each foot being the lead foot.
- Break down a movement that involves shifting body weight into smaller parts so that it is easier for the client to perform.
- Remind the clients to tighten their buttock muscles when shifting weight in order to maintain body alignment.
- Have the clients use good posture when standing and sitting.
- Use movements that are done forward, backward, side-to-side and diagonally in order to reinforce moving around objects and on uneven surfaces.
- Progress from being able to stand and balance, to being able to walk, then finally on to being able to reach for an object and walking around obstacles.

Resistance (Strength) Training

When the terms *strength training* or *weightlifting* are mentioned, the image of bulky muscular people comes to mind. These individuals lift an enormous volume of weight for several hours on a daily basis to gain those muscles.

Strength training for older adults is used to strengthen the muscles in order to help the client complete everyday tasks. Researchers have found that older adults who have been involved in weight training exhibit increased mobility, muscle tone and balance, which translates to fewer falls and a decrease in the potential for certain injuries. The strength training component may be done utilizing various modes of resistance such as a piece of elastic band.

There are many commercial types of elastic resistance bands available from those with a very light resistance to ones with a much heavier resistance. Various lengths are also available. One-liter water bottles or one-quart milk jugs half full of water weigh about one pound and can be used in place of commercial weights. As the clients progress, water can be added to the containers to make two-pound weights. Two-quart containers can be used for weights up to four pounds. If vinyl-covered weights are available, they may be preferred to elastic bands or jugs of water. Small vinyl-covered weights (1 to 5 pounds) are available for reasonable prices at various sporting goods and discount department stores.

Tufts University researchers asked nursing home residents (average age 87) to participate in an exercise program on weight machines three times a week. The participants of the exercise program increased their walking speed by 48 percent and leg strength by over 170 percent. In another 6-week, 3-times-a-week study of 60- to 90-year-old nursing home clients, the researchers found significant gains in strength, speed and endurance (Rimmer, 1994, p. 30).

The type of older adults this book is designed for will never be lifting large amounts of weight. However, even people who seem frail and are confined to wheelchairs can participate in these exercises. How the movement is completed is extremely important in strength training. Whether the client is using jugs, bands or weights, good posture is essential. Although there are a few exercises listed in the next section, this list is by no means complete. Consult with an exercise specialist or a physical therapist and read additional material on strength training before adding this component to the exercise program.

Tips for Strength Training

- The stretching portion of the program should precede the strength training portion.
- Use light weights—plastic drink containers partially filled with water are a good way to start.
- Make sure the clients maintain normal breathing during the exercises (they have a tendency to want to hold their breath).
- Complete the exercise taking the muscle through the full (pain-free) range of motion.
- It is better to do more repetitions with lighter weights than a few repetitions with heavier weights (10–15 repetitions are recommended by the ACSM for anyone over 50 years old).
- Watch that the person is exhibiting good posture throughout the exercise.
- Avoid holding weights and completing an aerobic component at the same time. For example, do not have the client hold weights and march in place.
- Engage in a year-round program on a regular basis. Older adults should use some type of resistance training at least one time a week and a maximum of three times a week.
- Make certain that movements are completed in a slow, controlled motion.

- Where possible, utilize resistance training machines, such as Nautilus, versus free weights, because the machines will make the person use the correct posture.

The Exercise Session

It may seem as though setting up an exercise program is a difficult task. It could be, if you try to have everything in place for the entire program before you start the first session. However, if you have the general idea of what you want the program to include, it can be planned like any of the other recreation programs—one or two sessions at a time.

There are relatively few exercise specialists who have the experience working with the type of older adults we are working with, especially the mentally impaired and physically frail clients. But, do consult them when possible, for their experience and expertise in the field of exercise science is valuable. It is important to involve the clients in activities that increase flexibility, mobility, balance, coordination, and strength. Although most of the recreation professionals know a great deal about the client, we often know relatively little about the mechanics of an exercise as well as those of the human body. Try to establish an agreement with an exercise specialist. Teach him or her about the strengths and needs of the older adults, while he or she teaches you about exercise and body mechanics.

The main thing to remember while planning the exercise program is that an exercise session is most beneficial to the clients if it follows a format similar to this:

- Greeting/introduction;
- Warmup
- Stretching (flexibility)—at least one exercise per muscle group;
- Aerobic activity and/or strength (resistance) training;
- Balance exercises;
- Stretching (flexibility);
- Cool down; and
- Closing/thank you.

Exercises to Avoid

There is an impressive amount of research being done in the field of exercise and its benefits for older adults. Recreation professionals need to keep up-to-date with the current findings if they are to provide a program that is of the greatest benefit to their clients. Because an exercise is used in a video or in a manual does not mean that it is suitable for use with older adults. That is why we are including a list of practices that should be avoided because they are harmful to the participant:

- Tilting the neck back (lowering the neck forward is okay).
- Fast arm circles (keep them slow and controlled).
- Any fast swinging arm or leg motions (slow and controlled is the rule).
- Bouncing in a stretch (hold all stretches motionless).
- Forcing a person's muscles to stretch further (hold at a comfortable stretch).

Exercise Session Suggestions

This section gives the recreation professional some exercises and movements to utilize with older adults. It is in no way a complete list. Always remember, if a movement is painful or uncomfortable it is not a good movement for the clients. If it causes any dizziness, lightheadedness or a loss of balance, stop doing the exercise. The clients will let you know if something is not comfortable.

As previously discussed, older adults should exercise on a regular basis. Exercise sessions should be held three times a week for a period of 45 to 60 minutes. Since older adults do best with a routine, the format of each session should include a greeting, a warmup, stretching, aerobics, balance exercises, strength training, stretching, cool down, and closing.

The warmup should be a minimum of five minutes with the stretching portion being a minimum of five minutes also. You should aim for a 15–20 minute aerobic portion, although 10 minutes for a beginner class is more realistic. Follow with a 10–15 minute strength training component, then five minutes each of balance, stretching and cool down exercises. These are suggested times, and you will need to determine the best timing for your clients.

If the program goal is to increase flexibility and balance, a larger portion of the program will be devoted to the warmup, stretching, balance and cool down periods. Remember, people who have been exercising will be able to tolerate a longer and more intense session than those who are just beginning.

Exercise programs seem to work best if they are scheduled for six- to eight-week periods. At the end of that time, give the participants a certificate for completing "Exercise I" and begin another group of sessions called "Exercise II" (or use any creative name that works for your clientele). This helps the clients feel they are really accomplishing something, and they won't feel they are signing up for a lifetime commitment to exercise sessions. New clients may want to join the group and will feel inadequate if they feel the group is too advanced. Offer beginner and open house sessions on a regular basis to encourage new members. The following are suggestions for the various segments of your exercise sessions. Be sure to review the tips for exercising material before utilizing the exercises.

Greeting

Each session should begin with a greeting and an introduction of the instructor as well as each of the group members. Any health concerns that might interfere with the exercise program should be discussed. If taking resting heart rates or blood pressures, they should be administered at this time.

Warmup

When working with older adults in a warmup, it is important to begin slowly and progress to a faster pace within the session. For example, begin to walk slowly without the arms moving, then begin to move the arms with the legs, then after a few minutes increase the speed of the walking. Warming up with mild cardiovascular activity increases the blood flow to the tissues and increases the body temperature, therefore reducing the chances of injury during the stretching and flexibility phase. This warmup phase should last approximately five minutes. Remember, this is to be mild cardiovascular activity to prepare the body for a more strenuous work session. Here are some suggested activities for the cardiovascular warmup segment:

- Walk, swinging arms gently (walking can be done in place or seated).
- March, arms moving gently up and down (marching can be done in place or seated).
- If clients cannot coordinate arms and legs, have them use their legs, then their arms.
- If seated, run in place, moving arms.
- Jog in place just using an arm motion or use an arm ergometer (it is like a set of bike pedals for the arms).
- Punching motion with arms (make certain the motions aren't "jerky").
- If seated, pull with both arms as if using a rowing machine.
- Conduct an orchestra, using both arms.

Stretching and Flexibility

When stretching with older adults, complete at least one exercise per muscle group. The following stretches are written for the client who is seated. Complete each stretch slowly three to five times. Focus on the muscles where tightness is common such as the shoulders, thighs, hips, calves, and ankles. Women should pay attention to stretching and strengthening the upper back muscles because they have a tendency to have rounded shoulders. It is important to encourage all of the clients to sit erect.

Many older adults can walk, but have difficulty with standing. They may be lacking the flexibility, strength, and/or balance to stand up. This segment of stretching may vary in terms of time, based upon the type of clientele and how many weeks this group has been exercising. Here are some helpful stretching activities:

- Nod head forward and back into place (do not tilt head back).
- Turn head from side to side as if to say, "No."
- Slowly tilt head from side to side, as if you want to place your ear onto your shoulder.
- Raise both eyebrows and lower.
- Open eyes wide, close, then open and look right and left.
- Push eyebrows down and release.

- Yawn wide, with mouth open, move jaw right and then left.
- Wrinkle your nose.
- Make strange faces like filling cheeks with air and blowing it out.
- Shoulder shrugs.
- Bend arm across chest, grasp the elbow of the bent arm with the other hand, and slowly pull to stretch the bent arm to feel the stretch at the shoulder. Reverse and stretch the other side.
- Bend arm and raise it over head, grasp the elbow with the other hand, gently pull the bent arm toward the back of the head. Keep the bent arm as close to the ear as possible. This is stretching the under side of the upper arm.
- Close and open fingers.
- Touch each finger on each hand to the thumb and release.
- Bend and flex the wrist gently.
- Turn slowly from side to side at the waist.
- Slowly tilt from side to side at the waist.
- Bend from waist as if to touch toes.
- Flex and point the toes.
- Ankle and wrist rotations.
- Buttocks hold.
- Feet flat on floor, turn toes out as if duck footed, then turn as if pigeon-toed.
- Slowly stand up, and then sit back down. Complete the movement several times slowly. Work up to being able to stand up and sit down 10 times. This is an excellent activity for those clients who can walk but need to strengthen their leg muscles.

Aerobics

It is difficult for many older people to work hard enough or move quickly enough to raise their heart rate very much. It is also difficult to obtain an accurate heart rate as it is difficult for the leader to get around the room quickly enough to take the clients' heart rates. It is also more difficult to hear an older person's heartbeat without a stethoscope.

Never take an older person's heart rate at the carotid artery as the pressure from the fingers can lower the person's heart rate too quickly, limiting the flow of blood to the brain and causing dizziness.

Although many older adults can take their own heart rate, others may create a number based on the number given by the person beside them. A better way to determine whether or not the client is overworking is to utilize the Rate of Perceived Exertion (RPE) as explained earlier under Tips for Aerobics.

While seated, the aerobic component can include:

- Marching, running, or walking in place.
- Marching Band or group-developed routines to march music. Can use homemade pompoms to combine arm movements with marching. Clients can march for a portion of the song, then use arms for a portion if they cannot coordinate both.
- Holding onto the sides of the chair, alternate kicking one leg then the other.
- Pushing both arms forward from chest, and pulling them back in.
- Punching a pretend punching bag.
- Rowing a boat.
- Jogging, with arms or with legs only. Use in combinations, if possible.
- "Image" exercises—which are listed under a separate heading—can often be utilized as an aerobic activity without the client thinking about exercising.

Balance Exercises

Balance activities are new to the exercise program, but an extremely important addition to the session, especially for older adults in terms of being able to stand, walk, and transfer. *Balance exercises may be the most important portion of the session for your clients.* Remember, it is important to divide the following activities into small segments and remind the clients to hold onto something, at first.

Repeat each activity several times, remembering to give each foot an opportunity to be the lead foot and rest about 10–20 seconds between exercises. In some ways, these exercises take more concentration than many of the others. It may be best for some groups not to play music during this section. Here are the activities:

- Stand holding onto the back of a chair, shift weight from one foot to the other without lifting the foot off of the ground.
- Walk in place, trying not to hold onto the chair. A more advanced move would be to walk around the chair.

- Stand with both feet slightly apart, weight distributed evenly (starting position), slowly point one toe forward, then back to the neutral position. Complete several times, then repeat with the other foot. Work toward being able to lift the foot off of the floor slightly.
- Use the same starting position as above, but point the toe to the back and return, each foot in turn.
- From the same starting position, point to side and return with each foot.
- From the same starting position, point diagonally to the front with each foot and return.
- From the same starting position, shift the weight to one foot, lift the other foot slightly to the front and hold, then back to place. Repeat using the other foot. Repeat with each foot, lifting to the back and to the side.
- From the same starting position, step to the side, bring other foot beside the first. Cue by saying, "Step, together, step." Reverse to the other side. Then do the same thing stepping forward. A more difficult version is to do this step to the rear.
- From the same starting position, slowly lift foot off of the floor, bending the knee, lift knee to a comfortable height; work toward being able to lift the foot as high as the chair seat.

Strength Training

The following are a few examples of strength or resistance training exercises for older adults, and please remember this list is not exhaustive. Review the section on strength training for important tips such as reminding the clients to breathe, starting with very low weights, such as plastic water or milk containers (with very little water in them). Review the material on tips for exercising before utilizing the following exercises:

- Bicep curls (arms down at side, slowly bend the elbow bringing the weight up to the shoulder and then lowering).
- Shoulder press (weights at shoulder height, elbows down, slowly lift arms overhead and lower).
- Front raises (arms by side, slowly lift straight arm forward until it is at chest height and lower slowly).
- Wheelchair push-ups. This can be done in an armchair or wheelchair. With wheelchair locked, hold onto the arms of the chair with elbows bent, slowly straighten arms and tighten buttocks, hold for three seconds, then rest. Repeat 5 to 10 times. This helps to maintain the muscles that are needed for standing and transferring.
- Broomstick windup. Use a 12-inch section of broomstick with an 18-inch cord attached to the middle of the stick. Attach a small plastic jug to the other end of the string (see illustration). Rotate the stick to make the string roll up until the bottle gets to the stick. Add resistance by filling the jug with sand or water.

J. H. Rimmer's *Fitness and Rehabilitation Programs for Special Populations* is an excellent resource specific to working with older adults in all forms of exercise and specific medical conditions. A. Feinstein's *Training the Body to Cure Itself* has clear sketches of various exercises being performed which are useful to the elderly population. Complete references for these titles can be found in the Bibliography.

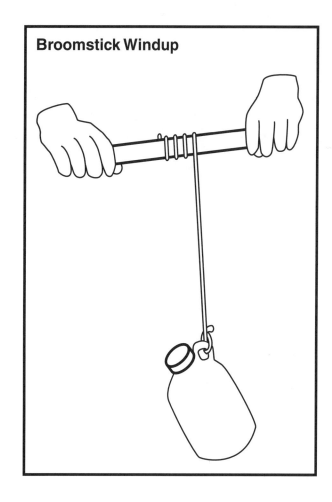

Broomstick Windup

Cool Down

Cool down exercises can be some of the image exercises listed later in this chapter and/or the activities in the aerobic section. The music should get progressively slower and more relaxed as this segment continues. Many clients enjoy imaginary trips to the beach, or some other place they find relaxing, and pantomiming the activities that would be associated with the area.

Stretching Cool Down

Complete some of the stretches from the earlier stretching section. The clients will enjoy the repetition from the beginning of the session. Try to vary the stretches from session to session to hold the clients' interest. These stretches may be added into the cool down section and done to very soothing music. The following are additional ideas to incorporate into the exercise program.

Music

Music can help to motivate clients to participate and to add enthusiasm for an exercise program. Music helps the clients establish a rhythm and forget they are exercising. The music should be upbeat and have a strong central beat. Some of the old-time songs like "If You Knew Susie" and "I'm Looking Over a Four Leaf Clover" are great because clients can sing along which increases the aerobic activity. A combination of songs with words and those without works well. Since reaction time for most older people is slow, the action should be repeated for at least 16 beats to give them time to internalize the action and to do it several times.

The confused client can usually only concentrate on one type of stimuli at a time. Since exercise is the main thrust of the program, try eliminating the music if the clients are not participating. If the clients continue to sit and watch, try eliminating voice commands and use body motions to demonstrate what the person should be doing. It may be necessary to complete every movement in a count of 32 beats instead of 16 because it takes confused clients much longer to catch onto the exercise. A routine approach to the program is imperative for the lower functioning client.

Image Exercises

Image exercises are completing movements that look more like charades, but everyone does them at the same time and they often do not realize they are exercising. Although many of these everyday moves are generally completed on only one side of the body, make sure the clients complete them on both sides. These exercises encourage their creative thinking abilities. Some of the image exercises work best in the aerobic section of the program while others might be better used in the stretching or warmup section. Analyze the movement in order to determine where it is best suited for your program. Image exercises can be used as a part of a discussion group or a dramatics group as well.

Some great image exercises that often bring a chuckle are:

- Beauty Queen (or King)—You have just been elected the queen (or king) of _____ (they decide of what) and you are riding in a fancy car (have them decide type) and you have to wave to all of the parade watchers, make sure you wave to both sides of the street.
- Gymnast—You have just completed a perfect _____ (have them fill in the blank) and your score was a perfect 10, so sit up tall, raise your arms over your head, arch your back slightly, lift your head high and beam at the judges.
- Golf Swing—This is the opportunity of a lifetime—you have a chance to play _____ (add the name of the golf course), you are on the fairway of the _____ (add hole), swing that club and hit that ball. Try it on the other side. Did you get a hole-in-one?
- Band Leader—Lead the band using the hands, unsharpened pencils, or short pieces of $3/_{16}$-inch dowel cut into 12-inch lengths as batons.
- Fly like a bird.
- Row your boat across a lake.
- Play an important concert on the piano (or pick another instrument).
- Tennis anyone?
- Baseball Game—Pitch, swing, catch and run in place to home plate.
- Flip pancakes.
- Construct a building—Saw wood, hammer nails, and lift heavy beams.
- Punch whatever brings stress into your life.

- Hygiene—Wash up for supper—don't forget the hands, arms, face and behind those ears! Put on aftershave lotion or perfume.
- Climb a very high ladder.
- Wake up—Big yawn, stretch and get dressed for the day.
- Cat—Stretch like a cat, scratch at a post, bat at a string.

Using Props

One of the best things about using props is that the clients forget they are exercising. They tend to concentrate on the prop instead of the exercise. Of course the opposite is true too, clients may be paying more attention to the prop and will not watch their form. If the client is confused, it may be difficult for him or her to use a prop and follow an exercise at the same time. There are many possible props including ribbons, scarves, squeeze balls, dowel rods and/or clay. Try not to utilize too many props within the same session. Just a few of the many ideas follow.

Balls

Small soft balls can be used for finger exercises such as squeezing the ball for finger mobility and lifting the ball with the toes. A larger ball can be held in both hands off to one side. Keeping elbows straight, slowly move the ball down through an arc in front and up the other side. Reverse. Balls can be passed or tossed to another participant for exercise. Make sure everyone has a ball in order to maintain participation. The stress reliever balloons work well here.

Brooms or Dowel Rods

Some people like to complete stretches, particularly waist tilts, from side to side utilizing a 3- or 4-foot piece of broomstick. An alternative to the heavier broomstick is a 3-foot length of $1/2$-inch dowel rod or $3/4$-inch PVC pipe. The pipe is much easier for the arthritic client to hold. We do not encourage the use of brooms, PVC pipe, or dowels for exercising with large groups or low-level clients, due to the possibility of clients accidentally hitting each other.

Additional Materials and Suggestions

Clay

To exercise their hands, have the clients pinch small bits of clay utilizing each hand and then roll the clay out into logs on a table using the palm of each hand in turn. Try rolling the clay into a log between the palms of their hands.

Flag Waving

Lightweight scarves or 3-foot lengths of brightly colored flagging tape or ribbons attached to ends of $1/2$-by-18-inch dowels are needed for each person. Music used for marches as well as relaxing music such as "Claire de Lune" are great for flag waving in a lively or relaxing manner.

Rice

To strengthen fingers and/or toes, place small objects like marbles, jacks, and small toys in a bucket filled with uncooked rice and have clients pick an object out of the bucket. Obviously, this is not an activity to try with confused clients who might eat the objects or the rice. It is not an activity for large groups either, due to the amount of equipment, but it is good for a novelty or to strengthen those fingers or toes on an individual basis.

Scarves and Large Handkerchiefs

Scarves make a nice prop because they are inexpensive, easy to store and easy to use. They can be twirled, waved, rolled, dropped, and swung. They are colorful for the lower level client. Occasionally, a client will forget to exercise and will watch the others' scarves, so keep reminding the clients to move their scarves.

Portable Bike Pedals and Steppers

Portable bike pedals are available from various companies. They are nice because the clients may be able to obtain a higher level of cardiovascular activity; however, they are very lightweight. The biking pedal machine is used while seated on a chair. Caution should be emphasized when using these machines with the clients because the apparatus could tip over. This is a good activity, however, for a one-on-one exercise session.

Portable stepper machines without handles are not very safe for the older adult. The client needs to stand in order to operate the stepper and it is very easy for the client to lose his or her balance on these portable steppers.

Other Ideas to Encourage Exercise

Aquatic Exercise

Water is an excellent medium for older adults. Because people have greater flexibility in water, it is easier for the older client to move sore joints and muscles. Clients have more range of motion and increased flexibility in water and there is no pounding on the joints. There are many sources regarding aquatic therapy. We have included a few references in the resource section.

A hint for working with water is that clients will benefit from different water temperatures. For example, clients with multiple sclerosis (MS) can fatigue easily so the water should be cool for them. Water is an excellent medium for the person with MS, but it is important to keep the pool temperatures a cooler 70°–78° in order to prevent premature fatigue. On the other hand, the client with arthritis should have warmer water to exercise, with a pool temperature between 85°–90°. It is very important to evaluate the client's needs before utilizing a pool. Remember to use approved flotation devices with the clientele.

Many agencies do not think about utilizing water because they lack a swimming pool. Most YMCAs and YWCAs that have swimming pools already have an aquatic exercise program in place and are a good source for ideas as well as pool usage. Many colleges and universities with pools offer courses in Adapted Physical Education or Recreation With the Disabled and can offer volunteer assistants.

Stress Reliever Balloons

The making of these balloons is covered in Chapter IX, Craft Fun. Use them for hand exercises or just squeeze them to relieve stress. This can be done in the stretching portion of the program at the beginning and/or the end or as a part of the cool down. Their use can be combined with face exercises and other stretches to become an entire relaxation session.

Walk Across the Country

"A walk across the country" is an excellent event for the entire facility. Have the clients decide upon the final destination. This might be done in a Resident's Council meeting, travel discussion group or in an exercise session. Post a map with a highlighted line showing the route that will be taken to reach the destination. Assign mileage figures to physical activities that will help the participants move toward the destination. Mark the map in another color as the mileage is completed. Participation in the exercise program would be worth points as would additional walking or other activities. This can be a major theme event running for a short, or long, period of time. Include additional events such as dinners, discussion groups and trips (see Chapter X, Theme Events, for additional information).

Older adults need to exercise in order to maintain and increase their functional ability. Work with other therapists to design the program and exercises that work best with the clients. The efforts to design an exercise program are worth it when the clients report the results of feeling better mentally and physically.

Chapter VII

Melody and Melodrama

Say It With Music

Music has been a part of most of the clients' lives and they continue to enjoy the old songs (and even some of the modern ones), but activities relating to music should include more than weekly sing-alongs. Tape and CD players can provide music in the clients' rooms. Radio and other "piped-in" music may also be available to the rooms in many residential agencies. Music on a full-time basis is as undesirable as too little music. Like all programming, music and related activities should be a part of the overall program balance. Try some of these music-related programs along with your sing-alongs to add variety.

Music Boxes   Sm Grp

Participants should be asked to bring a music box with them. In a residential facility, ask families and staff to loan music boxes for the day if clients do not have them in their rooms. Play the songs one at a time and where feasible, pass the box around to see if participants can guess the song. Lead a discussion regarding music boxes, asking how many have a music box, when they received it and if they have ever given one as a gift. If there is a locked glass case, display some of the more unusual boxes with the names of the owners.

Whistle 'n' Hum   Sm Grp

The leader should be prepared with a list of old-time songs that everyone knows, to use as suggestions, to get the activity under way. Have the group seated in a circle. The leader hums or whistles a few bars of a tune and the clients guess the song. The person who guesses the tune gets to go next. If the person cannot think of a song, show him or her the list. If someone can't hum or whistle, pick a volunteer or since you're the leader, hum another tune. After using the activity several times many of the clients will find that they can hum and/or whistle as well as guess the tunes.

Variation:
Play the first few bars of a song on the piano, dulcimer, harmonica or portable keyboard and have the group guess and/or sing along.

Daily Song   Any Number

Consider having a special song to begin and end each day at adult day-care centers and Alzheimer's disease units. A song is also helpful at the beginning and at the end of an exercise or discussion session. Make up the words to a simple tune that the lower level clients can remember. Perhaps some of the more musically inclined higher level clients can help with ideas for the tune and the words.

Rhythm Band   Sm Grp

A few years ago almost every senior citizen group had a "kitchen band." They haven't been as numerous in recent years, but the people who participated in them enjoyed the experience. Some of the bands had quite sophisticated "instruments" like washtub basses, broomstick cellos, and kazoo trombones. An expert pianist was the key to the band's success.

Most of the clients can still feel the beat of the music and have some semblance of rhythm. Make some of the following rhythm devices and let the clients use them to keep time to the music. You can use the "instruments" while you're working one-on-one or with small groups of clients. After a little practice the group may decide to perform for a special event.

Sticks

Make the sticks from ⁵/₈-inch dowel rods. Hardware stores have them in 36-inch lengths. Cut each dowel into four 9-inch lengths. Each "musician" will need two sticks. Four pair should be enough to start.

Shakers

We like to use 35mm film canisters which you can usually get from one-hour photo developing centers at no cost. Put a few dried beans or a teaspoon of rice in each canister. We have seen these used with up to 100 people, but you should be able to get by with five or six shakers for your group.

Sandpaper Blocks

You will need two sandpaper blocks for each person, so four sets should get you started. Cut eight pieces, approximately 3-by-4 inches, from ³/₄-inch soft wood such as pine. Sandpaper comes in 9-by-12-inch sheets. You will need two sheets of medium grade paper. Cut each sheet into four pieces and fit one to each block. Staple the sandpaper to the edges of the blocks and wrap masking tape around the edges to cover the staples. Remember, no staples or tape on the face of the block. Rub two blocks together gently to get the sound you want.

Bongos

Number 10 cans or 5-pound coffee cans make great bongos. Hold one of them upside down between your knees and use your fingers and palms to tap out the rhythm. Three or four of these should be enough for a small band.

Drums

Select several old pots and pie tins. Tap each with a pencil to determine which of them has the sound you like. Try a little larger stick to see if that makes a difference. Choose three or four to be used with the rhythm band.

These are enough "instruments" to get your group started. Show how the sound is made on each of them and hand them out to the participants. If you don't have a piano or portable keyboard, use recorded or taped music. Choose music with a good beat, like marches or Dixieland and let the band play along. You can have different members lead the band, even give them a baton to do it. When the band has practiced a few times, have it perform as part of a theme event for a larger audience. When working with lower level or individual clients, have them try using different instruments.

Girl Songs   Any Number

This activity may be used several ways. Play the tune and have the group guess the name of the girl and tune or use it as a paper and pencil activity where each person tries to fill in the blanks with the proper girl's name. A third way is for the leader to read the title or lyric section saying, "Blank," for the girl's name and having the group call out the name. Here are some "girl songs;" maybe you can add some more:

> When You and I Were Young _____
>   (Maggie)
> Sweet _____ Malone (Molly)
> _____ O' My Heart (Peg)
> _____ Rooney (Annie)
> Good Night _____ (Irene)
> My Little _____ (Margie)
> If You Knew _____ (Susie)
> _____, The Dawn Is Breaking (Marie)
> Every Little Breeze Seems to Whisper
>   _____ (Louise)
> _____ Marlene (Lili)
> Come, _____, in My Flying Machine
>   (Josephine)
> I Love All the Charms About _____
>   (Linda)
> _____ Is a Grand Old Name (Mary)

_____ of Washington Square (Rose)

Second Hand _____ (Rose)

Come Away, _____, in My Merry Oldsmobile (Lucille)

Oh, _____ (Susanna)

I Dream of _____ (Jeannie)

Sioux City _____ (Sue)

Has Anyone Seen My Sweet _____ (Gypsy Rose)

It was _____, but she's only a dream (Laura)

Oh, my darling _____ (Clementine)

Variations:

- Use as a first-comer activity or part of a theme event.
- Instead of girl songs see how many songs have a color in the title such as "*Yellow* Rose of Texas" and "That Old *Black* Magic."

Row, Row, Row Your Boat   Any Number

Here is a "quickie" that is fun and challenging. Practice it yourself several times before you try it with a group. The object is to have the group sing the song "Row, Row, Row Your Boat." Sing it again and leave off the last word, "dream." The next time leave off "a." Keep singing the song, leaving off another word each time, until the last time you will only sing the word "row" and stop. Now, try it again, only faster this time.

Variations:

- Sing the song with actions:
    - Row—Do rowing action.
    - Boat—Steer a boat.
    - Stream—Wiggle hand with "fish" movement.
    - Merrily—Both hands held head high.
    - Life—Fold arms at chest.
    - Dream—Hands in prayer position beside one ear.
- The action version also works well as part of an exercise group.

Other Motion Songs   Any Group

Use some of the motions songs that are used in nursery schools and kindergarten so that the clients will know them when there is an intergenerational program. Songs like "Itsy Bitsy Spider," "Rock-a-Bye Baby," "The Wheels on the Bus," "I'm a Little Teapot," and "He's Got the Whole World in His Hands" are some examples.

Musical Balloons   Sm Grp

You will need five or more inflated 8-inch balloons and some lively music (tapes, CD, record player or piano). Seat the group in a closed circle. Start the music and pass a balloon around the circle. Stop the music suddenly and whoever has the balloon must hold it in his or her lap while the game continues with another balloon. Players caught with a balloon when the music stops continue to play, they just have to keep the balloons they "earn" in their laps. It gets hilarious when the players have two or more balloons in their laps and have to keep passing the new balloon.

All the World Is a Stage

It may not be possible to put on a three-act play with your clients, however, there are many activities related to the field of drama which may be adapted for use in your facility. Some of the stretching and relaxing activities suggested in Chapter VI, Move It or Lose It, are dramatic in nature and can be used as a warmup activity for the dramatics group. The activities in storytelling are enjoyable and relatively easy to adapt for dramatics. Dramatics is more than having skits or plays presented by a group. However, with the proper approach, it is possible to have many of the clients preparing and presenting dramatic sketches for the other clients. Dramatics offer the clients an opportunity to express various emotions as well as utilize their creative abilities. Here are some ideas to get you started.

Mirroring   1:1, Sm Grp

Mirroring is used as a warmup exercise for dramatics classes in many schools. It can be an enjoyable activity to use with your clients.

Two people sit facing each other. One acts as the reflection in a mirror for the other's actions. Start with very simple arm and hand actions (remember, the "reflection" does it with the opposite arm), like moving the arm up and down and from side to side, opening and closing the hand. Then switch arms and finally use both arms at once. Raising and lowering the legs one at a time is another action. Don't forget facial expressions like smiling, frowning, grinning and blinking.

Charades   Sm Grp

Prepare cards, each with the name of an activity that most of the people would recognize, and give each participant one of the cards. Each person takes a turn doing a pantomime of the action described on the card. When finished, the rest of the group members try to identify the action. We have included some ideas to get you started:

> Washing a car
> Changing a light bulb
> Potting a plant
> Hanging a picture
> Making a pie crust
> Raking leaves
> Changing a tire
> Checking oil in a car
> Ironing a blouse
> Hemming a skirt
> Knitting a hat
> Milking a cow
> Saddling a horse
> Changing a diaper
> Making lemonade

Stand a Minute   Any Number

We often say, "Wait a minute," or "I'll be there in a minute," but do we know how long a minute really is? The participant may not look at a watch or clock during this activity. You can have the people stand and hold on to a chair. Tell them when the minute starts and tell them to sit down when they think the minute is over. Keep track of when the first person sits down and when the last one sits down (after about a minute and 30 seconds, if the group is not all seated, have the rest take their seats). If there are clients who cannot stand, have them keep their hands on the arms of their chairs until they think the minute has passed

and then fold their hands. It has been our experience that the first person sits after 15 or 20 seconds, and most are seated by the end of 45 seconds.

I Can't Pay the Rent   Any Number

Each person must have a paper napkin for this "melodrama." If it is a full-size napkin, it should already be folded in fourths as it comes from the pack. Show the participants how they can crumple a folded napkin between their thumb and forefinger to look like a bow tie, a hair ribbon, or even a villain's mustache. Explain to the group that there are three characters in this melodrama. *The first is the fair maiden* and when she speaks they are to hold the folded napkin to their heads like a hair ribbon. *The second is the villain* and when he speaks the folded napkin is held under their noses like a mustache. *The third character is the hero* and when he speaks the napkin becomes a bow tie.

The group members do the melodrama in unison so they will need to have a short "practice" session to learn the lines. (You say the fair maiden's lines in a falsetto voice, holding the "hair ribbon" in place and they repeat them. Then do the villain's lines in a deep voice using the "mustache" and have them repeat them, and finally the hero's lines with the "bow tie," which they also repeat.)

You have the idea, so here are the lines for the melodrama:

> Maiden: "I can't pay the rent, I can't pay
>   the rent, I can't pay the rent, today!"
> Villain: "You must pay the rent, you must
>   pay the rent, you must pay the rent,
>   today!"
> Maiden repeats her lines
> Villain repeats his lines
> Repeat maiden's lines again
> Repeat villain's lines again
> Hero: "I'll pay the rent."
> Maiden: "My hero!"
> Villain: "Curses foiled again!"

Don't forget the actions with the folded napkin and lead the group through it two or three times, each time doing it a little faster.

Variation:
Use as a skit with individuals playing the three parts.

Lion Hunt

Large Group

The lion hunt skit has been around for many years. In the early 1960s, Jerry developed this version which has traveled all over the world and been translated into at least four different languages. We have used it successfully with groups of all ages and recommend that you learn the words before using it with a group. It is especially effective when you have a group of children sitting on the floor in front of the clients. You have to be an enthusiastic leader and really get into the story and actions. You say the first line and have the group repeat it. Do the whole story line by line, doing the actions they are to repeat.

Practice this with the group. You say a line and they repeat it. When they have the idea, go on with the whole story, playlet, skit, song, or whatever you want to call it.

Refrain:

Goin' on a lion hunt
I'm not afraid. [Shake head]
Got my camera [Hold "camera" up to eyes]
And a roll of film, too [Tap pocket]
Goin' to get a picture, [Snap picture]
That's what I'm goin' to do!

Verses:

Open the door [Pull the door open]
Go outside,
Close the door [Close it]
We're goin' for a ride.

Walk to the Jeep [Tap knees alternately with hands]
And climb in. [Lift one leg and then the other]
Turn on the key [Turn it]
Put it in low [Pull back with hand, and to the right]
Let out the clutch [Lift left foot]
And here we go!

Do the *Refrain:* Goin' on a lion hunt . . .

Guess I'd better stop.
Put on the brake, [Right foot, remember?]
Turn off the key, [Turn it]
Get out of the Jeep [Just like you got in]
And walk to a tree. [Hands tapping knees, again]

Climb that tree [Use hands to pull yourself up]
'Til I get to the top [Keep climbing]
And then I stop
Look all around. [Shade eyes with one hand, but hold on with the other]
No lion anywhere,
So I climb back down, [Reverse hand climbing motion]
'Til I reach the ground.

Refrain: Goin' on a . . .

I walk along [Walking hands again]
'Til I come to a stream
There's a bridge [Use hands to hold "binoculars"]
So, walk on the bridge [Hit fists alternately on chest for walking sound]

Look over the side [Peer over the side]
And fall in! [Clap hands for splash]
That's OK,
Good day for a swim! [Swim with hands]

Climb out the other side [Stepping motion with feet]
And shake myself off [Shaking motion with body]
Walk through the mud [Sucking sound with mouth as feet are moved]
'Til I come to some grass

It's tall grass,
But I walk through [Slide palms together to make swishing sound]
That's what I do. [Keep sliding palms back and forth]

Refrain: Goin' on a . . .

There's a hill [Point to it]
We'll climb that hill [Use hands to tap
   knees alternately and slowly]
It's a hot day! [Say it slowly and wipe
   "sweat" off of brow]
It's a long way! [More slowly and droop
   tired shoulders with a sigh]
Slo-o-ow down-n-n [Say this part
   slowly]

Refrain: Goin' on a . . . *[do the refrain about
half speed]*

Here's a cave
Let's go inside [Hold cupped hands over
   mouth]
It's mighty dark in here, [Talking into
   cupped hands for muffled effect]
I can't see a thing! [Talk into cupped
   hands]

Refrain: Goin' on a . . . [Talk into cupped
hands]

[After end of refrain, say:]

Stop!!
Two eyes, [Reach out with index fingers
   to touch lion's eyes]
Shaggy mane! [Use hand to feel it]
Long back, [Pat lion's back with hand]
Big tail . . . [Use hand to feel length of
   tail]
It's a LION! [Suck in breath]
He's in the cave with ME! [Take deep
   breath]

[Speed things up, now]

Run out of the cave, [Alternately tap
   knees fast]
And down the hill. [Keep running]
Don't look back, [Keep running]
He's following still! [Run some more!]

Through the tall grass, [Swishing sound
   with hands]
And through the mud. [Sucking sound
   as you pull feet from mud]

Run across the bridge [Alternate fists
   thumping chest]
And fall in! [Slap hands for splash sound]
Go for a swim [Crawl stroke with hands]
Climb back out,
And shake myself off. [Shake body]

Run to the tree [Running motion]
Climb to the top [Climbing motion]
And then I stop [Pant, 'cause your out of
   breath!]

Look all around [Hold on with one hand,
   shade eyes with other]
No lion anywhere.
So I climb back down [Climbing motion]
And walk to my Jeep. [Walking motion]

Climb in [One foot at a time!]
And turn on the key. [Turn it]
Put it in low, [Stick shift, remember]
Let out the clutch [Lift left foot]
And home we go! [Don't forget to steer]

Been on a lion Hunt [Still driving home]
I wasn't afraid!
Stop! [Slam on the brakes]
It's a LION! [Scared look!]
Two eyes [Reach behind seat to feel
   them]
Shaggy mane [Feel it?]
Big back [Feel it, he's in the back seat!]
Long tail [Feel how long it is]
He's in the Jeep with me!

Jump out of the Jeep
And run to the house ["Run"—hands tap-
   ping knees or stomping feet]
Open the door [Do it]
Run inside ["Run" some more]
Close the door [Close it]
Run and hide!
Jump under the bed [hands forward and
   bend down]
Safe at last! [Breathe sigh of relief]

Been on a lion hunt *[say it quietly]*
I'm not afraid
Had my camera [Show it]
And a roll of film, too [Hold it up]

Forgot to snap a picture [Look sad]
Like I was goin' to do
Been on a lion hunt

Stop! [You're frightened!]
Two eyes, [*Whisper this and the next few lines*]
Shaggy mane, [Same motions as before]
Big back,
Long tail!
It's a LION! [Very frightened]
He's under the bed with me!
[Leader ends it with the following lines that the group does not repeat, because they'll be laughing]

But it's my pet lion, Herman
And he's STUFFED!

Remember the leader says a line and does the actions, then the group repeats them except for the last two lines.

Plays From Stories   Sm Grp

What is nice about this activity is that the dramatics group members can create their own stories and build them into a play that can be performed as a special event for a larger crowd. Developing short or long skits to perform is an activity that can be repeated several times a year with the dramatics group. The leader asks each member of the group to fill in the blank for a topic such as "My favorite vacation would be to go to _____," "My favorite meal is _____," or "The worst tasting thing I ever ate was _____."

You can ask every person within the group the same question or vary the questions. Remember, not all of the questions have to be positives. Combine the answers into a simple story that may be humorous to read and make into a skit. Make sure everyone has a role to play in the skit. Include lines for someone to say like, "The curtain rises for the first act." Use the clients' comments and ideas about being an older person that they find humorous.

The key to the success of this event is letting the clients develop their own plays and skits. Using this technique helps them to remember their lines. Have fun with it and keep it light and fairly short. Scenery and props can be created by members of the dramat-

ics group as a part of dramatics or during crafts sessions. Scenery isn't even necessary for most of the performances. Someone will have to take the clients' ideas or one-liners and make them into a skit. After developing and writing a few skits, a member of the group may be able to write and develop the skits for the entire group.

Calendar Travel   Sm Grp

Collect calendar scenery pictures of well-known tourist destination sites. After looking at the pictures, the group decides which site(s) is to be visited on this particular trip. Have the group help make a list of questions that need answered before the "trip" can be made.

Here are some sample questions to get you started:

Where are we going to go? (List the destinations.)
How long do we want the trip to take? (Number of days.)
What time of year do we want to go? (Decide what season would be best.)
How are we going to travel? (Auto, plane, RV, or combination.)
What all will we need to take? (Clothes, camera, traveler's checks.)
Where will we stay while we're there? (Hotel, motel, bed-and-breakfast.)
What souvenirs do we want to shop for? (Things related to the site.)

After we have answers to all of our questions, it is time to make up a series of skits about getting ready, what happens on the way, what we see while at our destination, problems with reservations and anything else about the "trip" that might make an interesting skit. After a few practice sessions, the production should be ready for presentation as a part of a special event.

Shoebox Dramatics   Sm or Md Grp

A shoebox (with five or six unrelated items in it) is prepared for each group of five or six participants. Each box should have different items. We've used things like mousetraps, sink stoppers, toilet rolls, apples, oranges, soup cans, scrub brushes, and anything else that will fit in the box. Each group of participants is given a box of items and a length of time, say ten minutes, to use all of the things (including the box) to prepare a skit. Each group then presents its skit to the other groups.

Joke Dramas   Sm Grp

Start a collection of jokes that can be used as mini-skits. We copy them from magazines like *Reader's Digest* and we use large type to print them on 4-by-6-inch cards. List the number and gender of the characters needed on each card. Select participants to fit the characters and give them the "script" and a few minutes to prepare. These mini-skits are great for use at special events or as fillers anytime. Here is the type of joke we mean:

New Hearing Aid—Two characters—Any gender

Person #1: "I hear you purchased a new hearing aid."

Person #2: "Yes and it's great but it was really expensive."

Person #1: "Really, how much did it cost?"

Person #2: "Three thousand dollars, but I can hear everything perfectly!"

Person #1: "Three thousand dollars! What kind is it?"

Person #2 (looking at wristwatch): "It's 4:15"

Nursery Rhymes   Sm Grp

Nursery rhymes have great possibilities for skits based on their ready-made plots. The plots can be easily embellished and a variety of endings can be developed. It's up to the imagination of the group. Several small groups can work on producing these nursery rhyme skits and then sharing the results with each other. These are great to present as a part of an intergenerational program.

Chapter VIII

Sweet Treats

Let's face it, most of us really enjoy something sweet as a treat. There is all of this discussion about how older adults lose their taste buds, but have you ever known an older adult to turn down a dessert? Older adults retain their taste for sweets longer than any other taste sensation. Judy tells stories about outings that would have been disasters had they not stopped for ice cream. Suddenly the problems had become adventures. We have included some ideas for special treats for your clients. Some take little preparation time and can be served as a treat during a special event, while others can be made as part of a food preparation activity.

Food can be a great motivator for clients to attend events. Animals and children, particularly baby animals and toddlers through first graders, are also great motivators for older adults. We caution you to use food as a motivator on a selective basis as many of the clients are on strict diabetic or restricted calorie diets.

We reviewed one facility's monthly activity schedule and found that out of 32 events, 28 of them involved food. That is probably about 20 too many for one month. Select events such as the birthday party and/or welcoming tea and possibly the monthly special event for regularly scheduled food activities. Avoid the trap of serving food at every event. Keep in mind that a small amount of food is all that most of the clients need because of their sedentary lifestyle. A coffee klatsch might serve as a special treat once a month and the baking group should be charged with making goodies for events such as the welcoming tea instead of preparing everything for their own immediate consumption. For those special times you want to try something a little different, try one of the following sweet treats.

Breads and Cakes

Amish Friendship Bread

It is unusual to think of using a starter dough for an older adult baking project, but older adults are a perfect group to make this tasty bread. They remember potato starters on the back of the stove, because yeast was limited, and making homemade bread, so it is a good reminiscence topic. Although yeast is now easily available, it is really fun to watch the starter and have a ready-to-use supply.

A starter is something to watch and it gives the clients some responsibility, yet it is not a time-consuming project. This starter needs to be stirred daily, fed on day 5, then used for baking on day 10. This is not a good recipe for the diabetic client because of the sugar, but the bread it makes is delicious. You may want to experiment with other starter recipes besides the one we have included.

Making the Starter
Ingredients:
>   2 cups of flour
>   1 packet of yeast
>   1 teaspoon of salt
>   2 cups of lukewarm water

Mix the ingredients on day 1 and store in a glass or plastic container with a loose cover. Use a wooden spoon to stir the mixture. It is suggested that you do not store the starter in the refrigerator; however, it is possible to store it there if you make sure the starter is beginning to bubble before putting it in. On days 2, 3, and 4 you stir the mixture one time with a wooden spoon.

On day 5, stir these additional ingredients into the starter:

1 cup of flour
1 cup of granulated sugar
1 cup of milk

On days 6, 7, 8 and 9 stir the mixture once with the wooden spoon.

On day 10 stir in the following ingredients:

1 cup of sugar
1 cup of flour
1 cup of milk

The tradition is that on this day you are to divide the starter into three parts, using one-third for making bread and giving the other two parts to friends. If you wish, use two thirds of the starter and bake extra bread, then use the last third to begin again.

It is not necessary to add the ingredients every five days and bake it every ten days. We have gone as long as 10 days without adding to the starter and three weeks without baking. It is also possible to put in half of the ingredients if you are getting too much starter. Just remember to stir it once a day with a wooden spoon, and keep it covered. Use the starter to make the Amish Sweet Bread described here.

Amish Sweet Bread

Ingredients:
    1 to 2 cups of starter
    1 cup of oil
    3 eggs
    1 cup of sugar
    2 cups of flour
    1 teaspoon of vanilla
    1 teaspoon of cinnamon
    $^1/_2$ teaspoon of baking soda
    1 teaspoon of salt
    1 large (5.1-ounce) package or 2 small (3.4-ounce) packages of vanilla instant pudding

To make the loaves of sweet bread, add the oil (substitute applesauce if you want to reduce the fat), eggs, vanilla and sugar to the starter. Mix the flour, cinnamon, pudding mix, baking soda, and salt together and

add to the batter. The batter is rather thick when everything has been mixed together.

Grease and sugar two loaf pans (if you wish to substitute a spray for the grease, then do not use sugar on the pans). Bake 40 to 50 minutes at 350°. Cool the bread 10 minutes before removing the loaves from the pans.

This bread has a sweet, unusual flavor. For variety, add raisins, Craisins (dried sweetened cranberries), nuts, and/or bananas to the batter before baking. It is also great with fresh fruit like strawberries or blueberries served on top or even canned pie filling. It is a nice dessert to serve at a strawberry festival or Fourth of July party. It is worth the effort to make this bread.

Baked Bean Bread

Although the thought of baked beans in a sweet bread does not sound appealing, this bread is delicious with a really nice texture from the beans. This recipe is not good for diabetic clients due to the amount of sugar in the recipe.

Ingredients:
    1 (16-ounce) can of pork and beans (drain off the liquid)
    2 cups of granulated sugar
    3 eggs
    2 cups of flour
    1 cup of vegetable oil
    1 teaspoon of cinnamon
    $^1/_2$ teaspoon of baking powder
    $^1/_2$ teaspoon of baking soda
    1 cup of raisins
    1 teaspoon of vanilla

Drain the baked beans; mix with sugar, oil, and eggs. Mix until smooth. In a separate bowl combine the flour, soda, baking powder, and cinnamon and add to the bean mixture. Stir in the vanilla and raisins. Bake in a 325° oven for 45–55 minutes. The bread is done when you can stick a toothpick in the loaf and it comes out clean. The baking time depends on the size of the pan or can. The bread can be baked in two loaf pans that have been greased and floured.

Part of the novelty is baking the bread in the bean cans. Remove both ends of the cans, rinse and dry the cans thoroughly, making sure there are no rough edges when the lids are removed. Grease and flour five 16-ounce cans. Place the cans on an ungreased cookie sheet. Fill each can approximately two-thirds full of batter. Be careful not to overfill. This makes a great treat for a western theme or camping event.

Homemade Bread

It is easier to make homemade bread than ever before because of the bread recipes for bread machines. Many of the older people will remember kneading the bread and will enjoy watching a bread machine do all of the work. Although bread machines are becoming more reasonably priced, rather than purchasing a new machine, borrow one to show the clients. Bread machines can also be used as a mixer for other types of breads such as banana, baked bean and pumpkin bread, to name a few.

If it isn't possible to borrow a bread machine, why not try a few of those frozen loaves of bread that are found in the freezer at the grocery store. Simply thaw, grease a pan, let it rise, and then bake.

Flowerpot Muffins

For an unusual looking muffin, use small, clean clay flowerpots (no larger than a 2-inch pot). Grease and flour the inside of the pot and use any muffin mix or use your own recipe. Place the pots on a cookie sheet so no batter will leak out while filling them two-thirds full. Bake them in a 350° oven. They are done when tested with a toothpick that comes out clean. Baking time varies due to the size of the pots. Use an assembly line approach with the clients to mix the batter, and grease, flour and fill the pots.

The muffins can be taken out of the pots once they are done baking, but they look so cute in the pots that the group usually likes to put the pots right on the table. They are a great treat for a theme event, such as a garden party or spring fling. Decorate the pots with a ribbon or even add a gummy worm as a decoration after the muffins are baked.

Be sure to use *lead-free* pots for baking. They are available at many specialty gift stores. Package a few pots to make a nice gift or an item to sell in the gift shop.

Herman

Herman is another type of starter. It is very similar to the Amish Friendship Bread starter; however, the recipes are different. You can use the Herman starter for the following recipes and also for the Amish Sweet Bread described earlier.

Starter:
> 2 cups of milk
> 1 cup of sugar
> 2 cups of flour
> 2 envelopes of yeast

Stir all of the ingredients together in a nonmetallic container. Keep in a warm place and stir once a day every day for five days. Herman can be kept in the refrigerator, but does not have to be kept there.

On the fifth day, add:

> 2 cups of flour
> 2 cups of milk
> 1 cup of sugar

Continue to stir one time per day. On the tenth day, use Herman in one of the following recipes. We think that you will want to try all of them.

Herman Applesauce Cake

Ingredients:
> 2 cups of Herman
> 1 cup of brown sugar
> 1 cup of margarine
> 1 cup of applesauce
> 2 eggs
> 2 teaspoons of cinnamon
> 1 teaspoon of nutmeg
> 1 teaspoon of allspice
> 1 teaspoon of baking soda
> 1 teaspoon of salt

Glaze:
> 2 tablespoons lemon juice or orange juice
> $1/4$ cup of confectioners' sugar or granulated sugar

Cream the sugar and margarine, add the eggs, applesauce and Herman. Mix dry ingredients and add to the batter. Bake in a greased 9-by-13-inch pan in a 350° oven for 40–50 minutes. Mix juice and sugar together to make glaze; drizzle on the warm cake.

Herman Chocolate Cake

Ingredients:
    1 cup of Herman
    $^2/_3$ cup of oil
    $1^2/_3$ cups of sugar
    $1^3/_4$ cups of flour
    $^1/_2$ cup of cocoa
    $^3/_4$ cup of water
    1 teaspoon of baking powder
    $1^1/_2$ teaspoons of baking soda
    $^1/_2$ teaspoon of salt

Mix the oil and sugar. Add the Herman, cocoa, vanilla and water. Mix dry ingredients together then add to the batter. Pour the batter into a greased 9-inch square pan, bake in a 350° oven for 30 minutes.

Herman Coffee Cake

Ingredients:
    2 cups of Herman
    2 eggs
    $^2/_3$ cup of sugar
    $^2/_3$ cup of oil (or applesauce to reduce fat)
    2 cups of flour
    $^1/_2$ teaspoon of baking soda
    $1^1/_2$ teaspoons of cinnamon

Optional:
    $^1/_2$ cup of chocolate chips, nuts, raisins, peaches, apples or Craisins

Topping:
    $^3/_4$ cup of brown sugar
    2 tablespoons of cinnamon
    2 tablespoons of finely chopped nuts
    2 tablespoons of butter

Mix the eggs, sugar and oil together. Add the Herman, flour, soda, cinnamon and any nuts, chocolate or fruits. Pour into a greased 9-by-13-inch pan. Cream the brown sugar, cinnamon, nuts and butter together and sprinkle over the batter. Bake in 350° oven for 30 minutes.

Sissy's Cinnamon Rolls

Ingredients:
    1 loaf of frozen bread dough, thawed
    $^1/_4$ cup of softened butter or margarine
    2 tablespoons of cinnamon
    $^1/_2$ cup of granulated sugar

Glaze:
    1 teaspoon of vanilla
    $^1/_8$ cup of milk for thinning
    $^1/_2$ cup of brown sugar
    $^1/_4$ cup of melted butter

Roll thawed loaf of frozen bread into a $^1/_2$-inch thick rectangle. Spread the softened margarine, sugar and cinnamon over the bread dough. Make a roll starting with the long edge. Slice to desired thickness, remembering they will rise. Melt the butter or margarine and mix with the brown sugar, vanilla and approximately $^1/_8$ cup of milk for the glaze. Spread the glaze in the bottom of a 9-by-13-inch pan and place the sliced rolls on top of glaze with a sliced side down. Cover with a towel and let rise in a warm place. When the rolls are doubled in size (in about 20 minutes), bake in a preheated 350° oven for 20 minutes. Let them cool in the pan for 5 minutes before removing. Sissy measures her ingredients by eye, so you may want to adjust the amounts to your groups' taste.

Variation:
For an even quicker method, use a can of refrigerator biscuits and a muffin pan. Cut each biscuit into four parts and roll into small balls. Roll each ball in a mixture of 1 teaspoon of cinnamon to 4 teaspoons of sugar. Put four balls in each muffin cup and bake at 400° for approximately 10 minutes.

Dirt Cake

A dirt cake is easy and everyone likes the taste, especially after they have heard the name. Make this one for a Halloween party in a 9-by-13-inch pan and add candy corn and other candies for decorations. Another suggestion is to make it in shallow lead-free flowerpots. Decorate them with gummy worms crawling out of the dirt and insert a plastic flower in the center.

Ingredients:

 1 (16-ounce) package of Oreo cookies, crushed
 8 ounces of cream cheese, softened
 $1/_4$ cup of margarine, softened
 1 cup of powdered sugar
 1 (12-ounce) carton of Cool Whip
 2 (3.4-ounce) packages of vanilla instant pudding
 $3^1/_2$ cups of milk

Mix the softened cream cheese, margarine and powdered sugar. In a separate bowl, mix the Cool Whip, pudding and milk. Blend the contents of the two bowls. Put a layer of crushed Oreos on the bottom, then a layer of the pudding mixture. Continue the layering process, ending with crushed Oreo cookies. Don't forget to add gummy worms, flowers or other decorations.

Easter Basket Cupcakes

Place cupcake papers (foil liners may be used) in muffin tins; fill them with your favorite cake batter and bake as usual. Use your favorite canned or homemade icing. Make the cupcake into a basket by taking one half of a twist of licorice and forming it into a handle. Sprinkle shredded coconut that has been dyed green with food coloring to look like grass on the cupcake. Press jelly beans or other candy into the top of the basket. These make nice gifts for children visiting the clients or they may be used as a treat at an Easter event.

Ice Cream Cone Cupcakes

Ingredients:

 1 box of sugar cones (the ones with the flat bottoms)
 1 box cake mix (any flavor, prepare batter as per package instructions)
 1 can of frosting
 Jimmies or other decorations

Mix the cake mix according to the package instructions. Fill each individual ice cream cone two-thirds full of batter. Place the cones into a muffin pan or a mini muffin pan. Bake in a 350° oven 15 to 20 minutes or until a toothpick inserted into the cake comes out clean. Let cool, then frost and decorate. This recipe makes approximately 24 cones. These cones

are great as an unusual treat to be shared with children or as a part of a special event. They are best when eaten the same day they are made.

Microwave Coffee Mug Cake

What a fun and quick way to create individual cakes. We often make these for dessert for ourselves because they are so easy, but they can be made for any number of people.

Ingredients:

 1 box cake mix (any flavor, prepare batter as per package instructions)
 Baking spray for the cups
 8- or 12-ounce ceramic coffee mugs (no gold or silver trim)

Optional:

 1 can of frosting (any flavor)
 Sprinkles, jimmies, or other decorations

Spray the coffee mugs with cooking spray. Mix cake mix as directed on the box. You may want to substitute applesauce for the oil, in order to cut down on the fat. Fill the coffee mug $1/_2$ to $2/_3$ full of cake mix. Be careful not to overfill the cups as the cake will rise and spill in the microwave. Microwave on full power for 1 minute and 20 seconds for a larger mug and 1 minute for a smaller mug. Test with a toothpick and if it comes out clean the cake is done. It will look and taste very moist. Decorate as desired. Sometimes we poke holes in the cake after it is done and drizzle coffee or melted chocolate in the holes. These cakes are best eaten right away, just serve them in the mugs. If necessary, they can be saved for a day or two. If working with a small group, prepare half of the mix at a time.

Peach Dump Cake

This cake is so easy to make and it's wonderfully delicious. It makes a nice treat to serve at a welcoming tea or coffee hour.

Ingredients:

 1 (20-ounce) can of peaches
 1 butter pecan or yellow cake mix
 1 cup of pecans

1 cup of shredded coconut
$\frac{1}{2}$ cup of melted margarine
Whipped topping (optional)

Pour the peaches (juice included) into the bottom of a greased 9-by-13-inch pan. Sprinkle the dry cake mix over the top of the peaches, distributing the mix carefully, but don't try to even it out. Cover the top of the cake mix with the pecans and then the coconut. Pour the melted margarine over the top of the mixture. Again, do not worry about spreading the margarine to all edges. Bake in a 325° oven for 1 hour (watch to make sure it does not burn). If the coconut is getting too brown, but the cake is not done, cover the top with aluminum foil. The cake is done when a toothpick stuck in the cake comes out clean. If desired, add whipped topping as the cake is served. Leftovers are best stored in the refrigerator.

Variations:
• Substitute cherry or apple pie filling for peaches for a different flavor.
• You can leave off the coconut and/or substitute crushed pineapple.

Turtle Cookie Dough Cheesecake

Ingredients:
    1 package of refrigerated chocolate chip cookie dough
    1 box of no-bake cheesecake (prepared as per package instructions)

Optional toppings:
    2 ounces of melted chocolate chips
    1 ounce of melted caramel, butterscotch, English toffee or white chocolate chips

Slice the chocolate chip cookie dough into evenly sized slices as if making cookies. Place slices in a 9-inch pie pan, pressing them together to form the crust. Bake 9–11 minutes in a 375° oven. The cookie dough should still look a little soft. Mix the cheesecake using the recipe from the box and pour it onto the cookie dough crust. If desired, drizzle the top with melted chocolate chips and/or other topping. Refrigerate until firm. Other toppings, such as cherry pie filling can be used. You can make this with your favorite cheesecake recipe (which requires baking), but it takes longer.

Individual Cheesecakes

Ingredients:
    1 box of vanilla wafers
    1 jar of strawberry jam or 1 can of cherry pie filling (other flavors may be substituted)
    1 tub of whipped cream cheese
    2 teaspoons of vanilla (optional)
    Muffin cups

Place one vanilla wafer in each muffin cup. (If using vanilla, thoroughly mix into the cream cheese). Fill the muffin cups two-thirds full of the whipped cream cheese. Top with a teaspoon of jam or cherry pie filling. Serve immediately, or chill. For variety, try a graham cracker instead of the cookie in the bottom of the cup.

Candy

Old-Fashioned Taffy Pull

Judy's image of a taffy pull was two lines of people pulling this tough, sticky confection. Jerry tried the taffy with classes of fifth graders and thought it would be too messy for older adults. Well, we were both wrong. This has proven to be a great activity even for older people with arthritis, adults of all ages and for kids eight and older. The following is an easy-to-prepare recipe for taffy we obtained from an older woman in Mercer, Wisconsin.

Ingredients:
    2 cups of granulated sugar
    1 cup of light corn syrup
    1 tablespoon of vinegar
    1 teaspoon of vanilla
    1 tablespoon of butter

Mix all of these ingredients together in a pot, stirring constantly over a low heat until it reaches the hard ball stage. (There is a category on a candy thermometer known as "hard ball.") You have reached this stage when you drop a tiny bit into a glass of water and it rolls into a ball, versus running. Let it cool in the pan until the edges are solid and the middle is warm to the touch. This part takes about 30 to 45 minutes.

Higher level clients can be involved in the preparation phase. Use the cool down time to reminisce or discuss other homemade candies or desserts. For those clients who have a short attention span, cook the taffy ahead of time and have them participate in the pulling phase only.

Prepare the area for the actual taffy pull by spreading a sheet of waxed paper on the table in front of each person and having a large supply of stick or tub margarine. The messy part of cleaning sticky hands can be alleviated by having each person wear a pair of vinyl or latex gloves. They don't have to wear gloves but their hands will become quite sticky without them. Have the "pullers" coat their gloves (or hands, if they don't wear gloves), both front and back, with margarine.

Give everyone a small piece of the taffy mixture about the size of a golf ball. When first working with the taffy, it will be very warm for the clients. Each person does his or her own pulling. They should hold onto their pieces with both hands and pull it until it is about 6 inches long, then fold the piece in half and pull again. If it sticks to the pullers' fingers, add more margarine to the hands, but be careful about adding too much because the taffy becomes stringy and slippery if there is too much margarine. Keep pulling and folding until the taffy lightens in color (it should be almost an ecru color). It will also thicken and appear shiny. When you feel it is ready, twist the taffy in a strand about $1/2$- to $5/8$-inch thick. If it is still too thin fold it and twist it again before it cools, then lay it on a clean piece of waxed paper to let it harden. When it is a bit cooler, cut it into smaller taffy-size pieces and wrap the individual pieces in wax paper. Twist the ends of the paper as they do for commercially made taffy. Remember you are making soft taffy and it should not become "rock" hard.

We have shared this taffy recipe with many professionals who work with older adults, and everyone has raved about it. It really works!

Cream Cheese Candy

This is a noncook sweet candy, which the older people who have made it seem to enjoy making and eating. This candy is quite sweet, but very good for a lower functioning group to make because the dough is like Play-Doh and you don't have to be concerned if the clients eat it.

Ingredients:
   3 ounces of cream cheese
   $2 1/2$ cups of powdered sugar, sifted
   $1/2$ teaspoon of peppermint flavoring
   Food coloring

Cream the cheese. Add 1 cup of powdered sugar, the flavoring and a few drops of food coloring until the desired candy color is obtained. Continue to add powdered sugar until mixture is stiff enough to knead. Roll into 1-inch balls. Place on a cookie sheet that has been covered with wax paper. Stamp with cookie stamp, press into a candy mold, or just flatten with the palm of your hand. Refrigerate until set.

If you want to use a rolling pin, place a sheet of wax paper under the dough and one on top, and that will make it easier to roll out flat. Roll it to about a $1/4$-inch thickness and cut shapes with small cookie cutters. You can also use commercial candy molds and press the mixture into them instead of using the stamp.

Variations:
   • Make chocolate candy by omitting the food coloring and adding 3 teaspoons of cocoa to the recipe (the cocoa reduces the sweetness).
   • Use vanilla or peppermint flavoring. There are many other flavorings available in candy supply stores.
   • Another variation is to melt $2 1/2$ cups of white button chocolate and mix with the cream cheese, powdered sugar, and flavoring. Try different variations for different types of events.

Cookies

Cake Mix Cookies

Ingredients:
   1 box of cake mix (any flavor)
   $1/2$ cup of margarine or butter
   1 teaspoon of vanilla
   1 egg

Optional:
   Pecans, sprinkles, coconut, cinnamon for decorating

Blend the cake mix and margarine until creamy. Beat in the egg and vanilla. Add cinnamon, nuts, or any extras you would like. The dough will be rather sticky, so we found it best to use teaspoons to put the dough onto an ungreased cookie sheet. Bake 8 to 10 minutes in a 375° oven. The cookies will rise in the oven, but may fall when removed. Let the cookies sit on the cookie sheet for 1 or 2 minutes before removing. Try adding chocolate chips and coconut to a chocolate cake mix for a very rich cookie. Sprinkle on cinnamon and place a whole pecan on each cookie to use for a special tea. These cookies are thin and chewy.

Cookie Stamps

Cookie stamps are ceramic, glass, or wooden presses that you use over and over again. Press the greased stamp on the cookie prior to baking. Stamps come in a wide variety of designs and can be purchased in a price range from $2.95 to $6.50. More decorative stamps with handles are now available for $13.00 to $20.00. They are easy to use and so much fun. They make great cookies for teas or holiday events.

Each stamp comes with directions and recipes, but you can use other recipes as long as they do not contain baking soda or baking powder, in order to preserve the impression made by the stamp. Prepare the recipe as usual, roll a bit of dough into a ball and press the cookie stamp into the dough. It does not take much pressure to form a nice impression in the dough; however, the deeper the impression the more likely it will be retained during baking. Baking the cookies at 325° allows the cookie to maintain most of the impression. A hint to help ensure successful cookies is to roll the cookie dough in granulated sugar before utilizing the press. That way you don't have to worry about the dough sticking to the stamp. If it does stick, clean the stamp and spray with a cooking spray.

Although more expensive, the Brown Bag Cookie Company produces beautiful cookie molds. This company's molds are generally very large, but the cookies or ornaments made with them are great to hang on a theme or Christmas tree. The molds can also be used to make molded paper. If clients function at a very high level, they can make beeswax ornaments using the molds (these techniques are discussed in Chapter IX, Craft Fun). There are a lot of ideas in *The Idea Book* from the Brown Bag Cookie Company (the address is in the resource section).

Flower Saucer Brownies

These are similar to flowerpot muffins. Prepare your favorite brownie mix, but grease and flour a clean clay flowerpot saucer. Pour the batter into the saucer and bake at the same temperature as you normally would bake brownies. It does not matter whether a box mix is utilized or you use a recipe from scratch. Baking time varies based on size of the saucer. This novel way to bake makes a great gift. To prepare the gift, mix up the dry ingredients, write the recipe on a card along with the baking instructions, put the saucer, recipe and mix in a small plastic bag, tie with a ribbon and add a gift card. Saucers and pots that are *lead-free* are available at specialized gift stores.

Oatmeal Craisin Cookies

If you have never made anything with Craisins this is a great recipe for beginners. Craisins are cranberries that have been soaked in sugar and cranberry juice and dried. They add a really great flavor to this cookie and are now available in most grocery stores in the same aisle as the raisins or baking items.

Ingredients:
  $1/2$ cup of sugar
  $1/4$ cup of brown sugar
  $1/4$ cup of softened margarine
  $1/4$ cup of shortening
  $1/2$ teaspoon of baking soda
  $1/2$ teaspoon of cinnamon
  $1/2$ teaspoon of vanilla
  $1/4$ teaspoon of baking powder
  $1/4$ teaspoon of salt
  1 egg
  $1^1/2$ cups of quick oats
  1 cup of flour
  1 cup of Craisins
  $1/2$ cup of finely chopped pecans

Mix the sugars with the shortening and margarine. Mix the cinnamon, baking powder, salt, baking soda, and oatmeal with the flour. Combine the flour mixture with the sugar and shortening mixture. Add the pecans and Craisins. (Walnuts and raisins can be substituted for the pecans and Craisins.) *Note:* This dough can be very crumbly, giving a "granola"-like texture to the cookies, so add another egg if the dough is too crumbly. If the clients cannot eat nuts, leave them out or add chocolate chips instead of the nuts. Bake on an ungreased cookie sheet for 8 to 10 minutes in a 375° oven.

Sugar Cakes

Judy once worked in Lancaster County, Pennsylvania, and in 1976 she was introduced to these large, cake-like, soft, mild cookies, and is thrilled to share the recipe for these wonderful cookies which are perfect for the older adult.

Ingredients:
   2 eggs
   2 cups of granulated sugar
   $^1/_2$ cup of melted margarine
   1 cup of milk
   $1^1/_2$ teaspoons of vanilla
   $1^1/_2$ teaspoons of soda
   $1^1/_2$ teaspoons of baking powder
   4 to $4^1/_2$ cups of flour
   Granulated sugar to sprinkle on top

Mix the sugar, margarine, eggs, vanilla and milk. It is okay to use an electric mixer. Add 3 cups of flour slowly, mixing thoroughly. Add the soda and baking powder to one cup of flour, and slowly add this mixture to the batter. Add additional flour as needed. The batter should be thick, but not stiff like a traditional cookie.

Lightly spray the cookie sheets with cooking spray and preheat the oven to 375°. Using a tablespoon, place the batter onto the cookie sheet. Leave some room between each cookie because these cookies rise and spread. Sprinkle sugar on top of the batter before baking. Bake 6 to 8 minutes. The cookies are baked when the bottoms are golden brown with the tops remaining lighter. The recipe makes approximately $3^1/_2$ dozen cookies. Jerry likes to sprinkle a little extra sugar on the top when the cookies come out of the oven. These are soft, light and not overly sweet cookies.

Ice Cream

Plastic Bag Ice Cream

Homemade ice cream is a treat, but it always seems to be messy and take so long to make. Plastic Bag Ice Cream is quick to make and not messy. The clients will really enjoy the novelty of making this treat. It is a good activity to do with older folks and children together. Each plastic bag makes one cup of ice cream.

Ingredients per 1-cup serving:
   1 pint-size Ziplock-type storage bag
   1 gallon-size Ziplock-type storage bag
   1 cup of milk
   1 tablespoon of granulated sugar
   1 teaspoon of vanilla
   6 tablespoons of table salt
   Ice cubes to fill a gallon bag three-quarters full

Put the milk, sugar, and vanilla in the pint-size bag. Make sure the bag is securely sealed. Put the 6 tablespoons of table salt in the gallon bag and fill with ice cubes until the bag is three-quarters full. Put the sealed pint-size bag inside the gallon bag that has the ice and salt. Seal the gallon bag and begin to shake. The more vigorously the bag is shaken, the quicker the mixture will turn into ice cream. It takes about five minutes of shaking the big bag until the ingredients form into ice cream. When it is the consistency you are looking for, remove the pint-size bag from the larger one. Wipe the salt from the outside of the pint bag with a paper towel. Then enjoy the ice cream. The ice cream can be eaten right from the bag or put in a bowl. You can add toppings such as strawberries, chocolate and jimmies. The ice cream will be soft, so it should be eaten immediately. You may want to add more sugar or vanilla to the recipe to suit the tastes of your clients.

Bag shaking may be shared by two people, but it means there will be smaller servings. However, it can be less tiring on the individual. Your clients may want to wear gloves when shaking the bags because of the ice. Plastic Bag Ice Cream is a nice treat at a picnic or a fun snack on a dreary winter day.

Variation:
Use a one-pound coffee can instead of the pint-size storage bag and a five-pound can instead of the gallon bag. Make sure you put a lid on each can before shaking.

More Treats

Applesauce Apple Butter

Many of the clients who were raised in the country will remember making homemade apple butter in the fall. Making apple butter in a crockpot or an oven is quicker and is so much easier than the cleanup after making it over an open fire in a copper kettle. Have the clients tell you about making old-fashioned apple butter while they work on this simpler version of an old favorite. The smell is wonderful and will permeate throughout the area and stimulate the clients' sense of smell. The apple butter is well worth the time it takes to make it.

Ingredients:
> 1 pint of apple cider or apple juice
> 1 large (50-ounce) jar of applesauce
> 2 cups of granulated or brown sugar (less if using sweetened applesauce)
> 2 or 3 tablespoons of ground cinnamon (to taste)
> 1 or 2 tablespoons of ground cloves (optional)
> 4 or 5 ($^1/_2$-pint) canning jars and lids

Boil one pint of apple cider or apple juice in a saucepan until it is reduced to a half pint. Pour the applesauce and the reduced cider in a crockpot. You can add the 2 cups of sugar right away or wait for a couple of hours. Add the sugar to taste. If the sweetened applesauce is used, you will need less sugar than for unsweetened applesauce. Cook the apple mixture in the crockpot on low for about 24 hours, or on low for 8 hours then on "high" until it thickens (approximately 3 more hours). Remove the lid from the crockpot when cooking on "high" to help it thicken faster, but remember it may "spit" when you start to stir it on "high." Make sure a staff member or a higher level client does the stirring with a long handled wooden spoon. Stir the mixture often to help it darken evenly. Add the cinnamon and cloves when the apple

butter is almost done. Stir the spices in thoroughly and heat for a few minutes. Taste and adjust seasonings. Remember it is always possible to add spice, but difficult to take it out, so add the spices slowly until the apple butter tastes right for your group.

The apple butter is done when you put a spoonful on a plate and no ring of juice separates from the apple butter. Another old-time way to test it is to place some on a metal spoon and let it cool a few minutes. The apple butter is ready when you turn the spoon over and the apple butter does not fall off of the spoon. The apple butter should be a beautiful dark color with a bit of a sheen. If you do not reduce the apple cider or juice in a saucepan before putting in the applesauce, your apple butter will be a much lighter brown. Ask the clients for their methods of testing the apple butter. Serve the warm apple butter on pieces of fresh bread or on saltine crackers.

To speed up the process, boil the cider down before the clients arrive, or involve just one client with a volunteer in that first step. Since making apple butter can take almost a day and a half, start the evening before and cook it in the crockpot on low overnight, then on high in the morning. While the apple butter is cooking it is best for it to be a drop-in time for the clients to check on the progress. When it is finally time to add the spices, the group can get together to participate in the tasting and canning process.

To can the apple butter, use clean half-pint or pint jars with canning lids and rings (jars, lids and rings may be purchased at most discount department stores). Put the lids in hot water several minutes prior to filling the jars. Fill the jars to within $^1/_4$ inch of the top. Wipe off the rim of the jar with a damp cloth, place the lid on and secure with a canning ring. Make sure the ring is as tight as possible and place the jar lid side down to cool. When completely cool, the jar is sealed if the lid remains depressed. If it has "domed up," the jar of apple butter will have to be refrigerated until used.

Serve the apple butter as a treat at the end of a holiday party or festival. Apple butter seems to taste best in the fall when the cider is freshest; however, it can be made any time of year using apple juice instead of cider. It is a great addition to a fall festival or Halloween event. The apple butter can be put into jars such as pint canning jars or even into baby food jars and given out at a bazaar. If the jars are sealed, the apple butter does not have to be refrigerated.

However, if you reuse small jars such as baby food jars, refrigerate the apple butter. This is a good project to involve a few higher level clients for a longer period of time. The group can be making homemade bread to serve while the apple butter is cooking. Or if you want to extend the process over two days, make the apple butter one day and the bread the next.

Homemade Jelly

Many of the clients will remember canning and have lots of stories about their experiences. This jelly is quick and easy to make. Remember it is very sweet and not a good idea for most of the diabetic clients to eat a lot of it. The juice mixtures such as cranberry raspberry and cranberry peach make excellent jelly.

Ingredients:
- 4 cups of unsweetened fruit juice (100% juice mixtures work well)
- $1/_4$ cup of lemon juice
- 4 to $4^1/_2$ cups of granulated sugar (less if the juice is sweetened with other fruit juices)
- 1 ($1^3/_4$-ounce) package of pectin

Pour the fruit juice and lemon juice into a large pan. Heat slightly, and then add all of the pectin. Give it a minute or two to dissolve, and then continue to heat the juices and pectin mixture over a medium-high heat until it comes to a rolling boil. Stir frequently. High-level clients may be able to do most, or all, of this work since it does not boil very long. Stir in the sugar and return the mixture to a full rolling boil, stirring frequently. Continue boiling the mixture for one minute, stirring constantly (a staff member may want to stir during this last minute). Remove from the heat, skim off any foam that forms and pour the jelly into jars. Baby food jars make good containers, but remember unless the jar seals (see the apple butter section on canning) you will have to store the jelly in the refrigerator. A batch makes approximately 6 half-pints. Making homemade jelly is a good way to instigate reminiscence with the clients about their jelly making and canning experiences.

Homemade Butter

Ingredients:
- 1 pint of room temperature heavy cream (not whipping cream)
- 2 empty plastic jars with screw-top lids (peanut butter jars are good)
- 4 heavy rubber bands
- Table salt to taste (optional)

Pour one half of the heavy cream into each jar. Screw the lid on tightly and put two rubber bands around the jar to make it easier for the clients to grasp. Have the clients take turns shaking the jar. Keep shaking the jar and passing it from one client to another. While they are shaking the jar, the group members may talk about making homemade butter, other items they canned, and favorite memories. When the butter "balls up" within the jar and there is just a small amount of liquid left, the butter is ready. Someone will want to drink the buttermilk, so don't throw it away. Place the butter in a small bowl and wash it in several changes of cold water until the water is clear. Mix a small amount of salt into the butter and serve over crackers or bread. It really tastes great and can be done with lower level clients and/or with children and older adults.

Herb Butter

Soften butter or margarine until it is easy for the clients to manipulate. It is even possible to use whipped margarine or butter. Chop either fresh or dried herbs (favorites are basil, dill and parsley) into very small pieces. Mix with the softened margarine or butter. Press the margarine or butter into a butter mold and place it in the refrigerator until the butter hardens. Remove it from the mold and serve it with homemade bread, mashed potatoes, corn on the cob or other vegetables. A butter press can be used by letting the butter harden slightly, then rolling it onto wax paper. Press the molded press into the butter. Trim the excess butter away and then refrigerate the butter "pats" until ready to serve. If you do not have access to either a butter mold or press, use a small cookie mold or put small portions into small plastic cups. The dietary department should be able to help you obtain small cups. It is best to utilize only one herb at a time versus mixing several together.

Tips for Making Treats With Groups

Baking groups always seem to attract a lot of participants. Many of the clients may say, "I'm just here to eat," but we suggest getting everyone involved. That means, "Unless you help to make it, you can't taste the treat when it is ready." Here are some tips for making baking and cooking groups easier to supervise:

- Keep the group small enough that everyone can be involved.
- Have several topics to discuss as you bake, so those who are not completing a task are still involved in the activity.
- If the group is lower functioning mentally, it is best to keep conversation to a minimum so the clients can stay focused on the task.
- Break up the tasks so everyone has something to do.
- Try to seat everyone in a semicircle or circle so all can see what is occurring. It is best to utilize a round table for this activity. If there must be two tables for seating everyone, have a leader working with each table and make sure two batches or two different recipes are being made.
- Keep a supply of moist towelettes like Wet Ones around to help the clients clean their hands before, during, and after baking.
- Copy the recipe(s) to be used on a copier, enlarge the print as needed. This preserves the cookbook.
- It may be helpful to tape the enlarged recipe to index card stock to make it easier for the clients to handle.
- If the group functions at a high level and can work somewhat independently, have them help prepare the dough to be chilled overnight. Put the dough into a large food storage bag and tape a copy of the procedure for making the dough into cookies on the front of the bag.

- While two people are making cookies from the dough and filling the cookie sheets, have the rest of the group working on a different cookie recipe.
- Have clients work in teams of two to mix a recipe, one to read and get the ingredients ready and one to add and mix them.
- In many cases it works best to break down the process into one task for each person. For example, someone creams the butter and sugar, another adds the flavoring, yet another adds the eggs, and so on until everyone has a task. The cookie stamps work well in the assembly line approach, as they add another step.
- When using the assembly line approach, remember to rotate the tasks so the same person does not always do exactly the same thing. The clients sometimes want to claim ownership of their tasks and have difficulty letting anyone else try. It is best to start with a different task for each person, each session, until everyone has done each job.
- Make a list of who has done each job. You think you will be able to remember, but so many things happen between sessions it is best to write it down.
- It is better to hold smaller, shorter sessions than it is to have one long large group session.
- If a recipe calls for softened margarine, try the squeeze-bottle-type to make it easier for the clients to work with the margarine.
- To reduce the cholesterol from the eggs try Just Whites, from Deb-El Foods Corporation. The can of dried egg whites is found in the baking section of the grocery store and you cannot tell the difference in cakes, sweet breads or coffee cakes.
- Applesauce is a great substitute for the oil in many cakes and sweet breads.

Note: All of the recipes in this chapter have been used successfully by professional recreation leaders and volunteers working with older adults possessing limited physical and/or mental capabilities. We feel that you can use the recipes in your programs with the same results.

Chapter IX

Craft Fun

Fun or Busywork?

We once visited a nursing home where the craft leaders worked from 7:00 A.M. to 3:00 P.M. and had $2^1/_2$ hours for coffee before the first group was scheduled. No work was done outside the craft room and the project for the day of our visit was wrapping coat hangers with yarn (they sold them in the agency gift shop). It was evident that the gift shop was overstocked, based on the activity we observed. The residents were seated at a long table. On one side of the table clients were wrapping coat hangers with yarn and the clients on the other side were unwrapping the yarn and winding it back into balls! Was the program therapeutic or diversionary?

We feel that the term *diversionary* should not be used by any agency providing care for an aged clientele. Recreation programs and especially crafts programs should provide a challenge, use the strengths of the client to make something of value, and above all be an enjoyable experience. That philosophy has prompted us to collect and share the projects and activities in this chapter. We hope they will be of value as you develop a crafts program that has real value for your clients.

Picture Frames

Making frames for photos provides a sense of accomplishment for the client and is an inexpensive alternative to purchasing them. Some of the clients may need help to cut the opening for the picture, but the remainder of the project can usually be accomplished with minimum assistance.

Cardboard Frames

Materials per frame:
> 5-by-7-inch photo
> Two $6^1/_4$-by-$8^1/_2$-inch pieces of cardboard (cereal boxes work well)
> $^1/_2$-inch double-sided mounting tape
> Paper cutter
> Scissors
> Exacto knife
> 12-inch ruler
> Pencil
> Cutting board

Directions:
Use a paper cutter to cut two pieces of cardboard $6^1/_4$-by-$8^1/_2$ inches for each frame. You may want a couple of clients to help do this part of the project ahead of time.

The clients making the frames should start with the piece that is to be the front and using the ruler, draw lines $^3/_4$ inch from the edges that are to be the sides and top of the frame. Draw a line 1 inch from the bottom edge of the frame (remember to check the photo to determine whether the bottom should be the wide or narrow edge of the frame). With the rule for a straight edge, use a sharp knife to cut out the center of the frame along the lines carefully (don't forget to use the cutting board).

On the piece of cardboard that is to be the back of the frame, carefully place strips of mounting tape along the two sides and the bottom (the top must remain open to insert the picture). Next, peel off the mounting tape's protective paper, exposing the second sticky side. Place the frame front on the tape, making sure that the edges are even on both pieces and that the top of the front piece is toward the edge with no tape. Press the edges firmly together, and the frame is ready to decorate. The photo may need to be trimmed slightly to fit in the frame.

Variation:
Take a few painted puzzle pieces and glue them together in an interesting design. Glue a pin on the back for an unusual brooch. The clients can add glitter, sequins or even spatter paint on the pieces to make interesting pins.

Frame Decoration With Puzzle Pieces

Materials:
> Wood or cardboard picture frame
> Discarded puzzle pieces
> Masking tape
> Paint and/or spray paint
> Paintbrushes
> Glue or glue gun

Directions:
Attach the puzzle pieces to the sticky side of a wide piece of masking tape to hold them while they are being painted. Use spray paint or a brush to paint the tops and edges of the pieces (don't paint the backs). Paint the frame and let it dry. After the paint has dried, remove the puzzle pieces from the tape and use a glue gun to fasten them to the front of the frame taking care that they don't protrude into the picture area (or past the bottom edge, if the picture is to stand on a surface). You may have to scrape a spot bare on the frame in order to make the glue hold. The pieces are used as decorations, a few on each side, not covering the entire frame.

Button Decorated Frames

Materials:
> Buttons of various shapes and sizes
> Picture frames or small boxes
> Glue gun
> Paint
> Brushes

Directions:
After painting the box or picture frame, use the glue gun to attach a variety of buttons as decorations. Remember, don't let any of the buttons protrude beyond the bottom edge if the picture frame is to sit on a stand.

Jar Lid Photo Frames

Materials:
> Two-piece canning jar lids and rings
> Photos to mount
> Small magnets
> Heavy cardboard
> Glue gun
> Scissors

Directions:
Use the lid as a pattern and trim the picture to fit inside the ring. Place the picture, faceup, on the lid and insert it in the ring. Cut pieces of cardboard the same size as the lid and glue them in the ring. Glue the magnet to the backing. The cardboard backing should be thick enough that the magnet will be flush with the back edge of the ring. The completed picture and frame can serve as a refrigerator magnet or can be mounted on any metal surface.

Egg Coloring

Coloring eggs is fun and a tradition for several holidays in many cultures. It gives an opportunity for the clients to exercise the small finger and hand muscles, and often leads to significant interactions between the clients and staff.

Tips for Preparing Eggs

- Boil eggs in a stainless steel or glass pan. Do not use iron or aluminum pans as they will affect the dyeing process. Let the eggs cool to room temperature in the water.
- Dry the eggs on paper towels or in cardboard (not Styrofoam) egg cartons.

Batik Eggs

Materials:

>Hard-boiled eggs, cooled to room temperature
>White crayons
>Food coloring or commercial egg dye prepared
>as per instructions
>Bowls
>Large spoons

Directions:

Batik is a method that uses wax to block off areas that are to be left natural after dyeing.

Use a white crayon to draw designs on a hard-boiled egg. Dye the egg by placing it on a spoon and lowering it into the dye solution made with food coloring. The designs will remain the original color of egg.

Easter Egg Dye Bags

Materials:

>Hard-boiled eggs, cooled to room temperature
>Commercial egg coloring bags
>Cup
>Large spoon
>Paper towels
>Cardboard egg cartons
>Newspaper to cover work area

Directions:

Fill a cup half full of water (being careful not to use too much) and submerge the egg in the water. Lift it out and let excess water drip off on a paper towel. To make the colors brighter, add a tablespoon of white vinegar to the water.

Twenty coloring bags come in the commercial kit and each bag can be used to color several eggs. Gently lower an egg into a bag and pat or lightly squeeze the bag to transfer the color to the egg. Hold both ends of the bag and carefully press the bag around the egg. Open the bag and slip the egg onto a cardboard egg carton to dry. We have found that each bag can be used to color three eggs if the eggs are not too wet before they are put in the bag.

Complete directions come with the kits and contain suggestions for creating multicolor eggs and for making designs on the eggs. The kits are available at discount department stores.

Variations:

There are sponge paint and glitter egg-dyeing kits available. Look for them in discount department stores.

Gift Ideas

We tend to forget that our clients like to give gifts, as well as receive them, and often would like to make gifts for family members. Schedule a series of workshops to create gifts for birthdays, Valentine's Day, Easter, Passover, Hanukkah, and Christmas.

Gift ideas which are described in this or our earlier book include greeting cards, pressed flower notepaper, homemade paper, molded paper, bean layers, sand art, candies, flowerpot muffins, bird feeders, sachets, sun catchers, picture frames, tree ornaments, toys and games.

Gift Bags

Materials:

>Scraps of remnant material
>$1/_4$-inch wide ribbon or colored string
>Pinking shears
>Sewing machine

Directions:

Create gift bags of various sizes by cutting two pieces of material to the desired size with pinking shears. Sew three sides of the bag with the wrong sides facing and then turn the bag right side out. Fill it with the desired gift item and tie the bag with a piece of ribbon or use colored string.

Greeting Cards

Materials:

>Old greeting cards
>Colored art paper or stationery
>Envelopes
>Glue
>Scissors

Directions:

Older people love to send and receive cards. Have volunteers bring in old greeting cards. Ask residents to donate any old ones they no longer want to keep. Cut out the verses and cut out the nice pictures on the front. Paste the pictures on the front and the verses inside of colored stationery or art paper that has been cut and folded to fit a standard-size envelope. We have even used homemade paper that we describe how to make on page 160 of *Recreation Programming and Activities for Older Adults.* Have the clients make up a supply of cards for themselves and for the recreation department of the agency, and make sure every client receives a card on those special dates like birthdays.

Christmas Ornaments

Materials:
> Clear plastic or glass ornaments (available from
>   craft stores)
> Various colors of water-based craft paints
> Egg carton separators to support ornaments
> Newspaper to cover work area

Directions:
Remove the cap and hangers from the balls and pour a small amount of paint into the ornament and let it make a streak down the inside of the ball. Rotate the ball about an eighth of a turn and make a streak of another color inside the ball. Make three or four lines with different colors in this manner, being careful not to let too much paint accumulate in the bottom. Place the balls at an angle on the egg cartons to dry. Rotate the balls a quarter turn about every 15 minutes for the first two hours. Then rotate them every couple of hours during the day for the next two days. Each turn of the ball changes the pattern and colors. Maintain a striped look by keeping the ball upright, or create swirls by turning the ball on its side. At the end of second day dump out the extra paint and let the rest dry. After the paint is thoroughly dry, replace the caps and hangers.

    The balls are fun to decorate and easy enough that the task can be accomplished by fairly low functioning clients with proper supervision. The ornaments make great presents for the clients to give to family members or they can be used to decorate the agency's holiday trees.

    Craft stores also have clear two-piece plastic ornaments that can be decorated with watered down white glue. The glue is painted on the inside of the

ornaments (small foam brushes work well; be careful that the clients don't use too much glue). When the painting is finished, sprinkle each half with glitter. Let dry overnight and paint the inside with colored paint. The glue dries clear and the glitter and color show through. Reassemble the ornament and attach the cap and hanger. More complete instructions are available at the craft stores where the ornaments are purchased.

Styrofoam or Satin Ball Ornaments

Materials:
> $1\frac{1}{2}$- or 2-inch satin or Styrofoam balls
> Sequins and/or buttons
> Scrap felt pieces, plastic eyes, and miniature
>   pompoms
> 14-inch ribbon
> Craft glue or glue gun
> Scissors

Directions:
Decorate the balls by gluing sequins or buttons on them. Attach a loop of ribbon for hanging. You can also make cute dog head ornaments by gluing on eyes, a pompom nose and two felt ears.

Cinnamon-Applesauce Ornaments

Materials:
> 2 cups of powdered cinnamon
> 1 to $1\frac{1}{2}$ cups of applesauce
> Rolling pin
> Mixing bowl
> Large cutting board
> Assorted cookie cutters
> Plastic drinking straw
> Narrow ribbons

Directions:
Add the applesauce to the cinnamon, mixing in the bowl, until the mixture forms into a rather dry ball. Roll out this "dough" onto a cinnamon covered surface until it is a little over $\frac{1}{4}$-inch thick. If the dough is too sticky to use, just add more cinnamon. Use the cookie cutters to cut out the shapes. Reroll dough until all of it is used. Use the straw to make a hole near the top of the ornament for hanging. The ornaments can be left to dry naturally or the process can

be speeded up by baking in a 150° oven for an hour or so. If the ornament starts to crack before it is dry, spread a little applesauce on the crack and let it dry. Insert a ribbon through the hole in the ornament and tie with a bow.

These ornaments smell great and can be used as decorations any time of the year. They can even be painted with craft paints if you desire. Another great gift idea!

Cinnamon Pomanders

Materials:

> 2 cups of powdered cinnamon
> 1 to $1\frac{1}{2}$ cups of smooth applesauce
> Mixing bowl
> Plastic drinking straw
> Ceramic cookie molds
> Scrap of wood
> Narrow ribbons

Directions:

Mix the cinnamon with a cup of the applesauce until the mixture is dry and crumbly. Add a little applesauce at a time and continue to knead until the mixture is the consistency of modeling clay. It should not be permitted to become sticky. Dust the cookie mold with cinnamon and use your fingers to press a golf ball–size chunk of the "clay" firmly into place. Make certain every part of the mold is filled and the back is as level as possible. If your fingers get sticky, dust them with some cinnamon. Use a knife to trim away any excess mixture from the mold.

To release the pomander, hold the mold in a vertical position and tap it against a scrap of wood (you don't want to dent your table!) quite hard several times. When the edge of the pomander starts to come away from the mold, carefully remove it and place it on a baking sheet. Use the drinking straw to cut a hole for hanging.

You can let them dry naturally or bake them in a 150° oven for an hour. Place them on a cooling rack until they become quite hard. Insert the ribbon and tie with a bow and you have your sweet smelling pomander. After some time the scent will begin to fade. When it does, just use a little sandpaper on the back, and it's ready to go again.

Let's Paint

Painting can be messy, and many agencies doing crafts with older people tend to stay away from any craft that uses paint. We have observed that agencies with successful painting projects have several things in common:

- They have plenty of old newspapers available to cover the areas where the clients will be painting.
- Large old shirts are available for the painters to wear as smocks.
- Fast drying water-based paints are used for ease of cleanup.
- Painting is done with very small groups, usually a staff member or volunteer working with not more than three clients while they paint.
- The projects are small enough that painting can be completed in a very short time in order not to tire the client.
- Care is taken to assure that the client has an acceptable product upon its completion and a pleasurable experience in the process.

There are so many creative ways to paint, some of which are quite easy for the clients to use. A few methods follow. They can be used on ceramic ware, wood, or fabric, and they meet the criteria for successful programming.

Press Design Painting

Press design is like stenciling only much easier. The best way to learn this type of painting is to purchase a starter kit. There are several brands on the market, each costing under $10 for a starter design. The kit includes instructions, foam presses, paint and a brush. You can purchase various designs or even the foam to create your own designs from a craft store. The technique is simple. Apply a thin coat of paint to the foam press, press it down onto scrap paper a few times to remove the excess paint then apply it to the object you want to paint. Like stenciling, you remove most of the paint before you start. Unlike stenciling, you don't have to worry about the paint running under a stencil or holding the foam press piece in place.

Spatter Painting

Materials:

Old toothbrush
Popsicle stick
One dark color and one light color of spray paint
Cardboard
Object to be painted

Directions:

What a fun way to create an old enameled look to an item. We used spatter paint on the chick feeders that we made into bird feeders (described later in this chapter). Paint the object with a dark color such as blue, plum, or forest green. We used flat spray enamel paint and painted it in stages letting the feeders dry between coats. When the last coat was dry we were ready to spatter paint. We experimented with several different methods and found the following the easiest to use with the clients.

Be sure to cover the area where you will be working with newspaper. The painter should wear a smock or apron to protect from any errant spatters. Spray a small circle of flat white enamel on a piece of heavy cardboard. Wet the tips of the toothbrush bristles in the pool of enamel. Hold the Popsicle stick a few inches above the object to be spattered. Pull the toothbrush across the Popsicle stick. It works best to pull toward yourself. Little bits of paint will land on the object. Some clients may find it easier to hold the toothbrush steady and move the Popsicle stick across the bristles. Either method will achieve good results. We found it best to keep the arms extended while doing the spattering to avoid getting paint on us. Paint does get on hands, so the clients may want to wear disposable gloves. The base coat should be a dark color. Spatter with a lighter color, such as cream, ecru or white.

Crackle Painting

Materials:

Crackle medium (available at craft stores)
Dark and light acrylic paint
Brushes
Clean-up materials
Object to paint

Directions:

Crackle paint gives the item a cracked or aged look. This too can be done on wood, ceramics or fabric. Crackle paint only works with acrylic paint. Start with a darker color for a base coat. After it has dried, brush on the crackle medium. Once this dries, apply a thin layer of a light color acrylic paint and watch the paint begin the crackling process as it dries. Read the instructions on the bottle because some companies suggest you apply the top coat to a tacky finish and others to a dry finish within two to four hours of the application of the crackle finish.

Drip Painting

Materials:

Acrylic paints
Brushes
Clean-up materials
Objects to be painted

Directions:

This method is a lot of fun because it is so creative. This method of painting looks great on fabric such as aprons, T-shirts, and caps, although it can be used on wood or ceramics.

When working with fabric you do not need a base coat, but with other materials start with a light colored base coat. Again this can be sprayed on with flat enamel or brushed on with an acrylic paint. Once the base coat is dry, dip a paintbrush into brightly colored paint, hold the brush over the item to be dripped upon. The paintbrush should be held 2 to 4 inches above the item. Move the paintbrush in a slow steady motion and let the paint drip off onto the object. Change colors and continue to drip paint in swirling, circling or zigzag motions. Use as many colors of paint as desired, and as much paint as desired. Smaller amounts of paint dry faster, but larger amounts give more of a three-dimensional effect.

When painting on T-shirts, insert a sheet of cardboard inside the garment to keep the paint from bleeding through to the second layer of fabric.

Wipe Off Painting

One of the nicest features about working with stains is that they can be light or dark. The same can be done with paint to give a "washed" look. The technique works best with wood projects made from oak or other wood with what we call an "open grain." Spray flat enamel or brush acrylic paint on the surface of the project and immediately wipe it off with a clean cloth. Remove as much of the paint as you desire. This makes a good base coat for press-on designs or stenciling, but it may be that you don't need further decoration. When dry, spray or brush on a coat of clear finish to seal the surface.

Marbleizing and Stone Paint

Check with your craft or hardware store for a starter kit for these types of paints. The starter kits are approximately $10. Both use a base coat of spray paint plus a second coat that gives either the marbleized or stone finish. They can be used on a variety of surfaces and give a great finish, but remember they both involve spray paint and many clients find it difficult to press down hard enough on a spray nozzle. However, handles which fit on spray paint cans are available from many craft and hardware stores. These handles make it easier for the crafter to release and control the spray.

Stenciling

Stencil brushes and stencils are available from craft stores, along with directions for their use. Clients tend to get too much paint on the brushes and it runs under the edge of the stencil. We find that sponge brushes are easier for most clients to use. The brush should be tapped on a piece of cardboard several times to remove the excess paint before using it on the surface to be stenciled. It is better to get too little paint on the project and have to go over it a second time, than to get too much and have it bleed under the stencil.

We suggest you use colored pencils or crayons with the stencils for your less skilled clients. There are many reusable plastic patterns available from craft stores. Use masking tape to hold the stencil to the material. Teach the client to start the crayon on the stencil and move it onto the material. You can easily stencil on fabric and wood. With a little experience, you can even do shading.

Paper Doily Stencils

Materials:
   Placemat or other article to be decorated
   Paper doilies
   Spray adhesive
   Spray paint

Directions:
Place the doily facedown, on a table covered with newsprint, and spray with the adhesive. When dry, center the doily on the placemat with the adhesive side toward the mat or other article to be decorated. Press the doily onto the mat so that all parts of the doily are in contact with the surface. Shake up the can of spray paint and holding it 12 to 15 inches from the mat spray the entire surface. When the paint dries, carefully remove the doily and you will have a mat the color of the paint with the original color of the mat showing through the design.

Rubber Stamps

Rubber stamping is a desirable way of decorating a surface. There are more varieties of stamps and colors of ink pads on the market than ever before. They are easy to use, create great designs and are very versatile. They make great party invitation designs, and can easily be added to a newsletter or calendar before it is duplicated, or even after. Bookmarks and note cards are easy to make and usually sell well at a bazaar. Rubber stamping works best if you purchase the special rubber stamp ink and markers that have been created especially for rubber stamp art.

For a lower level client, pressing the stamp onto the ink pad and then applying it to the paper may be an advanced skill. However, we have found that it works very well for many clients in this category when used on an individual basis.

Show the more creative clients how to use a felt-tip marker (there are ones specifically for rubber stamping) to color in certain areas of the stamp prior to stamping on paper. It may work better for your clients to use the stamp with the ink pad and then color in various areas they want to have a different color.

Embossing with rubber stamps is like working with glitter. After stamping the design on the paper, pour some embossing powder on the ink. Dump any excess embossing material back in the bottle, then use a heat source to warm the paper until the embossing material rises and creates a sheen. We use a hair dryer set on low as our heat source. We also heat the paper from underneath so the embossing powder does not blow away. Commercial heat guns can be purchased for approximately $25 to $30, if funds are available.

Puppets and Dolls

Puppets and dolls may sound as though they are not age-appropriate. If used correctly, they can be a great addition to the program. In the days before you could buy everything at a store, parents used to make toys for their children. Making a puppet or doll will bring back memories of toys the clients' parents made for them, as well as challenging their dexterity. It could be a great lead-up to your next intergenerational program. The clients could put on a show for the children or give the toys as gifts.

Sock Puppets

Materials:
> Heavy socks (have each person bring one)
> Felt scraps
> Yarn
> Scissors
> Craft glue
> Button eyes
> Needles
> Thread

Directions:
Each person should place a sock on a hand and pull it up his or her arm. Push the toe of the sock between the thumb and the rest of the hand (like Shari Lewis and Lamb Chop). Make eyes (or use button eyes) and tongue from felt and glue in place. Use yarn to make hair and whiskers. Show the clients how to move their thumbs to make the puppets "talk."

Have the clients make up names for their puppets. Ask each person to introduce his or her puppet to the rest of the group saying, "Hello, my name is _____." The puppeteer should talk in the voice of the puppet and move the puppet's mouth at the same time. The leader should demonstrate with a puppet

and have his or her puppet call on the next person. Later, try to get the clients to ask questions of their own or other peoples' puppets.

Vinyl Glove Puppets

Materials:
> Vinyl or latex gloves
> Felt-tip pens

Directions:
A quick method for making hand puppets is to use a vinyl or latex glove. Have the clients place the glove on their nondominant hand and make a fist with the thumb on the outside. Use felt-tip markers to draw the features on the glove with the mouth being the opening between the thumb and first knuckle as shown in the illustration. Use the puppets in the same manner as described for the sock puppets. To make the gloves slip on easier, you can sprinkle a bit of baby powder in them.

Cornhusk Dolls

Materials:
> Dried cornhusks
> Twine
> Yarn
> Scissors
> Basin or bucket

Directions:
Collect the dry soft inner husks in the fall (or purchase husks at a crafts store). Soften them by soaking them in warm water until they are pliable. Tie about a dozen strips together at one end with string or yarn. To make a head, turn the husks back over the

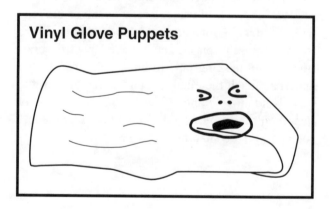

Vinyl Glove Puppets

knot and tie another string as shown in the illustration. Gather three husks on each side and tie for arms as shown. Tie the remaining husks for the body as shown. Divide the husks below the body and tie for legs. Make a skirt from husks for the female dolls by tying them with the husks over the head as shown and then bending them down while they are still damp. Use felt-tip pens to draw facial features and buttons. This project makes a great gift or sales item in the agency gift shop or bazaar.

Cornhusk Dolls

Just Paper

Paper Gift Bags

Materials:

    Plywood forms (different sizes)
    Heavy paper (old grocery bags)
    Glue gun or white glue
    Scissors

Directions:

You can make your own paper gift bags from used grocery bag paper which has been flattened and decorated using any of the methods which have been de-

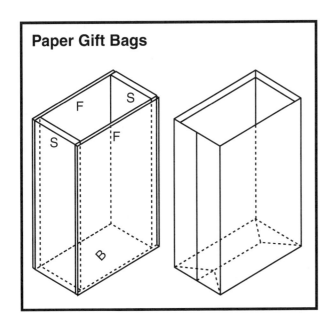

Paper Gift Bags

scribed previously in this chapter. Heavy giftwrapping paper can also be used.

Make several plywood forms the shapes and sizes of the bags to be constructed. Use $\frac{3}{4}$-inch scrap wood for the bottom (B) and sides (S). The front and back (F) can be made from $\frac{1}{8}$-inch hardboard or $\frac{1}{4}$-inch plywood. Fasten together with small nails, leaving the top open as shown in the illustration. We store our smaller forms inside the larger ones. Cut the paper so that it is 1 inch longer than the circumference of the box. The width of the paper should be the height of the finished bag, plus the thickness of the bag, plus 1 inch (for example, if the finished bag is to be 8 inches high by 6 inches wide by 3 inches thick, the width of the paper should be 8 + 3 + 1 = 12 inches; the length of the paper should be 6 + 3 + 6 + 3 + 1 = 19 inches).

Start by folding down and gluing a 1-inch border for the top of the bag. Now fold the paper around the form, keeping the fold next to the form and the edge even with the top. Wrap the paper around the form and overlap one inch on a narrow end of the form. The paper should extend beyond the lower end of the form enough to fold and glue for the bottom. Use the glue gun to cement the vertical joint, being careful not to glue the paper to the form. Turn the form upside down and fold the end of the bag sides (S) in against the form. Arrange the front and back pieces (F) so that they have 45° edges and fold the into place against the form. After creasing all of the edges, carefully glue the bottom of the bag (but not to the form!). When glue sets, remove the bag from the form.

Cut two pieces of ribbon and glue them to the inside edge of the top of the wide sides of the bag for handles. You now have a bag just the right size for that gift you didn't want to have to wrap. We know this sounds difficult, but once the forms are made and you make a bag on your own, you will see that it is easier to do than to describe.

Cookie Mold Plaques

Materials:
> Paper-mâchè (available at craft stores, or make your own)
> Unscented toilet paper
> Bowls
> Ceramic cookie molds
> Wooden spoon
> Wire drying racks
> White glue
> Artists' brushes

Directions:
Here is an easy method for making paper-mâchè. Have the clients tear paper towels into small pieces (about $1/2$-by-$1/2$ inches) and when you have about a bucketful, cover them with water and let them soak overnight. Put the saturated paper in a blender, a little at a time and blend into a pulp, adding only enough water to make it work. After blending the pulp, squeeze out most of the water until it is the consistency of bread dough. Now you are ready to use the cookie molds.

Lay a piece of dry toilet paper on the mold with the edges extending a couple of inches over the edge. Dampen a fine brush (like a #5 artist's brush) with a little water and gently press the tissue into all parts of the mold, trying not to tear it or get it soggy (little rips are not too troublesome).

Lay a second layer of dry tissue over the first and press it in place. There may be enough dampness from the first layer that very little water will be needed for the second. Keep adding layers of toilet tissue in this manner until you have a total of seven or eight layers. Now is the time to add two more layers, but instead of using plain water, use white glue

which has been diluted with an equal amount of water to dampen the tissue.

The tissue in the mold is now thick enough to use a bigger brush (like a 1-inch flat artist's brush). Apply five or six more layers using the glue and water mixture but you don't have to press the tissue into the mold as carefully as before. Remember the paper-mâchè you made? Use it to fill the mold until the cavity is filled to the level of the back, pressing it firmly in place.

Cover the back with 8 or 10 more layers of the toilet tissue using the glue mixture to dampen each layer (be careful not to get it too damp). You have to make sure that you don't have pools of water at any stage of the process. Now you are ready to release your work from the mold. *Don't let it dry in the mold or you may never get it out!*

Lay a piece of brown grocery bag on the table and invert the mold on the bag. Strike the mold sharply several times with the wooden spoon. Hold the tissue that extends from under the mold with one hand and gently lift the mold off of the formed object. There might be a few tears in the surface of the object so wet the fine brush and smooth them out.

Place the objects on a drying rack for 24 hours and then trim the edges with a craft knife. You can then use watercolors or acrylic paints to decorate the figures and you may want to glue ribbons on the back for hanging them.

Marbleizing Paper

Materials:
> Glass or enamel pan (9-by-12-by-1-inch)
> Variety of oil-based paints
> Paint thinner
> Typing paper (20# weight)
> Popsicle sticks

Directions:
Fill a shallow glass or enamel pan to $1/2$-inch from the top with tap water. Use a Popsicle stick to put a few drops of oil-based paint on top of the water. Swirl it around carefully with the stick. Hold a piece of paper by opposite corners and lower it onto the surface of the water, making sure there are no bubbles underneath. Carefully pick it up by the corners and lay it on a flat surface, paint side up, to dry. The paper should remain the original color with swirls of

the paint color. A couple of different colors of paint may be used at the same time. Be careful not to swirl the color too much or apply too much paint to the water. The marbleized paper can be used for greeting cards or note cards. Usually three or four pieces of paper can be colored before changing the water and cleaning the pan. Use mineral spirits to clean the paint that adheres to the pan, and then wash with soap and warm water before refilling and starting again.

Spraying Paper

Materials:
Handmade paper or typing paper
Pump spray bottles
Food colors

Directions:
If you want to make paper see pages 160–163 in our book, *Recreation Programming and Activities for Older Adults* for directions. When the paper is nearly dry, use diluted food colors in a spray bottle (like the ones you use to spray window cleaners) to make designs on the paper. After spraying, place the paper between sheets of clean newsprint and press lightly to set the design. You can use stencils or cutouts to direct the spray or just freehand spray it.

If you are using typing paper, dampen it with a sponge and wait until it is almost dry before using the spray paints. Set the color the same way as when working with handmade paper. The decorated paper can be used for making greeting cards or notepaper.

Placemats

We have used the making of placemats as a first-comer activity for large group picnics, but it can be used almost any time to create a personalized placemat. Cut newsprint to placemat size, about 16 by 20 inches, and use sponge printing, fruit printing, finger painting, stenciling, bingo markers, colored crayons, or colored pencils to decorate the mats.

Variations:
• To make reusable mats, use poster board. Decorate them in the same manner as described earlier, but cover them with clear contact paper when the artwork is dry.

• Cover a table with newsprint and have the people decorate the area in front of them. After the paper dries it can be hung as a mural for everyone to admire.
• Use a theme for the mural or placemats such as animals, spring, or fruit.

Coffee Filter Butterflies

Materials:
Large (10-cup) paper basket-type coffee filters
Plastic spring-clip clothespins
Colored pipe cleaners
Felt-tip bingo markers

Directions:
Flatten a coffee filter and color it with bingo markers or other felt-tip pens. Fold in half with colored side out and pinch together in center. Clip with a colored clothespin. Fold a pipe cleaner for the antennae and insert it into the clothespin as shown in the illustration. If you wish, cement a magnet to the underside of the clothespin to make a refrigerator magnet. This is an ideal project for an intergenerational program.

Other Fun Projects

We didn't quite know in which category to include the following suggestions, but we think they are worthwhile activities.

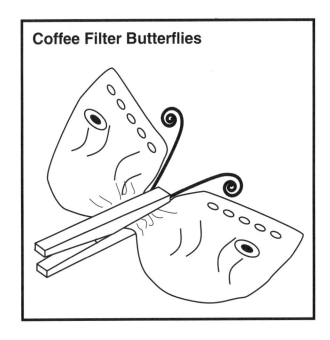

Coffee Filter Butterflies

Orange Pomanders

Materials:

    Oranges
    Whole cloves
    Powdered cinnamon
    $\frac{1}{4}$-inch ribbon
    Plastic bags

Directions:

Push the stems of whole cloves into the surface of an orange until it is completely covered. Put a teaspoon of cinnamon into a plastic bag, insert the orange and shake until the orange is covered. Remove the orange and tie a ribbon around it in a crisscross fashion so that it can be hung in a closet as an air freshener. The orange will shrink in size but will retain its scent for some time. This is another good gift item that clients can make.

Chick Feeder Bird Feeders

Materials:

    Chick feeders (6-inch round 8-hole feeders, available from farm stores for about $1)
    Quart mason jars
    Spray paint
    Old toothbrushes

Directions:

Spray-paint the feeders a medium to dark color with flat exterior quality paint. When the paint is dry, speckle or spatter paint with white or cream (see spatter painting earlier in this chapter). When the paint is dry, fill a quart jar with birdseed and screw onto the feeder as shown in the illustration. Create a hanger or just place it on a table outside. These usually sell really well at bazaars. We have seen them priced at $8 to $10.

Colored Sand Jars

Materials:

    Sandbox grade white sand
    Food coloring or dye
    Large margarine tubs
    Wooden sticks

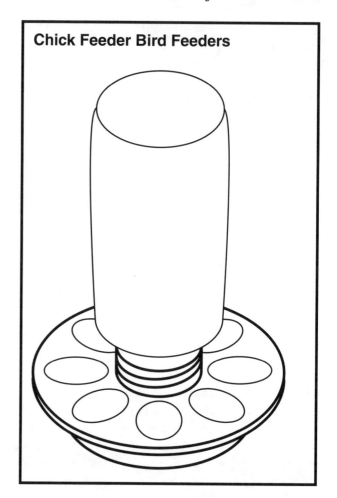

Chick Feeder Bird Feeders

    Pint jars with screw-type lids
    Large paper clips
    Large spoons

Directions:

The first part of the project is to color the sand using food coloring or dye. Prepare different colors in each of the plastic tubs, first by filling each one about half full of water, then adding food color. Carefully add sand to each tub and stir with a wood stick to make certain that the sand is covered. After several minutes, pour the liquid off and spread the sand on paper towels to dry.

After the sand dries, carefully spoon layers of different colors into a jar. The last layer should come up to the neck of the jar. Open a large paper clip until the wire is straight and push it down along the inside edge of the jar to make a design in the sand. Repeat this several times around the sides of the jar. When finished, fill the jar with more sand and screw the lid on tight. The sand-filled jar makes a good paperweight.

Bean Layering

Materials:

Different types and colors of dried beans
Pint jars with screw-type lids
Large spoons
Margarine tubs

Directions:

This is simpler than the sand jars and works well with lower functioning clients. Have the different types and colors of beans separated in margarine tubs. Spoon a layer of one type and then another layer of a different type until the jar is full of beans. If you want to create a pattern, push a pencil down the inside edge and let beans fall into the spaces created. For the more confused clients, or for those with poor use of their hands, have them pick up the beans one at a time rather than using a spoon (this will encourage finger exercise). If you wish, fill the jars with a variety of beans that can be used as a mixture for soup, to be given as usable gifts. Make a jar hat as described next to add a finishing touch to the jar that is being given as a gift or being sold in a bazaar.

Jar Hats

Materials:

Scrap cloth
Pinking shears
Ribbon or yarn

Directions:

Cut a small piece of cloth into a square about 4-by-4 inches, using pinking shears to make a nice edge. Center the square over the filled jar and lid and tie with a piece of ribbon or yarn. This quick little project adds a nice finishing touch to bean or sand layered jars, or even for a jar of jelly or apple butter that the clients have made.

Soap Molding

Materials:

Soap molding kit (available from craft stores)
Microwave oven
Sharp knife
Old mixing cup

Directions:

This is a more advanced craft and must be done with a very small group because there are not many tasks and the soap must be molded very quickly. Before investing a lot of time or money in soap molding, purchase one kit and have a staff or volunteer in-service on the activity in order to iron out all of the steps. The kit is not difficult to use, and it is fun. It requires the use of a sharp knife to make shavings from the soap, color, and fragrance blocks. It also requires someone to pour the very warm liquid into the soap molds.

Although this does not sound like the best activity for older adults, many of these clients did all of their washing in homemade soap and will enjoy the chance to compare the differences between the modern version and how they had to make soap. An address for a soap molding kit is listed in the resource section. Some of the larger craft stores do carry the kits you would need to get started, along with the additional supplies to continue using the craft.

We do not recommend the traditional making of soap as it requires the use of lye. The people stirring it in the hot grease can easily be burned, so we suggest you use the commercial product for this craft.

Stress Relief Balloons

Materials:

Small balloons (3 or 4 inch)
Wooden pencil with eraser
Flour
Spoon
Small funnel

Directions:

Insert the eraser end of a pencil in a balloon and use it to insert the balloon into a second one of the same size to make a double-walled balloon about 2 inches in diameter. Remove the pencil, insert a small funnel and fill the inner balloon with flour. Remove the funnel and tie the inner balloon securely. Now tie the outer balloon and work the knot back inside of the outer balloon. Use a permanent ink pen to draw faces on the balloons to make them more personalized. Use the balloons for hand exercises or just squeeze to release stress.

Tips for Working With Crafts

Paint and Glue

- Older adults tend to spill glue and paint, and want to use too much. Preserve these materials by using margarine tub lids. They are hard to tip over and are easy to clean for reuse.
- Cut an egg carton into sections to make small pots for glue or paint.
- Beauty wedges (located in the cosmetic section of a store) are great to use to conserve paint. They can be used instead of stenciling brushes or for any project where paint can be dabbed on the surface. A package usually sells for under $2 and the wedges can be washed and used repeatedly.
- Beauty wedges can also be used to apply makeup for face painting, clowning, and Halloween.

Project Assembly

- To keep all of the supplies a person needs to complete a craft project together, lay all of the pieces on a paper plate. This keeps the items organized for the participant.
- Consider using the assembly line approach for some craft projects so that everyone, even those with limited ability, can be involved.

Supply Sources

- Several craft supply stores now carry ceramic molds that are less expensive than the Brown Bag molds and are just as good for molding paper-mâchè and cinnamon-applesauce ornaments.
- Call other senior centers, nursing homes and day-care centers to explore the possibility of sharing ceramic molds.
- For older adults who have difficulty using scissors, there are new scissors available through catalogs for those with arthritic hands.
- Ceramic and plastic cookie stamps available in many craft and discount department stores work just as well as the higher priced ones found in specialty shops.

Chapter X

All Natural

It is a wonderful feeling of accomplishment for the clients when the seeds they have planted sprout, then grow into plants. Of course, they experience a different emotion if the chipmunks, squirrels, skunks, rabbits and deer eat the vegetables and flowers. Many of the clients have either been raised on a farm or have had a garden. Even city dwellers often reminisce about their gardening and bird-watching experiences.

This section explores ideas for enjoying nature and the natural environment. Many are hands-on projects that the clients can make, while others are ideas for nature observation. The purpose of this chapter is to help your staff become aware of some of the possibilities for introducing the clients to gardening, bird watching, weather-related and other nature-related activities.

Growing Things

Sunflower Seeds

Soak sunflower seeds in water for 5–15 minutes then place them between two layers of paper towels that have been dampened. Put a piece of waxed paper on a cookie sheet, then the dampened towels. Dampen daily as needed, until the sunflowers sprout, usually in two or three days. They can either be planted directly in the ground or in peat pots. You don't have to sprout them first, but it sure is a lot of fun to see the first growth as seeds begin to do their thing.

Sweet Potato Vines

Fill a wide bottom glass almost full of water. Insert the end of a sweet potato in the water and hold it in place by inserting round toothpicks into the potato so they rest on the edge of the glass. Keep the glass in a well-lighted place and in a few weeks roots will start to grow. Keep the water level constant and soon the vine will start to grow from the top of the potato. Set the glass on a windowsill and watch the vines grow.

Variation:
Try the same thing with carrots. Cut the bottom (the pointed end) off of the carrot, stick toothpicks into the sides of the carrot, place it in a glass of water. You must have a bit of the green top for the carrot to be able to grow. Many of the carrots found in the grocery store will work for this.

Grass Heads or Figures

Fill a cup with a piece of sponge that has been dampened in water and sprinkle grass seed on top. In a few days grass will begin to grow. Mist or sprinkle a bit of water on the sponge as it starts to dry out. It is fun to decorate the cup with a face prior to sprouting. The grass will look like hair. The clients can even cut the hair and it will grow back. Commercial products are available that look like faces and animals, or you can make your own designs using old margarine tubs or other containers. You can also fill the container with potting soil to grow grass hair. We like the sponge method—in case the container tips over, there is less mess. Kentucky blue grass is a bit more expensive than some other seeds, but grows nicely in containers.

Other things such as corn, beans, and peas can be sprouted in damp sponges, but remember they will not be able to continue growing like the grass.

Herbs

Herbs are easy and fun because they can be grown in small pots on windowsills, or in small or large garden plots. Select the type of herb carefully because some herbs like borage and peppermint will take over a garden. Apple mint and some of the more unusual mints are great because they have wonderful flavor, but do not spread as much. The mints are pleasant because they can be used in hot or iced teas and chewed as a breath freshener. They are also especially well-suited for sensory stimulation sessions due to their smell and taste. Parsley is great as a garnish, for herb butter (see Chapter VIII, Sweet Treats) and in tomato juice (see the following) and can easily be grown in pots in a windowsill, or in the garden. Another versatile herb is basil. Basil comes in some unusual flavors (such as licorice), which are great for the taste buds as well as for use in tomato juice and herb butter. We love fresh corn-on-the-cob with basil-herb butter. Yum!

Tomato Juice With Herbs

Crush a fresh herb like basil, parsley or chives and serve it in tomato juice. This gives the juice a nice flavor and uses some of the herbs you have been growing. A mortar and pestle can easily be obtained at a discount or department store. It makes crushing herbs easy, as well as providing a different activity for the clients to try.

Unusual Ways to Grow Flowers

Bleach Jug Planters

An alternative to spending a lot of money on planters for the clients is to use 1-gallon bleach containers as planters. One-gallon water jugs can also be used. Cut a $2\frac{1}{2}$-inch hole near the top of each side of the container (as shown in the illustration) leaving some

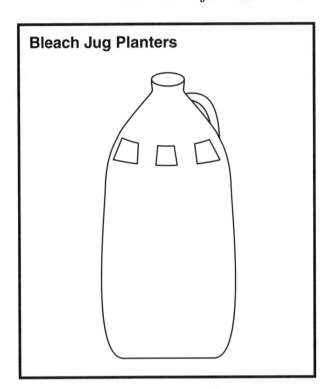

Bleach Jug Planters

of the piece connected at the top. Puncture a few holes in the bottom of the container for drainage. Put some loose gravel, charcoal briquettes or plant charcoal in the bottom of the container to keep from losing dirt when watering. Fill with dirt up to the bottom of the neck, and plant a plant in each hole. The clients may want to personalize and decorate the containers before they are planted. This can make a good winter craft project. The nice thing about jugs is that they can be easily moved and positioned for the clients to take care of. Some administrators may not appreciate having plastic jugs lining the facility walks, so consider utilizing these in a day room or enclosed courtyard.

Impatiens are good plants for these containers because they grow and spread out quickly. The double or single impatiens are beautiful. Other plants that work well are coleus, begonias, pansies, verbena, trailing lobelia and petunias.

Pouch Flower

These look terrible when they are first planted, but they are so much fun. Once the plants begin to fill in and around the bag, they are exceptionally beautiful. Visitors wonder how they are planted, so the bags are a conversation starter also. There is a specially made plastic bag that can be purchased for around $2

Pouch Flowers

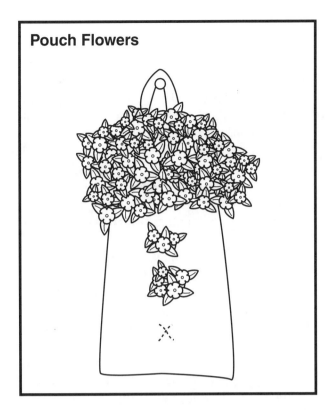

to $3 from your local garden center (an address for mail orders is in the resource section), but we made our own from bread bags.

You can make your own by cutting four or five holes on one side of a heavy-duty plastic bread bag as shown in the illustration. The holes should be X-shaped slits about 1-inch long. They should be fairly small because you don't want the dirt or water to come out through these cracks. For drainage, use a hole punch and make several holes in the very bottom of the bag. Fill the bag with dirt and lay it on its side with the slits up. Choose plants while they are still small and insert them in the slits. Take most of the soil off of the roots before planting. Poke a finger through the slits to make the hole for each plant and gently work the soil around the roots. Leave enough room at the top of the bag for a twist tie or two in order to hang it. Let the bag lay flat with the plants faceup for 3–4 days until the roots get established. Then hang the bag on a nail or plant hanger making sure the end with the twist ties is at the top. Remember there is a fair amount of weight to the bag so make certain it is securely supported. The pouches must be watered regularly, although they do retain moisture better than pots. Use the same types of plants as recommended for the bleach jug planters. The same planting methods apply to the commercial flower pouches.

The purchased pouches suggest putting a plant into the opening in the top and watering the plant at each hole. For clients, it might be easier to leave the top plant off and water at the top of the bag. These flower bags will really impress the rest of the staff.

Hints:
- If the holes are too large, use duct tape around the openings to hold the plants and soil in place.
- A few drainage holes in the bottom of the bag really help.
- After a few weeks the plants should grow enough to completely cover the pouches.

Upside-Down Pots

These are special clay pots that permit you to plant flowers when the pots are right side up, and then hang them as planters, upside down. They can be very expensive, but the novelty may be worth the expense.

An inexpensive alternative is to use a plastic wide-mouthed jar such as an industrial-size mayonnaise

Upside-Down Pots

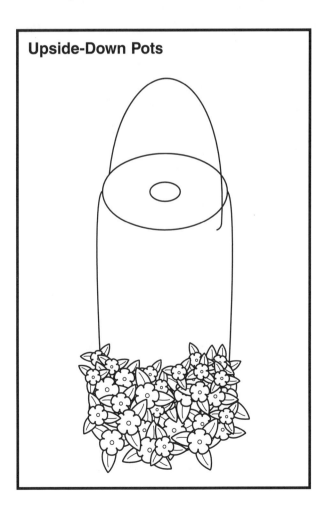

container. Cut a small hole about two inches in diameter in the bottom for watering and use coat hanger wire to make a handle as shown in the illustration.

You fill the very bottom with crumbled newspaper, then the dirt. Plant the flowers as you would any plant, water it, and wait one week. The week lets the roots take hold before you turn the planter upside down and hang it from a hanger. The plants will grow out and up the sides of the planter. It is particularly effective with plants that vine, such as nasturtiums, if you have a sunny location. Impatiens and petunias grow well in these pots, too. Water as usual. If you want to decorate the planters, it is easier to do so before you fill them with the soil.

Chimney Flue Planters

Although more expensive, a chimney flue can be filled with lots of gravel then potting soil and planted with annuals or perennials. They are a nice height and size for wheelchair users. Check with your local suppliers to see if they have any with slight imperfections that will prevent them from being used for their intended purpose. They might be willing to contribute them to your agency.

Tips for Growing Things

- The best thing to keep deer from eating your plants is a fertilizer known as Milorganite. It must be reapplied after a few rainstorms.
- Most plants grow faster and better when purchased and planted early in the growing season. Plants often become root bound (that means the roots are intertwined into a mass) and have a more difficult time growing if left in small pots too long.
- When planting flowering or vegetable plants, loosen the soil around the roots and put a few holes through the root mass with your fingers. This lets the roots get reestablished in their new environment instead of staying in a small cluster from the way they were growing before.
- When planting in pots, put loose gravel or charcoal briquettes in the bottom of the pot before planting. This helps drainage and prevents the loss of dirt through the drainage holes. All planters should have drainage holes to help prevent root rot that is caused by overwatering. If the pots

don't have drain holes, either drill some or add extra charcoal and gravel before adding the soil.
- Older adults tend to overwater plants rather than underwatering them. This causes them to become wilted and limp, making you think they need more water. Always feel the soil to make sure it is dry, before watering a plant.
- Most plants prefer soil that is thoroughly watered (water pours out of the drainage holes) then left to dry out almost completely before rewatering. The soil should be dry to the touch for several inches before rewatering. This helps prevent root rot.
- When growing seedlings, cover the top of the containers with a layer of newspaper after planting the seeds. This helps to hold the seeds in place and keeps the soil moist.
- Foam egg cartons make great starter pots for seedlings.
- It is better to mist seedlings than to water them. Misting is good exercise for the client's fingers. Sometimes they have difficulty completing the squeeze movement required from a spray bottle. Save a pump bottle from hair spray or window cleaner to use for misting.
- Raised garden plots or container gardening works well with older adults.
- The County Agricultural Extension Office is a good source to contact regarding local 4-H groups as possible volunteers for gardening (and pet therapy programming). They may be able to suggest sources for seeds and seedlings.
- Many commercial potting soils do not have enough perlite. It helps to keep the soil from compacting, so add perlite or vermiculite to the potting soil mixture to make it easier for the plant to grow.
- Soilless professional potting mixes dry out quickly so add potting soil and perlite to any professional mix you may be using.
- Potting soil can be reused if it is sterilized. To sterilize the soil, place it in an old shallow pan and bake it in 325° oven for an hour.
- Force bulbs such as hyacinth, daffodil, Dutch iris and paper white narcissus to grow and bloom inside. Purchase bulbs when they go on sale at the end of the season and store in a dry, cool place until you are ready to use with the clients. Fill a terra cotta saucer from a planter with stones or white marbleized rock, available at the garden

center or an agricultural store. Water without totally covering the top of the rocks. Surround the bulbs with the rocks and water as needed. Don't let the rocks get dry, but be careful not to have too much water on the rocks. Keep out of direct sunlight. Filtered light works best. The clients will enjoy watching the bulbs grow and bloom.

- To help chase away the winter "blahs," force forsythia, pussy willows, dogwood and cherry branches to bloom early by bringing small branches inside and placing them in a vase of water about 3–4 weeks prior to the usual time for blooming.
- Grow grass heads as a reminder that spring is coming.

For other ideas on gardening activities, refer to Chapter 19 in our earlier book, *Recreation Programming and Activities for Older Adults.*

Winter Nature Activities

Nature-related programs can, and should, take place any time of the year. As it gets colder, most of the activities take place inside, but they still relate to the natural world. We have included some ideas that will provide the clients with enjoyable activities that have therapeutic value during the cold winter months.

Feeding Birds and Squirrels

Bird watching is an activity that provides hours of enjoyment. If you are lucky, there is a large window looking out on a lawn or patio that has some trees and/or bushes nearby, for it is easier to attract our feathered friends if there is cover available. Set up some feeding stations anytime during the year in a location where they can be viewed easily from indoors. The birds can make good use of the food during the winter months, but keep on filling the feeders to attract the birds and squirrels for client viewing all year long.

Watching the birds and squirrels that come to the feeder the clients have built or filled with seeds brings a sense of wonder and enjoyment. The following are a few ways to incorporate this part of the natural world into your program. Helping to fill bird feeders is an excellent activity for the lower level clients and watching the birds is very relaxing.

First things first, so let's have the clients help prepare the food and build the feeders. These are fall activities that will help lead into the winter feeding regime.

Corn Shelling

Shelling dried corn off of the cobs is one of Betty's (Judy's mom's) favorite activities. It is one of the tasks she can stay on for over 30 minutes and she always has a smile when she is doing it. As with many clients' with memory problems, she likes to be useful and gains a sense of achievement from helping. She uses her fingernails to shell the corn, even though a butter knife works just as well. It is possible to purchase dried corn to be shelled from a feed store or some garden centers, but this method is very expensive. There is usually some corn left after the farmer has harvested the field. Just ask for permission to have volunteers or capable clients serve as "gleaners" and collect the corn.

Picking and shelling corn can be part of a theme event such as a fall festival, Halloween, or barn party. Corn shelling is an activity the children enjoy doing with the older adults. The stories the older adults tell during this activity fascinate the children. The shelled corn can be used to feed the birds and squirrels, but leave some of the corn on the cobs for one of the easy squirrel feeders we are going to suggest you use.

Sunflower Seeds

If you can find the space, plant sunflowers in the spring. The clients can enjoy them while they are growing. When the seeds have formed in the fall, bring the flower heads inside to dry. Place them on newspaper in an area where there are no mice. When the seeds have dried completely, the clients can pull them off of the heads and store them in containers to be used to feed the winter birds. If you do not grow your own seeds, you can purchase a variety of suitable seeds at most discount department stores and garden shops.

Large Bottle Feeders

Materials per feeder:
  Two disposable pie tins
  One 1-gallon plastic jug
  One wire coat hanger

Directions:

These are not the prettiest feeders, but they are inexpensive, easy to make, and do not have to be filled as often as smaller feeders. The jug will be hung upside down with a pie pan attached to the top and bottom of the feeder. Use a nail or an awl to make a small hole in the center of each pie pan. Drill or punch a similar size hole in the center of the bottom of the jug and another through the center of the cap.

Use a sharp knife to cut an opening in the bottom of the jug for filling the feed and three $\frac{1}{2}$-inch square flaps in the narrow neck so the birds can get to the seeds (see the illustration). The lower pie pan will catch any seeds that fall from the holes while the top pan keeps the rain out of the opening.

Straighten the wire and make a supporting flat loop about 3 inches in diameter on one end as shown. Insert the straight end of the wire through the bottom of the first pie pan so that the pan rests on the flat loop. Thread the wire through the jug cap that has been screwed onto the jug. Then thread the wire through the hole in the bottom of the jug. The last pie pan is placed on the wire in an inverted position to make a cover for the feeder. Now bend a hook in the wire about 6 inches above this cover (so you can lift the cover to fill the feeder). Leave the feeder plain or decorate it with felt markers or use sponge or spatter painting. It also helps to punch several small holes in the bottom tin to let any water through (the illustration shows an exploded view of the feeder—just push the parts together).

Mesh Bags

Use the mesh bags that items like onions come in and fill with old crackers, pieces of bread, or bagels. Hang a bag from a tree branch near the viewing window. The birds will enjoy the treat without the mess of crackers and bread lying all around. Commercial versions of these bags are available.

Soda Bottle Feeders

Materials:
  Commercial feeder base
  2-liter plastic beverage bottle
  Plastic margarine cup

Directions:

These feeders are nice because they recycle 2-liter beverage bottles. Obtain the feeder base to attach to the bottle from a hardware or discount department store. The cost is usually under $2. Some mail order catalogs also have these attachments. The directions that come with the base show how to assemble the device. A more expensive metal version is available for about $10. It does not work any better than the $2 version unless there are squirrels in the vicinity, for they tend to chew the plastic.

To make the bottle easier to fill, cut a 2-inch diameter opening in the bottom of the bottle (it becomes the top of the feeder) as shown in the illustration and use a plastic margarine cup to cover the opening. Fill with sunflower seeds or a bird seed mixture and hang it outside near a large window from which the birds may be observed and about 5 feet above the ground.

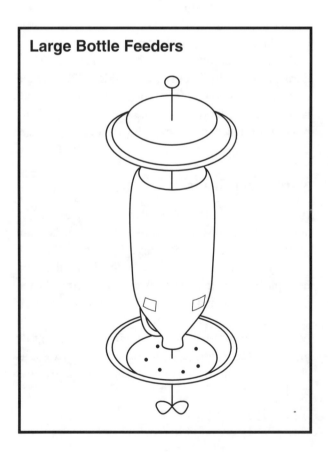

Large Bottle Feeders

Soda Bottle Feeders

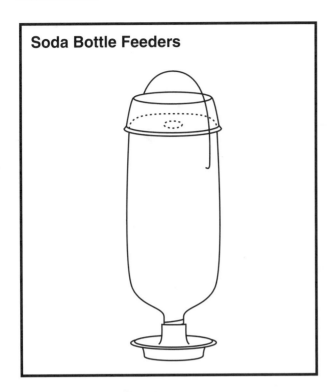

extra wire above the feeder is to permit the lid to be lifted for filling the feeder). We drilled a few extra holes in the bottom pan of our feeders to let any rain-water drain out. Fill the feeder with sunflower seeds and hang it up about 5 feet off the ground.

We've seen several different versions of this feeder at flea markets being sold for exorbitant prices and people were purchasing them.

Tips for Bird Feeders

- To make it easier for clients to fill bird feeders with limited staff assistance, use a clean laundry-detergent bottle (the new ultra-size ones are great). Remove the spout, fill the bottle with seeds, then put the spout back in. This provides a handy pouring spout so less birdseed is lost.
- A plastic garbage can is a good storage container for the seeds. Set it on a plant stand with casters to make it easier to move out of the storage area for the clients to fill the small containers used to fill the feeders.
- Use a small tin can to dip the seeds from the storage container and pour into the detergent bottle.
- If you only have a few feeders, a 5-gallon plastic paint bucket makes a good storage container.
- Make certain that you use rodent-proof storage containers.

Pie Pan Bird Feeder

Materials:

> Two 9-inch metal pie pans ($^1/_8$- inch holes through the center)
>
> 10-by-20-inch piece of $^3/_{16}$-inch mesh hardware cloth
>
> 6-inch plastic funnel or top of a $^1/_2$-gallon round plastic bleach container
>
> Heavy wire coat hanger

Directions:

This feeder turns two old or new metal pie pans into a screen feeder for sunflower seeds. It is a bit more squirrel resistant than most other feeders. Make a flat loop on an end of the straightened wire to support the lower pie tin. Insert the wire through the hole (from the bottom) of one of the pie pans. Place the funnel over the wire with the large end toward the pie tin to help push the seeds toward the mesh, making it easier for the birds to reach.

Make a 6-inch diameter cylinder of the mesh and use a piece of thin wire or small bolts through the overlapping portion to hold it together. Place the cylinder over the funnel as shown in the illustration.

Now place the second pie tin upside down over the center wire so that it becomes a cover for the cylinder. Make a loop in the wire about 6 inches above the cover for use to hang the feeder (the 6 inches of

Pie Pan Bird Feeder

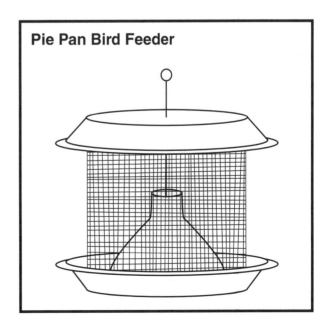

Suet Feeder

Materials:

Scrap plastic mesh bag
Stout cord

Directions:

Suet is available at most grocery stores in the meat section. If it is not available in your area, ask the butcher to save some for you. Mix sunflower and other birdseeds such as millet in with the suet and place it in the plastic mesh bag. Gather the ends together and fasten with a stout cord long enough to tie to a tree limb about 5 feet above the ground as shown in the illustration.

Although many birds enjoy suet, we especially notice the number and variety of woodpeckers that enjoy the treat and, since they are larger birds, they are easier for the clients to see. If you don't have the facilities to make your own feeder, you can purchase one at a hardware, discount department store, or gardening center.

Squirrel Feeder

Materials:

2-by-2-by-12-inch piece of scrap wood
1-inch screw eye
Four 16d nails

Directions:

Use a hacksaw to cut off the heads of the nails. Drill holes (in which the nails will be a tight fit) on each side of the wood. Insert the nails into the holes with the point sticking out (you can use a glue gun if the nails are loose). Put the screw-eye in the top to hang the feeder. Push an ear of corn on each nail and hang outside where the squirrels can find it.

As shown in the illustration, we added dowels to ours for the squirrels to hang on but we found they weren't really necessary. Clients enjoy watching the antics of the squirrels. We have seen as many as 15 squirrels at a time on our feeders.

Pine Cone Feeders

Materials:

Large coniferous cones
Peanut butter

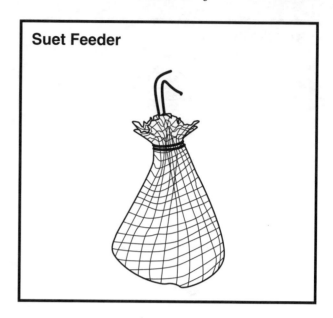

Suet Feeder

Birdseed
Narrow ribbon or string

Directions:

Cover the tables with newspaper and have your clients wear aprons, smocks, or old shirts. You might even consider plastic gloves for easy cleanup of the clients' hands. Give each of the participants a pine cone and let them fill the crevices with peanut butter. Be sure to pack it in as firmly as possible. After filling all of the crevices, roll the cone in birdseed. Tie a

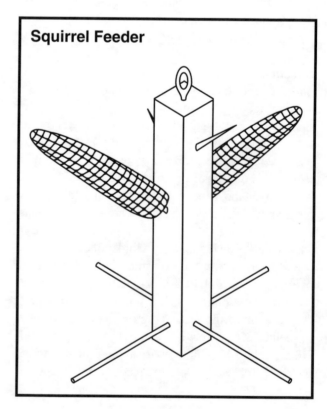

Squirrel Feeder

piece of ribbon or string to the top of the cone that is long enough to suspend the cone from a tree branch or other support.

Reindeer Food

Materials:
    Small plastic self-sealing bags
    Rolled oats
    Glitter

Directions:
Make "reindeer food" for children to sprinkle outside around the holidays. Reindeer food is actually rolled oats combined with glitter. Package small amounts sealed in plastic bags to distribute to children who come to sing Christmas carols or for the "adopt a grandparent" program. The glitter will light the way for the reindeer at Christmas and the oats are for the reindeer to eat. The winter birds will enjoy any of the oatmeal that Santa's reindeer don't eat.

Hummingbird and Oriole Feeders

There are so many commercial feeders on the market, many of which are reasonably priced, that it is best to purchase a feeder. Hummingbirds, orioles, and butterflies will often use the feeder. Don't be surprised to see a squirrel, or in the late evening a raccoon, trying to figure out how to get the juice out of the feeder. We even had a young bear drink all of the juice from our feeders on several occasions one summer.

Here is how to make the nectar: heat 1 cup of water warm enough to dissolve $\frac{1}{4}$ cup of sugar, let cool and fill the feeder. We usually mix up a quart of nectar at a time: 4 cups of water, 1 cup of sugar and a few drops of food coloring. Refrigerate any portion that is not used.

Note: Even though the birds that frequent your feeders do not need the nectar to be colored, it is often easier for the clients to see the feeder and to determine if it needs refilled when colored nectar is used. Use orange food coloring to color the oriole nectar and red for the hummingbirds.

Feeders for Butterflies and Small Animals

Many nurseries and garden centers are now recommending plants that will attract butterflies to your garden. The most commonly known flower is called butterfly weed. You may want to plant some flowers and hang a feeder in the middle of your garden.

Butterfly Feeders

A way to attract butterflies to your facility is to add a butterfly feeder to the ones you have for the birds and squirrels. Although it is sometimes difficult to locate these feeders, nature stores, garden centers and hardware stores are starting to carry them. Make sure you have an area with flowers to attract the butterflies. The feeders are generally made out of a heavy plastic and are shaped like flowers. Prices vary from $1.99 to $14.00. The resource section has addresses for sources if you can't find them locally.

Variation:
Instead of purchasing a butterfly feeder, try the sponge method. Dampen a colorful sponge with the butterfly nectar and place it on an old dish to attract the butterflies.

Butterfly Nectar

Nectar is easily made by heating 1 cup of water, warm enough to dissolve $\frac{1}{8}$ cup of sugar. Let cool, then fill the feeder. If you wish, you can make up a pint or more and store it in the refrigerator. We find that the hummingbirds enjoy this nectar, too, even though it isn't as sweet as their own (maybe it's just the weight conscious ones that visit).

Fruit Holders

In the summer use the squirrel feeders described earlier for fruit holders. Stick a small piece of fruit on the nails to attract hummingbirds, orioles and butterflies. Small slices of oranges, kiwi, watermelon, cantaloupe and banana work well. Fruit that is too ripe for the clients to eat is a treat for our flying friends.

Chipmunk Circus

After a visit to a local restaurant where they feed the chipmunks, Judy demanded that Jerry create a place for the chipmunks at their summer home. Jerry, being the creative guy he is, built an entire circus for the chipmunks out of bits of string, paper clips, and twigs. Our circus has evolved from a wire with strings to hold peanuts, to one with a merry-go-round, a seesaw, a trapeze, a climbing rope, and an old mailbox for a hiding place as shown in the illustration.

Your circus can be as elaborate or as simple as you and your clients decide. To hold the peanuts use large paper clips that have been opened to form a hook (with the end doubled back so the chipmunks don't get cut with a sharp edge). Fasten the hooks to the various devices with heavy string. Bend the hooks just enough to hold the unshelled peanuts. We made sunflower seed baskets from the bottoms of 2-quart plastic milk cartons and hung them with string. Our circus is attached to a length of rope stretched between two trees. The chipmunks learn very quickly how to get the peanuts and we usually have to replenish the circus at least twice each day.

Everyone who visits has enjoyed watching the antics of the chipmunks and several of our neighbors have built their own circuses. Chipmunks are amazing climbers, jumpers, and entertainers and they work for *peanuts!* The chipmunks will climb inside one of the suspended baskets and stuff their cheeks with seeds, peeking up and out as they do so. Our circus has been the topic of conversation on many afternoons and has led all of us to read everything we can on chipmunk behavior. If there are chipmunks near your facility, the clients will love a chipmunk circus.

Chipmunk Circus

Programming and Activities for Older Adults is a good source.

Miniature Christmas Tree

Materials:

> Evergreen branch
> Large potato
> Plates or large margarine tub covers
> Beads, ribbon, and glue for decorations

Directions:

Cut a large white potato in half and wrap it with aluminum foil and place it on a plate, flat side down. Insert an evergreen branch that has had its end cut to an angle into the potato to look like a tree. (*Caution:* Eastern hemlock branches lose their needles very quickly so try to use something else.) Decorate the branch with miniature decorations such as birds and bows. It is unnecessary to water this tree because the potato provides the needed moisture.

Nature Crafts

Most everyone enjoys using natural materials for craft projects. The few that follow will get you started and if you want more ideas, Chapter 17 of *Recreation*

Crystal Garden

Materials:

> Broken pieces of brick, charcoal, porous rock, or a cellulose sponge

6 tablespoons of ammonia
4 tablespoons of laundry bluing
6 tablespoons of water
4 tablespoons of salt
Food coloring (optional)
Shallow plastic or ceramic bowl

Directions:
Wash the bits of brick, porous rock, or cellulose sponge and charcoal and place them in a shallow nonmetallic bowl. Mix 4 tablespoons of each of the following: ammonia, laundry bluing and water. Pour the mixture over the wet articles and add drops of food coloring on top. Sprinkle 4 tablespoons of salt over the entire creation. Crystals will begin to grow overnight. Add 2 tablespoons of ammonia and 2 tablespoons of water after it starts to grow. The crystal garden will last for several weeks and will fascinate the clients as well as give everyone a topic to discuss with visitors. Although they are more expensive, commercial kits are available in almost every nature or science store to grow crystals that will last longer.

Press Dried Flowers

Materials:
Freshly picked pansies or other "flat" flowers
Waxed paper
Heavy book (for weight)

Directions:
Dry flowers such as pansies and violas (Johnny-jump-ups) by placing the fresh flowers between two sheets of waxed paper, then pressing them within the pages of a heavy book. The stems and leaves can also be pressed (or removed and paper stems added later). After several weeks, remove the dried flowers and use them to make bookmarks, nametags, invitations and stationary. Flowers that have just opened are easier to preserve.

Bookmarks

Materials:
Dried flowers
Colored art paper
Clear contact paper
Scissors or old pinking shears

Directions:
For each bookmark, cut a piece of art paper about $1\frac{1}{4}$-by-6-inches. Place the dried pressed flower on the paper. Carefully cut two pieces of clear contact paper a little larger than the art paper. Cover the front, pressing the contact paper securely over the flower and around its edges. Cover the back with contact paper, also. The contact paper should then be trimmed using scissors or pinking shears. If writing is desired, it should be done on the art paper before covering with the contact paper.

Nametags and Invitations

Materials:
Same as for bookmarks

Directions:
Cut the art paper to size and lightly glue the flower to the paper. Complete the writing, then cover the nametag or invitation with clear contact paper on the front only.

Sun Catchers

Materials:
Pressed dried flowers
Clear contact paper
Scissors or old pinking shears
Hole punch
Narrow ribbon

Directions:
For a sun catcher, place the dried pressed flower directly onto a piece of clear contact paper and cover the front with an additional piece of the same. Be sure to press out any bubbles. If bubbles persist, use a pin to prick a small hole to let the air escape. Cut to the desired shape with the scissors or pinking shears and punch a hole near the top. Insert a piece of ribbon and tie in a loop with a pretty little bow. The sun catcher is now ready to hang in a window.

Sand Dried Flowers

Materials:
Fine sand
Shoebox

Freshly picked flowers
Floral wire and tape

Directions:
Put fine sand in a box until it is about 3 inches deep. Leave about 2 inches of stem on the flowers you wish to dry and insert the stems in the sand until the flowers are even with the surface. Carefully sprinkle thin layers of dry sand over the flowers until they are completely covered. Place the box in a warm dry place for two weeks. When the flowers have dried, carefully pour off the sand. Attach a stem of floral wire and hold in place with the floral tape. Zinnias, marigolds, and dahlias are particularly pretty when dried using this method.

The flowers can be distributed as gifts to brighten the clients' rooms or used as corsages. They can even be made into floral bouquets for special events. See Chapter 19, Growing Things, in *Recreation Programming and Activities for Older Adults* for other methods of preserving and drying flowers and plants.

Flower Jars

Materials:
Modeling clay
Small jars, such as baby food jars, with lids
Small dried flowers

Directions:
Place a small amount of modeling clay in a baby food jar lid. Set a small dried flower in the clay and carefully screw the jar onto the lid to protect the flower. If the flowers are small enough, make an arrangement. Turn the jar over so the glass portion is now the top. These make nice gifts for the clients to create. If you choose to use larger jars, dahlias, zinnias, marigolds, Queen Anne's lace, and coneflowers are some of the types of flowers that can be used.

More Nametags and Gift Tags

Materials:
Seed catalogs and/or old greeting cards
Scissors
Glue
Small plastic margarine tubs
Clear contact paper
Colored art paper

Directions:
Make nametags, place cards, name plates for doors, or gift tags by cutting the pictures from old seed catalogs or greeting cards with nature pictures. Cut out the flower or scene and use it to create an interesting design. Glue it on the art paper that has been cut to the desired size. Use clear contact paper to make the project more permanent. Remember to complete the writing on the card or nametag before applying the contact paper.

Birdseed Squiggles

Materials:
Bird seed
String
White glue
Wax paper
Paper plate

Directions:
Squeeze a series of interconnecting loops (about $\frac{1}{8}$-inch wide and thick) on a piece of wax paper with a dispenser bottle of white glue. Use a paper or plastic plate under the wax paper to help keep the squiggle stable. Use a spoon to sprinkle birdseed over the design making sure all of the glue is covered. Let it dry overnight, then pour the extra birdseed back in the container. Peel away the wax paper from the squiggle and tie a string onto one of the loops and hang it in a tree for the birds to enjoy.

Tongue Depressor Tags

Materials:
Tongue depressors
Permanent markers
Clear acrylic spray

Directions:
Use these tags to identify plants and their owners. The tongue depressor can be used vertically in a planter, or horizontally if fastened to a dowel rod or stick to make it easier for the clients to see.

Spray the stick with the clear spray to seal the wood before writing or drawing on it. When finished with the design and lettering, spray the stick again to protect the design.

Take a Walk

Whenever the idea of a walk to enjoy nature comes to mind, we automatically think of a steep, hazardous hill or the groomed paths of a garden show. However, a walk around the grounds of the facility, or even around a courtyard can be a lovely way to enjoy nature close to home.

Wildflower Walks

Although wildflowers can be seen in any season, some of the best viewing is in early spring. The nicest thing about wildflowers is that many are becoming more common in the garden. It is possible to purchase a wildflower mix or even a carpet of wildflower seeds to be utilized at the facility. Clients may be able to wander through a wildflower area with family or tours can be arranged. For lower functioning clients, asking the person to find a yellow flower may be stimulating to the senses. Meanwhile, a higher level client may have a wildflower identification book to look up the names of the flowers.

Games and activities such as Nature Bingo, Flower Match, and I Spy can be a follow-up activity after touring the garden. Flower arranging, flower pressing, and drying flowers to be used as place cards, stationary and in arrangements can also occur. A local herb society or garden club may be able to offer assistance in terms of volunteers, seeds, plants and sources for more information.

Nature Walks

If your facility does not have an area nearby for enjoying nature, we encourage you to approach your administrator about having one developed. Jerry and Judy began working together to provide quality programming for older adults when Judy asked Jerry to help design a nature trail that could be navigated by wheelchairs at the 600-bed nursing home where she worked as the Director of Therapeutic Recreation.

A nature area does not have to be expensive nor large. A section within a courtyard or an area on the grounds can be utilized. If you are lucky enough to have a wooded area or a pond, plan a trail with benches for resting. Judy contacted a local service club and building supplier and asked them to donate time and materials for the trail at her facility. Don't be afraid to pitch your idea to the various service clubs and retailers in your area.

If possible, make a circular trail. This makes it easier for the clients to utilize the area. Make sure there are benches with backs located at short intervals along the route because the older adults get tired easily. Leave room in the resting spots for a wheelchair. Even if most of the clients use wheelchairs, the benches designate that it is a rest area. The family member or volunteer who is pushing the wheelchair appreciates the opportunity to relax and chat with the client at these spots. Nature questions and signs along the trail help to stimulate conversation.

Hike and Guess

This is a nice activity when each client can go with one volunteer or family member. Everyone takes a bag and gathers a nonliving item of interest. When the group gets back together each person describes the color and shape of his or her item without opening the bag, to see if the others can identify it from the description. Ask someone in the group to place his or her hand in someone else's bag and describe the item by feel, if no one has guessed it from the earlier description. The items can then be revealed and each person should be asked why that particular item was chosen.

Other Ideas for Enjoying Nature

The following items are available commercially and are good for helping to initiate discussions on a daily basis. They can be useful on one-on-one visits as tools for orienting the client to reality or as a diversion for the disoriented client.

Rain Gauges

Keep track of rain amounts on a daily, weekly, and monthly basis. If the clients have lived in a farming area or a resort area where weather is the daily topic of discussion, entire reminiscence discussions can occur about crops and recreational activities. Ask the clients about the worst rainstorm they ever experienced. Ask such questions as "When you were a child, what did you do during a rainstorm?" "Did you like to play in the rain?" "What if it began to thunder and lightning?" "Have you ever seen a tornado?" or "Were you ever in a flood?" These can be the basis for some interesting discussions.

Snow Stick

If you are in an area where there is snow, fasten a yardstick to a post in an open area where the clients can measure the amount of snow that falls. Keep a record of the first snow, the most snow in one day, as well as the amount of snow for the week, month and season. If there is no snow, watch TV weather reports to see how much snow is falling elsewhere. If some of the clients are willing, build a snowman where everyone can see it. If you can't go out, build a snowman out of Styrofoam balls or paper-mâchè. An entire large group event can be built around a snow theme. Think about a Snowball Dance, a Winter Carnival, or Winter Olympics.

Sundials

Although a bit more expensive than the other items listed in this section, a sundial can lead to a discussion about clocks, watches and older methods of keeping time. A sundial is a really classy addition to a courtyard. An outing to a watch museum or a display of watches would make a nice event. A summer solstice party can be held with all types of activities relating to the sun. For example, the decorations can be paper suns with shelled sunflower seeds being part of the snack.

Thermometers

Thermometers come in all sizes and shapes, from extra large outdoor models that can be read from a distance to the newer indoor digital types that show the outdoor and indoor temperatures. Recording the temperature on a large chart every morning is an ongoing task that should appeal to some of the clients. Observing the day-to-day changes provides oppor-

tunities for discussion about the weather. What was the coldest winter you remember? What about the hottest summer? Were winters colder when you were growing up?

Weather Sticks

Weather sticks are available at many specialty shops. Install one where it can be seen by a majority of the clients. The stick predicts the weather by dipping down when there is a lot of moisture in the air and points up when it becomes a dry sunny day. The sticks are great because they remind people of weather folklore. The clients will enjoy answering questions regarding weather lore. Have you ever seen a person do a rain dance? Do you know anyone who could find water with a divining rod? What weather sayings do you remember? Here are a couple from Jerry's childhood that his grandfather used:

> "Red sky at night, Farmer's delight. / Red sky in the morning, Farmers take warning."
> "When the wind is in the North, it's not fit to sally forth, / When the wind is from the East, weather's not fit for man or beast, / When the wind is in the South, blows the bait in the fish's mouth, / When the wind is in the West, that's the time that it is best."

Wind Chimes

Wind chimes make a delightful sound as they jingle in the wind. There are many types available, from soft sounding ceramic chimes to those made from the ends of old oxygen tanks, which sound like loud bells. It is best to borrow several different types to try before purchasing, to make sure that you have one most of the clients will feel has a pleasant and soothing sound. Some people who are highly stressed seem to mind the sound of a wind chime, so be careful about using them on one-on-one visits. Chimes are best placed in a courtyard or garden area where the sound will not be too loud for most people.

There are further suggestions in the Resources to help you develop an outstanding nature-related segment for your total recreation program.

Chapter XI

Theme Events

Most everyone looks forward to special days. Holidays, birthdays, and anniversaries are the obvious times for special events. Special events are an important part of a well-rounded recreation program. They are different from the regular schedule and give clients as well as staff something to look forward to. Remember, special events, just by their name, mean they are different from the regularly scheduled events. They should be a part of the monthly schedule, but shouldn't be the entire schedule.

Ideas for special events are endless and should revolve around a theme. A theme gives everyone a starting place for planning the event and helps to keep the program focused. Without a theme, the staff tends to play the regular games such as bingo and indoor bowling at the special events because these are activities they know the clients like. With a theme, the staff and clients stay focused so that even if favorite activities are to be played they must relate to the event.

Bowling is a great activity for an Olympic day or carnival; and bingo can be changed to names of flowers for a summer festival. There are several ways to find ideas for theme events. The newspaper or an atlas will list special dates and publications like *Ideals* and *Chase's Annual Events* are very helpful in determining unusual events which can be celebrated with your clients.

List the special events in the monthly calendar using graphics to draw attention to the various themes. In this age of computers, it is relatively easy to make flyers that can be posted to advertise the event. Naming the event in a way that the clients will want to know more about it, even to the point of initiating conversation with the staff and amongst themselves helps to promote enthusiasm. In the field of recreation, just like in the field of business, we have to

market and advertise our product if we expect success. The following suggestions will help you with ideas for theme events for your calendar.

Food-Related Events

It seems that many of the special events have food as a central feature. It is true that food, animals and children are great motivators for most older adults. That doesn't mean that all events should have food. In fact, many of the events would be easier to plan if the staff didn't have to worry about snacks or dietary restrictions.

Careful planning of the events where food is to be served is of utmost importance due to dietary restrictions. Another concern is the amount of food consumed by some of the people, whether it is eaten at the event or being "squirreled" in their purses or pockets to be taken back to their rooms. Here are some ideas for food-related events; just handle the planning and supervision with care.

Birthday Parties

It is impossible in most facilities to have a party for all of the residents on their actual birthdays. Each person should get special recognition on that day whether it is a card signed by the staff, his or her name announced on the public address system or listed in the daily bulletin, or a combination of these.

A good theme event would be a monthly birthday party, luncheon or tea, that has special invitations to all of those people who have birthdays during that month. Computer generated invitations can be made by volunteers and delivered to the invitees a few days in advance of the event. At the party each guest should be recognized and asked to share a favorite birthday memory. If you don't want a large cake, individual cupcakes (made and decorated by the cooking group) can have a candle for the person to blow out. The food doesn't have to be elaborate, just different from what is being served in the dining room. The activities should be related to the birthday theme, yet be a little different each month to keep the staff from becoming bored.

Family Dinners

On special holidays like Valentine's Day, Mother's Day, and Thanksgiving, ask for volunteers to help serve a fancy meal to the clients and their families. Charge a fee to cover family members' meals and limit registration by taking reservations. Families want to include their loved one in a celebration, but often cannot take him or her home. Have the meal at noon so the families can still have an evening meal at home and the staff and volunteers will not have to work too many extra hours.

Decorate the tables and use real dishes. The meal can be served buffet style because the family members can help prepare their relative's plate. Entertainment, such as music, adds a nice touch.

Small Group Dinners

If a person seems particularly depressed or needs a boost, ask him or her to invite two or three friends or relatives for dinner or a special snack. If you have the facilities to prepare the food, have the group plan the menu. Obtain some of the basic materials from the dietary department and, if possible, take the clients shopping for the rest of the ingredients. The group then works together to prepare the food, set the table, and enjoy good conversation while eating. This special attention always helps to bring a smile to all of the participants' faces.

Newcomer's Tea

Call it what you wish, but it is a special event to welcome the new residents. Actually, it should be a series of teas or events for the new arrivals. It helps them to become acquainted with each other and to

express any concerns they may have about becoming accepted as members of the larger group of residents. Social work staff should help with these events and be on hand to participate in the discussions that take place. A personalized invitation should be presented to the person several days prior to the event. Make sure that the administrators and a representative from each department attend. Use the activity portion of the event to help the clients relax and enjoy each other in their new surroundings. Some agencies invite family members to the welcoming tea and/ or hold a dinner or tea for the new families.

Mystery Dinners

Sign up a small group to go on a mystery dinner. Take them to a restaurant near the facility. They have seen fast food restaurants advertised on TV, so they often want to go there. Schedule the trip on off-peak hours. It is a good idea to get copies of the menu ahead of time so that it will be easier for them to order at the restaurant.

Suggestion:
If you are taking low-level clients it is best to visit a restaurant that has pictures on the menu so they can point to their choice.

Mother-Daughter Tea

Organize events such as these on Saturday or Sunday afternoons when daughters and granddaughters can visit and help transport the clientele. You won't need to schedule as many of your regular volunteers and it gives family something to do together. A short program, some cookies or cakes made by the cooking group, and a little tea is all that is necessary to spark an afternoon of conversation.

Slow Eating Contest

This is called a contest, although it is really just a programming technique to be used at a picnic or other special event when some of the clients want to "gulp" down the treat. We use graham or soda crackers and have a contest to see who is the last person to put the last bit of cracker in his or her mouth (everyone must keep chewing and take another nibble as soon as they have swallowed). You can do the same thing with ice cream, pudding or any other treat. Select foods that are difficult to choke on and provide bibs for the contestants. Always make sure you have Handi Wipes or something for spills. This may not be a special event in itself, but certainly qualifies as a special activity for something like an ice cream social or a picnic.

Food and Themes

It only takes a little imagination on the part of the staff to coordinate the snacks to be used at a special event with the theme of the event. The cooking group can make the snacks and have them ready for the big day. Several ideas that are mentioned in Chapter VII, Sweet Treats, include Dirt which would be ideal for Halloween, Easter Basket Cupcakes for Easter and Flowerpot Muffins for a Gardening Party.

Anytime Events

Fashion Show

If your agency is given clothing for the clients, as is the case in many nonprofit homes, it is often difficult to get the clients to choose an outfit from the selection. Judy solved this in her agency by periodically having a fashion show. Her staff chose both male and female clients to be the models. Each of the models chose one of the outfits to wear (with staff help, of course). The models then had a training session to teach them how to show off their outfits to the best advantage (this provided another opportunity to encourage client interaction). The fashion show notices were posted and all interested clients were invited to attend. Soon after the show there were many requests from the clients to visit the clothing shop.

A variation on this idea is to have a program where the clients use newspaper, doilies, colored paper and lots of tape to make costumes for a "fashion show." In small groups they choose a person to be costumed and the group cooperates in preparing the model. After the models are "dressed," have a fashion parade.

Many commercial clothing agencies will come to your facility to sell clothing to the clients. They will often be willing to help you produce a fashion show.

Cultural Events

Having special days to celebrate the diversity of the agency's clients has tremendous program possibilities. Wherever possible, have the clients participate in the planning. A Mexican Day, an Irish Day, an Ukrainian Day and a Scandinavian Day are some of the possibilities. Have relatives or volunteers loan items that reflect the culture. Use stories and activities that relate to the culture. If some of the clients have ever lived in the country, have them relate some of the things they remember about their life in that country. Serve a snack that is common to the culture.

Decorative Trees

If there is a small tree near the main entrance or on the terrace that can be seen by residents and visitors, consider decorating it for the different months of the year. If there is no tree that meets the qualifications outside, use one of the small trees that are in the facility or even decorate trees inside and outside.

Work with the clients to decide a different theme every month, for example: ice-cream cones for June, flags for July, schoolbooks for September. Gumdrops can be covered with clear plastic wrap. Tie them to the tree branches with colored yarn. Draw different food items on poster board, color them, cut them out and laminate them for another type of decoration. Small foam cups can be easily decorated with felt-tip permanent markers and hung upside down like small bells. Make paper-mâchè ornaments (see Chapter IX, Craft Fun) for another type of decoration.

Involve the clients in an assembly line approach making the decorations and have them help with placing them on the tree. These assembly line projects are fun for the clients. It gives them an opportunity to feel helpful and stimulates conversation among the workers.

Tree-Decorating Contest

Several facilities we have visited have tree-decorating contests several times a year. Sometimes they do it with a small tree on each unit and other times the contest is for individuals who have decorated tree branches (see Chapter X, All Natural). Have the staff vote on the best trees in several categories like the most colorful, the most original, and the best theme.

Make up certificates on the computer to give to the winners in each category.

Some agencies have used tree decorating as a fund-raiser. A collection box is placed in front of each tree and the tree that collects the most money is the winner.

Other Ideas

In addition to holidays there are opportunities for all kinds of theme events. Ideas are only limited by the imagination of the staff and volunteers. Why not hold a brainstorming session to make a list of themes that would be applicable to your clientele? Include your higher functioning clients in the session. Start with ideas like Dinosaurs, Pirates, Life in the Country, Amish Life, and Dress-up Day and keep going until you have a page full of ideas. Write the ideas on a chalkboard and don't elaborate on any until the list is completed (set a time limit for the brainstorming). Next have the participants select the top three or four ideas they would like to try first. Assign a couple of people to work on each idea and bring suggestions to the total group. The ideas can then be refined and further planning for the special event can continue. Try to delegate the responsibility for planning and have a time schedule so that there won't be that hectic last minute "toss it together" mess we sometimes have.

Here are some you may have used, but try them again while you are getting the ones that you brainstormed ready to schedule. Higher level clients enjoy giving the staff some ideas for recreation programming so be sure to include them in brainstorming sessions.

Flag Day

Secure small flags to distribute for everyone to wave as they sing along to patriotic songs. The waving is a good aerobic activity and encourages the clients to be active participants, even if they don't remember the words to the songs. The flags can be used on Flag Day, the Fourth of July, Election Day, and any other time you use patriotic songs.

For special Olympic-type events, have the residents make flags to represent their "country" or team. Flags can be made of paper and taped to small dowels. We used the sticks that came with the flower ar-

rangements that were donated to the facility after a funeral service. Sometimes we just attached residents' hankies or bandannas to the sticks so they would have something to wave or carry when we had the entry march for the event.

Intergenerational Programs

Most residents look forward to having a visit from a nursery school or kindergarten group. It is important that the program length be such that it doesn't tire the residents or go beyond the attention span of the children. Often the children will have a little skit or other type of program to present. Another activity that goes over well is to have the residents read a story to the children, or the children read one of their books to the residents. This works best on a one-on-one basis. Sometimes the children bring a toy or something they have made to show residents on a one-on-one basis. We have included many ideas for activities involving children and older adults throughout this book.

Baseball Outing

Take a group of your baseball fans to see a local team play. Before Judy became the Therapeutic Recreation Director, they used to take residents to major league games. They found that it was difficult to get them into the stadium and they were tired before the game was over. Judy discovered that there was more interest in watching local teams play because there was less travel involved and they could take comfortable chairs in which to sit. They were closer to the action and it was easier to get to the transportation when it was time to leave. Once Judy's clients attended a local baseball game and an aluminum bat broke when a player made a home run. The clients talked about that bat breaking for weeks, so even hometown or Little League games can be very successful outings.

Going to the County Fair

It became a tradition at Judy's agency to take as many people to the county fair as wanted to go. The number of volunteers that were scheduled was equal to the number of clients that would be attending at one time. Three bus trips were run each day for four days. The clients spent a little over three hours at the fair. There was about enough time for them to go through most of the exhibit buildings and enjoy some food. Over 200 residents attended the fair each year. A program like this takes very careful scheduling of staff and volunteers.

On such an outing it works best to assign volunteers to the clients. This leaves the professional staff free to handle bathroom trips and any emergencies that might occur. There must also be a great deal of coordination with the entire facility staff to be able to run such an event. It can only happen when everyone is dedicated to client-oriented programming, and it is really worth the effort.

Fishing

You might be able to take your clients fishing at a private pond where licenses are not required. However, if you are going to use public waters each client will need a license. Contact the local waterways patrol office to ask about the special licenses for persons with disabilities. In some states these licenses are free and in others a small fee is charged for a lifelong license. There are fish-for-free days in some states and people may fish on these days without a license.

Also, check on how much assistance a volunteer can give the disabled person without the necessity of the volunteer having a license. Several years ago, some of Judy's volunteers were cited for baiting the clients' hooks without having a license. It resulted in the state's regulations being changed, but be sure and check the regulations in your state.

Besides licenses, fishing poles and bait, the clients have to be prepared for the trip. Be sure you have heavy-duty sunscreen for each person and each should have long sleeves and hats. Don't forget drinking water and make sure that there are toilet facilities nearby. Also, don't forget the Wet Wipes.

By the way, there is a neat trick to keep the hooks from getting caught on everything and still leave them on the line when you store the equipment. At a one-hour film developing facility, ask for some of the empty film cartridges, or ask the facility staff members to save them for you. Use a sharp knife to cut a $1/_4$-inch slit in the top of each canister. Slide the fishing line just above the hook into the slit, drop the hook into the canister and snap the lid in place. Try it and you will find you save a lot of tangled lines.

Shopping

It seems that everyone wants to go on a shopping trip. Whether they buy anything else, the clients are going to have to stop at the snack bar for a cup of coffee or a dish of ice cream. Holiday shopping expeditions should be scheduled early in the day and not on weekends. When the stores are crowded the clients become very frustrated.

Have shopping trips throughout the year, not just at holidays. Schedule small groups of clients who are at nearly the same functioning level on the trip. Make sure that your volunteers are up to the task of pushing wheelchairs around the store. The volunteers must know where the elevators are and how to enter them with the clients. A staff member needs to be available to assist with toilet breaks and to handle any emergencies that might develop.

Clients always want to feel material and handle some of the items that they see. Perhaps the staff will have to be a little selective regarding what the clients are permitted to purchase. It helps if the client has a list and the volunteer has a copy of the items he or she wants to look at during the trip. Judy had a client that always wanted to buy a new wristwatch and he had never learned to tell time!

Nature Themes

Use flower or leaf stencils to decorate placemats or cover the table with newsprint and decorate it with vegetable prints. Divide the group into teams and name each team after a plant. Have relay races that use beans, walnuts or peanuts. Use fall leaves for decorations. Make leaf prints. Have sassafras tea for a beverage. On a warm day why not have the event outside, maybe even at a nearby park? Now, you have the idea—go with it!

Ongoing Theme Events

Theme events can range from a 1-hour special activity, to a half-day program of related activities, or they could be themes that run for several days or weeks. Here are a couple of ideas for ongoing theme events.

Armchair Travel

This is one that can last for several months and could even become a permanent part of the overall program. Every month have a different destination for the travelers. Show a movie, video and perhaps a slide show by someone who has been there. You can "visit" places in this country and even "travel" abroad. Find out how many of the residents have been to the place and ask what they remember about their visit. Perhaps some of them actually lived there. Have an activity common to the part of the country you are visiting. Prepare baked goods or crafts representative of the area. Plan a festival or a special meal, as a culminating activity to the visit.

Walk Across America

Plan a walking trip across the country. Secure a large map and plan the route with the clients. The clients realize that they can't actually walk the distance themselves so explain to them that it will be a team effort that will include the residents and the staff. Assign mileage figures to physical activities to move along the route.

Schedule related events that will add to the mileage to encourage participation. The staff can get involved by walking with clients or walking on their own during their break or lunch period to earn extra miles. If a resident wheels his or her own wheelchair, that counts. The length of a hall might count as a mile toward the destination. Ten minutes of exercise could count as 10 miles along the route. Make up a chart for each floor or unit with the names of the staff and clients and display it in a prominent location. Ask a person from each unit, staff or client, to keep it updated. Another person should be responsible for collecting the mileage figures from the previous day and updating the map each morning. Groups can do imaging exercises like "rowing" to cross the rivers and "skiing" to get over the mountains. This event can be run for short or long periods. To keep up enthusiasm, have a special party every time that you reach a major city or attraction along the way. Make sure to keep the map updated on a regular basis to keep the groups' enthusiasm high.

Variations:

- It may work best to begin on a small scale such as a walk across town or the county with programs which represent some of the businesses or highlights of the community. For example, our town has a nice bakery, a bicycle shop, several massage therapists, and a beautiful river. We could have an event with cookies from the bakery, songs such as "A Bicycle Built for Two," shoulder massages, and games that relate to taking items on a picnic if we wanted to combine several of the stops into one event. Or the group might walk across the state with a different event each week representing places to stop in the state.
- The event does not have to be exercise oriented. One agency did its event as a cruise ship with stops at various exotic ports of call. Use your imagination. This event can easily run with a variety of events for a week, month or season.

Club Events

There are or should be several clubs or special interest groups functioning among the clients in your facility. If they are not meeting presently, they need to be encouraged to do so. The baseball fans surely have several people interested in the same team. Besides getting together to watch the games on TV, get them together for a special event like a tailgate party before the All-Star Game. The gardening group should have some kind of a special event like a salad party when the lettuce and onions are ready to harvest. Another event could be a harvest fair when the vegetables are harvested. How about a crafts fair for the crafters? Soap opera fans could have a special soap opera trivia event. Use almost any excuse to get the residents involved with the planning and holding of programs that are related to their special interests. Client participation in planning these events encourages interaction and motivation and gives the group members something to anticipate.

Neighborhood Day or a Block Party

The residents come from a variety of towns or neighborhoods. A program that makes use of the diversity represented by the various groups can be the basis for a special theme event. It could last for a day with activities presented by each neighborhood, an afternoon bazaar, or become an evening block party. We've held block parties on nursing home parking lots on warm summer evenings with square and round dancing. Boy and Girl Scouts served as volunteers, danced with the clients, and did a great job. A public address system was used and Jerry furnished the records and served as caller (he used to call square dances professionally).

Square Dance

This is a great program for a summer evening. It is important to have a caller who has experience working with special populations. The local square dance club is fun for the clients to watch, but they are used to dancing complicated calls at a fast pace. They are great entertainment but are too complicated for the clients. In fact, after seeing them dance, most clients are reluctant to try to dance. So, make sure that the caller has worked with people with disabilities.

Here are some suggestions for a successful program:

- Do not have wheelchair and ambulatory dancers in the same dance (the wheelchair dancers tend to move too fast for the others).
- Each dancer should have a volunteer for a partner (clients often get confused as to which way to go).
- Keep the dances simple and short with no swinging. Clients get dizzy if they swing and they tire easily.
- Alternate wheelchair and ambulatory dances.
- Include some waltzes and slow polkas, even for the people in wheelchairs. They serve as a break for those who have been dancing and these dances are entertainment for all.
- Make sure the volunteers escort their partners back to the partner's "spot" when the dance is finished.
- Refreshments in the form of cool drinks need to be served several times during the program.

Breakfast on the Unit

We have seen this special event at several facilities. Using portable hot plates and food warmers, staff and volunteers have prepared and served breakfast to the residents on the unit. This is not a viable program that can be used on every unit or in every agency, but where it can be used, it will be very well received.

Variation:
Breakfast at the park. Most older adults love breakfast and enjoy preparing it in the outdoors. Send a staff member and volunteer ahead to prepare the grill, coffee and hot chocolate. The clients can crack and help scramble the eggs, make toast, and set the table.

Senior Prom

Often the local high school can provide you with a combo for the evening or the local Council for the Arts may be able to provide a grant to pay for a group. Sometimes a new group just getting started may be willing to volunteer for the event. It is important to review the group's repertoire to make sure they will include the old, familiar songs that the residents remember. Decorate the multipurpose room with balloons and tissue paper flowers (have the clients use a hand pump to blow up the balloons and make the flowers in craft sessions). Have everyone dress for the dance, even have dates if they want (could be a family member), give each lady a tissue flower corsage to be pinned on her by her "date." Chaperones can include the agency administrator, the head nurse and/or any staff members willing to attend (make a big "deal" about having to have chaperones).

Summary

Special events are an integral part of a well-rounded program. They should be scheduled on a regular basis, and vary in length as well as time of day. Client involvement in the events such as dances, fashion shows, and drama productions is just as important as the events where clients are only spectators being entertained.

Chapter XII

Working With the Low-Functioning Client

The key to success when working with one-on-one activities is to keep it simple. The program area must be kept uncluttered with as few distractions as possible. Some professionals suggest that we should even consider removing the salt and pepper shakers, placemats, flower arrangements, and napkin holders from the tables during meals to help keep the confused clients focused on eating. Activities should be planned to have simple directions, visual instead of verbal cues, with plenty of support and encouragement throughout the process.

There is some controversy as to whether the staff member should stand or sit when working with confused clients. Some agencies feel standing helps to keep the client focused on the activity. Other agencies feel that the staff member should sit with the clients especially if working with a small group seated in a circle. We suggest that your staff experiment with both ways to see what works best for your clients.

The important things to remember are:

1. Find out as much as possible about the client's background;
2. Many of the clients understand more than they can express;
3. They may be able to do more than the staff realize; and
4. What the person can do today may or may not be what he or she can do tomorrow.

Be sure to watch the clients closely, to see that they are not stressed by the experience.

The following one-on-one activities have been used successfully with a variety of low-functioning clients.

Cereal Box Puzzles

Preparation:
Cut the front of a breakfast cereal box (any well-known dry cereal) into 3 or 4 pieces with a pair of scissors. Make a frame to hold the assembled puzzle using a heavier piece of cardboard (that is 1-inch longer and wider than the puzzle) as backing. Glue a strip of the same heavier cardboard that is $1/_2$-inch wide along each side of the backing so that the assembled puzzle will fit inside the frame. Laminating the puzzle pieces will increase the durability.

Use:
Place all but one of the pieces in their proper places in the frame and give the client the last piece to insert. When success has been gained with one piece, have the client attempt to place two or more pieces with a goal of finally being able to assemble all the pieces correctly.

Hint:
Make several similar puzzles from different brands of cereal. When the client is able to have a successful experience with one puzzle, use another in a follow-up session.

Picture Puzzle

Preparation:
This is another simple puzzle idea. Select a colorful picture of a bird or animal from a calendar or magazine. It should be of a size that can be trimmed to 6 by 9 inches. Cut six 3-by-3-inch pieces of heavy cardboard. Align the pieces into a 6-by-9-inch rectangle

and glue the picture to the surface. Use a sharp knife to separate the pieces.

Use:
This puzzle is used in the same way as the cereal box puzzle.

Matching Lids

Preparation:
Collect different size plastic containers and lids (margarine, cottage cheese, etc.). It is best to have several of each size with several different products represented.

Use:
If you are working with a very confused client, use one container and a couple of different size lids and encourage him or her to find the correct lid for the container. Depending upon the ability of the client, you may be able to have several lids and containers of different sizes to see how quickly he or she can put the lids on the correct containers. Take time to discuss the contents that the container held and what might be kept in it now. Don't discuss the container's original contents while the client is trying to put on the lid.

Sorting Things

Preparation:
Collect a variety of things to sort. We've used playing cards, poker chips, checkers, buttons, screws, nails, washers, socks, washcloths, towels, baby clothes and lots of other things. Volunteers collected most of the things for us to use.

Use:
We found that many of the confused clients could sort things and not only enjoyed the activity but could keep on task for a longer period of time while engaged in a sorting activity. Start with a small number of familiar items like cards or poker chips for the client to sort by color. Nails, screws and washers should be sorted by size. Buttons can be sorted by size or by color or by the number of holes. Egg cartons are good containers to use for sorting the smaller items. Remember to use large items for sorting if the person might try to eat them. The clients may not

remember the activity the next day and the same items can often be sorted again. Please remember, don't dump the items that have been sorted into the storage container in front of the client!

Don't forget to keep the instructions simple, and show, rather than tell, the client what to do. You should not become frustrated if the client does well one day and is completely clueless the next.

Quilt Patch Pieces

Preparation:
Using scrap cloth with various patterns, cut out a series of quilt patches in different sizes and shapes. Preparation of the patches is a good project for the higher level clients. Cut out 3- and 4-inch squares and 3- and 4-inch triangles for a start. Use different prints and colors of material.

Use:
Have the lower level client sort the patches by size or color or shape. Be careful not to overwhelm the more confused client by giving too many choices. Two colors and two shapes are enough to start with for many clients. You should try to have them name the colors and the shapes, if they can, after they have completed sorting.

When working with clients who are a little less confused, we have had them sort the pieces into piles by shape and then by pattern or color. Some of the clients who had done quilting in the past enjoyed playing with the various shapes and colored pieces to create a design for a quilt.

Quilt Patterns

Materials:
    Duplicated sheets of quilt designs
    Crayons or water-based felt-tip pens

Directions:
There is some debate as to whether coloring with crayons or felt-tip pens is an age-appropriate activity for older adults. We would agree that it is not, if they were given young children's coloring books and were being treated like children. However, deciding on the colors and having to use fine motor skills to fill in quilt patterns is definitely a fitting as well as an enjoyable and creative activity.

Match It

Preparation:
Make a series of "go-together cards." Choose colored pictures of items that normally go with each other (e.g., coats and hats, scarves and gloves, cups and saucers, babies and bottles, cars and tires, cats and dogs). You can come up with some of your own as you look through magazines. It's a great assignment for a volunteer or student intern to prepare the cards. Use 4-by-6-inch cards and paste a picture on one card and the matching picture on another. If you want them to be used many times, laminate the cards.

Use:
If the client is very confused, start with three cards (two of them matching) and have the client point out the two that match. If he or she does well try it with two matching pairs and an extra card (five cards, in all). It may be necessary to show them how to make the match with one pair and see if they can make the second match. With clients on a little higher level, give them all of the cards and make it a game to see how many pairs they can match.

Photographs

Check with the family of the client with memory loss and if possible, secure a photograph of the person at the age he or she remembers the best. Make several copies and place one on the client's door and at his or her place at the table, to start. Several of the agencies that have used this technique have found that it works with many of their more confused clients.

Take photos on a timely basis of these clients doing activities and place the photographs on their bedside tables. This gives the staff something to talk about with clients.

Photo Albums

Request that families of clients who are confused create a memory photograph album of family and friends. They should include names and how the person(s) in the pictures are related to the client as well as when and where the photos were taken. Consider having pictures of the staff in the album also. Include pictures of the client and the relatives in their younger years, as well as current pictures. The staff

and relatives will find these albums useful in helping the person remember people and places.

Use the album with the client on a regular basis. Ask the client the names of the people and have him or her tell something about as many of them as can be remembered. Ask about the occasion where the photo was taken. We've used these memory albums every few days with some of the more confused clients with whom we work and find that some days a client's memory is very clear.

Greeting Cards

Encourage the clients' family and friends to send greeting cards on a regular basis. The cards may be of simple design and can easily be created on home computers. Keep the message simple and make sure that the senders include their relation to the client, like "your daughter, Jane," "your niece, Betty." The staff can use the cards to help stimulate the client's memory of the sender and even find a picture of the person in the memory album. No matter how confused the client may be, the cards are appreciated.

Collage

Take pictures of the confused client doing various activities. As a memory boosting technique, have the person arrange them on a piece of poster board and decorate the board with bits of greenery, bric-a-brac, lace, or yarn. Talk with the person about the various pictures and help him or her remember what was happening in each picture. Display the photo collage in the client's room so that the rest of the staff can help with the memory process.

A similar collage can be made with magazine or catalog pictures. Select a theme like a wedding, springtime, fall colors, Thanksgiving, or Christmas and create the collage. This can be an individual activity or a small group process.

Spell Your Name

Prepare for this activity by printing each letter of the person's first name on separate 3-by-5-inch cards. You may also have to print the whole name on a larger card in order for some clients to be able to complete the task. Have the client arrange the cards to spell his or her name. Ask the client if he or she remembers his or her middle name, maiden name, last name, and the names of his or her spouse, parents, and children. If possible, see if the client recognizes the names of family members that you have printed on 4-by-6-inch cards.

See if the client can still write his or her name. You may need to give encouragement or print the name for the person to follow.

Scrabble Spelling

Use Scrabble tiles with the clients to spell two- and three-letter words. Give them a *T* and an *O* and see if they can make *TO*. Try three letters if successful, then four. Spell out words for them to recognize. Have them spell their name and yours. If the Scrabble letters are too small, make your own on cards or use cut-out alphabets used to teach children. We have even seen some magnetic letters that would work well on a metal surface.

Show Your Numbers

This is an activity that works well for a small group. Prepare 3-by-5-inch cards each with a digit from 0 through 9. Give one card to each player. The leader calls a number such as *238*. Players hold up the correct cards. For your lowest functioning clients, it has to be a one-on-one activity where you see if the person can recognize the numbers or put two cards together to make a *20*.

SkipBo Cards

We mentioned these cards earlier as a game that can be modified for fairly low-level clients. Here are some more ideas for using these cards:

• Sort cards by color.
• Sort cards into groups of 12, in numeric order.
• With one set of 12 cards, put in numeric order.

Sensory Board

Use carpet tape to fasten 2-by-3-inch pieces of sandpaper, felt, carpeting, or plastic to a 12-by-16-inch piece of hardboard. This is a very good tool to use with sight-impaired clients. Have the client find the texture on the board that is closest to the texture of the person's sweater, bedspread, mirror, light shade, or rug or take the client outside and do the same with leaves, brick or lawn furniture.

We have used it with clients who couldn't speak or see and had them compare an object such as a leaf to a texture on the board. We could see by the looks on their faces when they were successful.

Sensory Stimulation Box

A heavy-duty shoebox works well for this activity. Have several items in the box (not too many to confuse the client). A small hand mirror, a bell, a Slinky, a squeaky toy, a stress reliever balloon filled with flour and a nylon scouring pad are some items you might consider including. Let the client take one item at a time out of the box. Talk to the client about the item before putting it back and taking another.

We have a larger box that we call the "country store." It has a "door" for the client to reach in and bring out an item. Some of the items we have included in the "store" are a can of soup, some hand lotion, a large spike, a bottle opener, and a corncob pipe.

The items should be representative of those found in the old neighborhood stores. Don't forget to have items that the men particularly remember.

Bird Feeding

Lower level clients enjoy a repetitive task like filling the bird feeders. The ones that use 2-liter bottles and screw-on feeder bottoms (described in Chapter X, All Natural) are great for sunflower seeds. Use the laundry soap detergent bottle suggestion for filling the feeders with sunflower seeds. The birds love the seeds and the seeds are large enough for the clients to use to fill the feeders successfully.

Screw-on feeders for plastic bottles are also made for feeding liquid food to orioles and humming birds. Directions for making the liquid are given in Chapter X, All Natural, also.

Homemade Play-Doh

Ingredients:

1$\frac{1}{2}$ cups of boiling water
$\frac{1}{2}$ cup of salt
2 cups of flour
Food coloring
2 tablespoons of alum
1 tablespoon of vegetable oil

Directions:

Dissolve the salt in the boiling water and add the food coloring, alum and vegetable oil. When everything is dissolved, pour the liquid into the flour in a mixing bowl and stir, then knead until smooth. The dough will keep for quite a while if stored in a tightly closed plastic bag when not in use.

Edible Dough

Ingredients:

$\frac{1}{2}$ cup of creamy peanut butter
$\frac{1}{4}$ cup of honey or syrup
$\frac{1}{2}$ cup of instant milk powder
2 tablespoons of powdered sugar (may want a little more)

Directions:

Mix and knead ingredients into a pliable dough. If it is too sticky add more powdered sugar. Use powdered sugar for "flour" when you roll the dough. The clients can roll out the dough and use miniature cookie cutters to make edible "cookies." Roll dough into 1-inch balls and use a cookie press to make designs. Press a small amount into candy molds to make "candy."

More Ideas for the Low-Functioning Client

The following activities and ideas for the low-level functioning client are described at various places in this book. All of them have been used successfully with a variety of lower functioning older clients. Many of them may not work for your lowest functioning clients, but they can be used as springboards to help you develop or adapt activities that will work. Most of the clients who are confused will need one or two clients to one staff member's assistance for many of the activities.

Confused clients often still want to be helpful. Setting or clearing a table for an event will often bring a great deal of satisfaction, because it is an activity that the person can still accomplish. The same is true of activities such as planting, watering or weeding a garden or flower bed. Although Judy's mother doesn't know who Judy is, she still can help her at mealtime by slicing bread, chopping vegetables and clearing the table. Don't rule out any activity—just try it several times with several approaches. This list is simply meant as a starting point.

Conversation Activities

Coordination Activities

Staff Tips

Throughout this book, we have tried to include various ideas and tips we have found successful when working with older adults. The following are additional tips and ideas to help you provide a well-rounded recreation program for your clients.

Programming Tips

- Don't rule out an activity because clients can't do all of the parts. Change it to meet your clients' needs. Learn how to be flexible and *adapt ideas.*
- Leaders need to be outgoing and good actors. Although it is sometimes difficult, the staff needs to learn how to act silly at times as well as enthusiastic at other times.
- Don't let staff stimulate too many senses at the same time when working with older adults. They process stimuli slowly so it is best to use just one sense at a time. This is especially true with the lower functioning client.
- It is easier for the client to process a visual cue than a verbal cue. Demonstrate the action you want the client to complete without verbal cueing.
- Older adults need affection. Don't be afraid to touch a shoulder, give a hug, or shake a hand.
- Compliment the client on how well he or she completes a task. Everyone needs praise.
- Clients like to feel they are useful. Ask them for help to complete a task, then offer praise. The smiles are worth the few minutes it takes to praise or thank the client.
- Often we take too much time transporting clients to an activity room for a program. Consider running the same program for smaller groups of clients and running the program more than once.
- Fifteen minutes can be a very long time for a one-on-one activity. Don't worry if a one-on-one session is short. Several one-on-one sessions in a week is more therapeutic for the client that one long session.
- Small group activities should be anywhere from 30–45 minutes in length. If the group is really enjoying the activity, then the program can be a bit longer.
- If it takes longer to transport the clients to the activity area than it does to run the program, then bring fewer clients and repeat the activity, versus increasing the length of the program.
- Small group activities should be comprised of three to five clients. We tend to make the group too large which discourages participation.
- Try to make sure the clients who will be attending a group session are not going to be pulled out of the group for other therapies before they join.
- Most small group sessions are the most therapeutic when the clients are seated in a circle or semicircle. If the clients are scattered all over the room, they feel no sense of belonging to a group.
- Some agencies feel it is better if the staff member stands to conduct the session, while others feel it is better for the staff member to sit within the circle. Experiment to see which works best with your clients. If the staff member does stand, he or she can get in closer to encourage and hear the clients' responses. Be careful not to have your back to the rest of the group too long.
- Use clients to create activities. The higher level clients will enjoy creating activities. Take in a game like Adverteasing and have the clients think

of as many slogans from commercials as possible. Have the group members decide what else they could do with the game. Give the clients an activity or idea and see what they come up with in terms of rules and modifications. Then run the activity utilizing their rules and ideas. This is best done with a very small group of three to four high-level clients, then run the activity with a slightly larger group.

- Older adults love children and enjoy their visits, but the children are often a bit shy, especially when meeting a large group of older people. Use small groups of children with small groups of older adults and have an activity ready for them to do together, for example, pudding painting (make vanilla pudding and mix it with food coloring then use as finger paint), making macaroni necklaces, egg shell mosaics, the Lion Hunt, songs such as "Row, Row, Row Your Boat" with arm actions, or another activity that the children and clients can do together.
- If a large group of children (such as those from a nursery school) are visiting, divide the group of older adults and children into smaller groups.
- Have a performance or "show and tell" for the entire group of children and older adults.

Awards

- Along with praise and thanks, awards for accomplishing a skill or task are essential.
- Awards can be simple. A ribbon for participating, a special luncheon, or a photograph work well as awards.
- Awards do not have to be trophies (they take up too much room anyway) or elaborate. A certificate or letter of thanks from the Administrator is appreciated more than a trophy.
- A simple award can be made by using pinking shears to cut out paper circles. Attach a ribbon with tape to each award.

Photography

- Check at the various photo development agencies for the best price. Ask if you can have a spe-cial rate because you are nonprofit and/or you take a lot of photos of your clientele.
- If given a discount, let everyone know where you get your film developed via a news release to your local newspaper and announcements in employee and/or family newsletters.

Wish List

- List large items such as a VCR, as well as smaller items such as special scissors. A laminating machine would definitely be on Jerry's list.
- If you have a pet at your facility, food for the pet should be on the list. Many zoos and rehabilitation agencies have an adopt-an-animal for a month program, and can give the cost of feeding the animal for a month.
- List the contributors' names on a plaque or in the newsletter. It is important to give the people who donate items or contribute money recognition in your newsletters.
- Don't forget that family members are often a good source for contributions.

Workbooks

- Create a booklet including ideas, list of materials needed and how a single program as well as a series of sessions can be run.
- Ideas for booklets include sensory stimulation, reminiscence, relaxation, exercise, gardening, or music. Create a format to be utilized with each booklet so they are easy to follow. Don't forget a table of contents.
- This is a rather large project to undertake, but can be completed by a dedicated volunteer or intern student. It can be broken into smaller parts by having a binder for each booklet you want to compile handy.
- As a staff member plans and/or runs an activity, which relates to one of the booklets, have him or her add his or her materials to the booklet.
- Include an index which lists group size, equipment, functioning level the activity is best for, and so on.

Special Events

- Every event needs an official introduction or opening and a closing or thank you.
- Decorations take a lot of staff time to create and are often difficult to store. Make decorations that can be used for more than one event.
- Keep the refreshments simple and appropriate for the event. For example, serve a punch at a square dance instead of hot chocolate.
- It is better to hold the same event for each unit or wing instead of jamming everyone into one room.
- Consider celebrations like parades that can take place through a unit or wing; this lets the people who would never attend an event off of the floor get involved.
- Keep special performances and entertainment to a maximum of an hour in length. Clients get tired and often need to use the rest room after an hour.
- Events that involve the client and/or staff as the entertainment are talked about and enjoyed more than any other type of special event.

Trip Hints

- Take an accurate head count as well as roll call before going on an outing to avoid stowaways.
- Take roll and a head count every time the clients get on and off the bus or van.
- Find out the clients' dietary needs and restrictions prior to the outing.
- Take clients who are at the same mental functioning level at the same time.
- If possible, take clients who all use wheelchairs or who all ambulate to the event. If this is not possible, take a small group.
- Be careful about taking more than one vehicle at a time to an event, especially if you are utilizing a full-size bus. It is often confusing for the clients and staff to keep everyone together.
- Carry a box of moist towelettes such as Handi Wipes or Wet Ones. They are wonderful for cleaning up sticky fingers or washing hands before serving a meal. Shout also makes a wipe that is excellent for removing stains from clothing.

- Take a jug of water and paper cups.
- Carry a big tote bag with all of the important things like a paring knife, first-aid kit, phone numbers of the facility, hospital, place(s) you are going, towels, plastic bag for garbage, diapers, Wet Ones, and Shout wipes.
- A paring knife is an essential item, especially when the group visits a farmer's market or fruit farm.
- Take along an extra list of the names of the clients going with you on the excursion.
- Have the names of some clients who are alternates. These are people who can go on the outing at the last minute. Make sure they are included on the list which the Medical Director signs giving the clients permission to attend an outing.

Marketing Your Program

- Clients love to see themselves in photographs and in videos. Take lots of videos and photographs and share them with the clients, family members, other staff and outside groups. Make sure you have a photograph release on each client before you show the photographs or videos to any group.
- Many of the clients who are confused will not recognize themselves in photographs and videos.
- Photographs and videos can be utilized to educate the other staff members and the public about your program and the goals you are trying to achieve.
- It is important to develop a positive image of your program. Often the recreation department is only seen as the fun and games people.
- Determine what the staff and outside groups think about your program. What you perceive your image to be may be very different than what others perceive.
- Many events such as the staff versus the client Wiffle ball game, the photography show, a crafts festival, or a tournament, may be the perfect opportunity to share facility activities with the general public. This may mean sending a news release to the local media or inviting the public to join in on the activity.

Resources

Publications

Alzheimer's Disease

Communicating with the Alzheimer Patient
P.O. Box 5675C
Chicago, IL 60680-5675
(800) 621-0379 in Illinois
(800) 572-6037
Ideas for communicating. First copy is free.

Innovative Caregiving Resources
P.O. Box 17332
Salt Lake City, UT 84117-0332
(801) 272-9446
Videos for low-level functioning client.

Newsletters for the Older Adult

Creative Forecasting, Inc.
P.O. Box 7789
Colorado Springs, CO 80933-7789
(719) 633-3174

Eldersong Publications, Inc.
P.O. Box 74
Mt. Airy, MD 21771
(800) 397-0533
(301) 829-0533

Publishers of Books on Recreation and Older Adults

Venture Publishing, Inc.
1999 Cato Avenue
State College, PA 16801
(814) 234-4561

Idyll Arbor, Inc.
P.O. Box 720
Ravensdale, WA 98051

Charles C. Thomas Publishers
301–327 East Lawrence Avenue
Springfield, IL 62703

Wellness Reproductions and Publishing, Inc.
23945 Mercantile Road
Suite KKATW
Beachwood, OH 44122-5924
(800) 669-9208

Cooking

Reduced Fat Ideas

Smucker's Baking Healthy
(888) 550-9555
Oil and shortening replacement for baking.

Just Whites
Deb-El Foods Corporation
Papetti Plaza
Elizabeth, NJ 07206
Dried egg whites recipe book. Just Whites are
    available in many grocery stores.

Cookie Stamps

Brown Bag Cookie Art
77 Regional Drive
Concord, NH 03301

Rrycraft
Cookie Stamps
4205 SW 53rd Street
Corvallis, Oregon 97333
(503) 753-6707
Also available in gift, craft and discount depart-
    ment stores.

Crafts

Craft Supplies

Economy Handicrafts
50-21 69th Street
Woodside, NY 11377-7598
(800) 216-1601

Creative Crafts International
16 Plains Road, Box 819
Essex, CT 06426
(800) 666-0767

Cross Creek Recreational Products, Inc.
P.O. Box 289
Millbrook, NY 12545
(800) 645-5816

Brown Bag Cookie Art
The Idea Book
L. R. Natkiel
77 Regional Drive
Concord, NH 03301
Ideas utilizing the cookie molds and presses.

Martha Stewart Sun Impressions Kit
Martha By Mail
P.O. Box 60060
Tampa, FL 33660-0060
(800) 950-7130

Egg Coloring Bags

Easter Unlimited, Inc.
Carle Place, NY 11514
Bags for dyeing eggs.

Soap Molding

Fields Landing Soap Factory
Environmental Technology, Inc.
Fields Landing, CA 95537
(707) 443-9323

Martha Stewart Soap Making Kit
Martha By Mail
P.O. Box 60060
Tampa, FL 33660-0060
(800) 950-7130

Discussion Ideas

Event and Discussion Ideas

Chase's Annual Events (published yearly by Con-
    temporary Books, Inc.)
The Day by Day Directory to 1996
Prudential Plaza, Suite 1200
Chicago, IL 60601-6790
(312) 540-4500
Events, birthdays of famous people, state facts—
    state tree, flower, bird, order states entered
    Union.

Extraordinary Origins of Everyday Things by
    Charles Panati
Harper and Row Publishers, Inc.
10 East 53rd Street
New York, NY 10022
Available at bookstores.

Rand McNally
Kids' U.S. Road Atlas (state maps, birds, flowers, trees, travel games)
U.S. Giant Discovery Atlas (capitals, state historic events)
Educational Insights
Dominguez Hills, CA

Leisure Education Materials

Creative Insights
Carrie Capes, CTRS
44 West 627 Route 38
Maple Park, IL 60151
Leisure education board games.

Picture Books for Discussion With Lower Level Clients

Anne Geddes
Cedco Publishing Company
2955 Kerner Boulevard
San Rafael, CA 94901
Available at bookstores.

Reminiscence

Bi-Folkal Publications
809 Williamson
Madison, WI 53703
(800) 568-5357
Materials for reminiscing.

Equipment

Beeping Ball

Flaghouse, Inc.
150 North MacQuester Parkway
Mt. Vernon, NY 10550
(800) 221-5185

Checkers

Jumbo Checker Game
Ventura Inc.
175 North Parkway
Fayette, GA 30214
Available at Cracker Barrel restaurants.

Exercise

Aquatic Therapy

Aquatic Therapy and Rehabilitation Institute (ATRI)
Aquatic Therapy Association and Symposium
RD 1, Box 218
Chassell, MI 49916
(906) 482-9500

Aquatic Therapy Programming: Guidelines for Orthopedic Rehabilitation by Joanne M. Koury, M.Ed.
ISBN 0-87322-971-1
Human Kinetics
P.O. Box 5076
Champaign, IL 61825-5076
(800) 747-4457

Nature

Bird Feeders

Wild Bird Feeder
RPM 7601 Bush Lake Road
Minneapolis, MN 55439
(612) 897-1110
Base for 2-liter beverage bottle.

Outdoor Products Marketing, Inc.
P.O. Box 2445
Minneapolis, MN 55424
(612) 926-277
Available in some hardware, grocery, and discount department stores.

Butterfly Feeders

Butterfly feeders are also available in some hardware, nature stores, and garden centers.

> Outdoor Products Marketing, Inc.
> P.O. Box 24451
> Minneapolis, MN 55424
> (612) 926-2770

> The Birding Company
> Yarmouth, ME 04096-0808

Flower Pouches

These are heavy plastic bags to grow flowers. They are also available at many garden centers.

> Al's Flower Pouch
> A.M.A. Plastics
> 1367 Oxford Avenue
> Kingsville, Ontario N9Y 2S8
> (519) 322-1397

Music

Companion Radio
Networx Corporation
1 Fishers Road
Pittsford, NY 14534
(800) 499-4040
Special radio programming.

Northword Press, Inc.
P.O. Box 1360
Minocqua, WI 54548-9978
Nature and soothing music tapes and CDs.

Radient Music
Kris Lee-Scott
1514 North Sherman Avenue
Madison, WI 53704
(800) 959-KRIS

Tools for Daily Living

adaptAbility
Products for Quality Living
P.O. Box 515
Colchester, CT 06415-0515
(800) 288-9941

Flaghouse, Inc.
150 North MacQuester Parkway
Mt. Vernon NY 10550
(800) 221-5185

Harriet Carter
Dept. 16
North Wales, PA 19455
(215) 361-5151

One Step Ahead Special Report
EKA Publications, Inc.
1050 Connecticut Avenue NW, Suite 1250
Washington, DC 20036
(800) 397-0533
(301) 829-0533
Catalog of resources for the disabled.

S&S Opportunities
P.O. Box 513
Colchester, CT 06415-0513
(800) 266-8856
Catalog of supplies for recreation.

S&S Primelife
P.O. Box 513
Colchester, CT 06415-0513
(800) 243-9232
Recreation activities for seniors.

Bibliography

Further Information

Alzheimer's Disease

Robinson, A., Spencer, B., and White, L. (1996). *Understanding difficult behaviors.* Ypsilanti, MI: Eastern Michigan University.

Crafts

Better Homes and Gardens incredibly awesome crafts for kids. (1992). Des Moines, IA: Meredith Corporation.

Fiarotta, P. (1975). *Snips and snails and walnut whales.* New York, NY: Workman Publishing.

Sunset creative fun crafts for kids. (1993). Menlo Park, CA: Sunset Publishing Company.

Cooking

Colvin, C. F. (1994). *A+ in cooking.* Memphis, TN: The Wimmer Companies, Inc.

Miller, J. (1997). *Cooking with Justin: Recipes for kids (and parents) by the world's youngest chef.* Kansas City, MO: Andrews and McMeel.

Ottum, B. (1995). *A day in an Amish kitchen.* Greendale, WI: Reiman Publications, L. P. (Country Books).

Better Homes and Gardens new cook book. (1989). Des Moines, IA: Meredith Corporation.

Shank, E. H. (1987). *Mennonite country style recipes and kitchen secrets.* Scottdale, PA: Herald Press.

Gardening

Burlingame, A. W. (1974). *Hoe for health.* Birmingham, MI: Author.

Groves, M. P. (Ed.). (1979). *Better Homes and Gardens complete guide to gardening.* Des Moines, IA: Meredith Corporation.

Exercise

Alter, J. (1983). *Surviving exercise.* Boston, MA: Houghton Mifflin Company.

Anderson, B. (1980). *Stretching.* Bolinas, CA: Shelter Publishing.

Biegel, L. (1984). *Physical fitness and the older person.* Rockville, MD: Aspen Publication.

Coven, A., and Sidelman, S. (1996). Dealing with medical emergencies in seniors' classes. *Idea Today, 14:9,* pp. 70–77.

Eller, D. (1993). Flex time. Once ignored, flexibility is now considered essential to fitness. *American Health,* April, pp. 68–73.

Feinstein, A. (Ed.). (1992). *Training the body to cure itself. How to use exercise to heal.* Emmaus, PA: Rodale Press.

Gardiner, J. (1996). Choosing music for seniors. *Idea Today, 14:1,* pp. 66–67.

Gardiner, J., and Prouty, J. (1996). Balance exercises for the mature adult. *Idea Today, 14:4,* pp. 23–26.

Jackowski, E. J. (1995). *Hold it! You're exercising wrong.* New York, NY: Fireside Books.

Kravitz, L. (1996). The age antidote. *Idea Today,* 14:2, pp. 28–35.

Kosich, D. (1997). Highlights from the 1997 IDEA World Research Forum. *Idea Today, 15:9*, pp. 36–43.

Lockette, K. F. (1997). Working with clients with visual impairments. How to think in terms of sound and feel, rather than sight. *Idea Today, 15:5*, pp. 36–42.

La Forge, R. (1996). Elastic tubing and seniors' strength . . . Circuit training and cardiac function . . . Bone health and strength training. *Idea Today, 14:4*, pp. 9–11.

La Forge, R. (1997). 1997 ACSM research update. *Idea Today, 15:9*, pp. 58–62.

Rimmer, J. H. (1994). *Fitness and rehabilitation programs for special populations.* Madison, WI: WCB Brown and Benchmark.

Rimmer, J. H. (1997). Programming for clients with disabilities: Exercise guidelines for special medical populations. *Idea Today, 15:5*, pp. 26–35.

Rizzo, T. H. (1996). Sweating it out. *Idea Today, 14:2*, pp. 80.

Wescott, W., and Guy, J. (1996). A physical evolution. *Idea Today, 14:9*, pp. 58–65.

Nature

Benyus, J. M. (1989). *Northwoods wildlife: A watcher's guide to habitats.* Minocqua, WI: Northword Press, Inc.

Cornell, J. B. (1998). *Sharing nature with children.* Nevada City, CA: Dawn Publications.

Harrison, K., and Harrison, G. (1985). *America's favorite backyard wildlife.* New York, NY: Simon and Schuster, Inc.

Stokes, D., and Stokes, L. (1986). *Animal tracking and behavior.* Boston, MA: Little, Brown and Company.

Recreation Programming

Creative recreation programming handbook: Ideas and year-round activities for children and youth. (1977). Alexandria, VA: National Recreation and Park Association.

Elliott, J. E., and Sorg-Elliott, J. A. (1991). *Recreation programming and activities for older adults.* State College, PA: Venture Publishing, Inc.

Therapeutic Recreation

Dixon, J. T. (1981). *Adapting activities for therapeutic recreation service: Concepts and applications.* San Diego, CA: The Campanile Press.

Kelland, J. (Ed.). (1995). *Protocols for recreation therapy programs.* State College, PA: Venture Publishing, Inc.

About the Authors

This book is a compilation of many people's kindness, talents and encouragement. As we went about writing this second book, we decided to tell you a little about our support team and us. Jerry is a retired associate professor from the Leisure Studies Department at the Pennsylvania State University. He is 76 years old and the creative genius behind this writing team. He is also extremely cost-conscious when it comes to purchasing materials, which is particularly useful to those departments with a limited budget. Judy is an assistant professor in the Recreation Department at Lock Haven University of Pennsylvania. She is the note-taker regarding the ideas and does the baking and gardening (with Jerry doing the tasting and testing).

We began working together in 1978 when we designed a nature trail at the nursing home where Judy was Director of Therapeutic Recreation. We served as presenters of programs at many conferences and for several years conducted in-service credit workshops on older adults and recreation. We had been married for a year when we published our first book, *Recreation Programming and Activities for Older Adults* which was based on the material we had used in our in-service programs.

For this second book, we tested the activities with clients in nursing and personal care homes. We tested our mothers, relatives and anyone else willing to try one or more of the ideas. Some worked really well for people like Jerry's mom, who still lived alone at 97, while others proved useful with the dementia clients like Judy's mom, who has no clue that Judy is her daughter. One of the most precious memories Judy will carry as a result of this book is watching her mom and 7-year-old niece, Stephanie, roll peppermint candy into balls to be dipped in chocolate (Grandma Betty had a chocolate candy business before her dementia became too bad).

Both authors have many wonderful memories associated with developing this book. We want to thank all of you who purchased the first book and encouraged us to research the ideas that have been used in this publication.

Other Books From Venture Publishing, Inc.

Inclusive Leisure Services: Responding to the Rights of People With Disabilities
by John Dattilo

Internships in Recreation and Leisure Services: A Practical Guide for Students (Second Edition)
by Edward E. Seagle, Jr., Ralph W. Smith, and Lola M. Dalton

Interpretation of Cultural and Natural Resources
by Douglas M. Knudson, Ted T. Cable, and Larry Beck

Intervention Activities for At-Risk Youth
by Norma J. Stumbo

Introduction to Leisure Services—7th Edition
by H. Douglas Sessoms and Karla A. Henderson

Introduction to Writing Goals and Objectives: A Manual for Recreation Therapy Students and Entry-Level Professionals
By Suzanne Melcher

Leadership and Administration of Outdoor Pursuits, Second Edition
by Phyllis Ford and James Blanchard

Leadership in Leisure Services: Making a Difference
by Debra J. Jordan

Leisure and Leisure Services in the 21st Century
by Geoffrey Godbey

The Leisure Diagnostic Battery: Users Manual and Sample Forms
by Peter A. Witt and Gary Ellis

Leisure Education: A Manual of Activities and Resources
by Norma J. Stumbo and Steven R. Thompson

Leisure Education II: More Activities and Resources
by Norma J. Stumbo

Leisure Education III: More Goal-Oriented Activities
by Norma J. Stumbo

Leisure Education IV: Activities for Individuals With Substance Addictions
by Norma J. Stumbo

Leisure Education Program Planning: A Systematic Approach—Second Edition
by John Dattilo

Leisure in Your Life: An Exploration—Fifth Edition
by Geoffrey Godbey

Leisure Services in Canada: An Introduction
by Mark S. Searle and Russell E. Brayley

Leisure Studies: Prospects for the Twenty-First Century
edited by Edgar L. Jackson and Thomas L. Burton

The Lifestory Re-Play Circle: A Manual of Activities and Techniques
by Rosilyn Wilder

Marketing for Parks, Recreation, and Leisure
by Ellen L. O'Sullivan

Models of Change in Municipal Parks and Recreation: A Book of Innovative Case Studies
edited by Mark E. Havitz

More Than a Game: A New Focus on Senior Activity Services
by Brenda Corbett

Nature and the Human Spirit: Toward an Expanded Land Management Ethic
edited by B. L. Driver, Daniel Dustin, Tony Baltic, Gary Elsner, and George Peterson

Outdoor Recreation Management: Theory and Application, Third Edition
by Alan Jubenville and Ben Twight

Planning Parks for People, Second Edition
by John Hultsman, Richard L. Cottrell, and Wendy Z. Hultsman

The Process of Recreation Programming Theory and Technique, Third Edition
by Patricia Farrell and Herberta M. Lundegren

Programming for Parks, Recreation, and Leisure Services: A Servant Leadership Approach
by Donald G. DeGraaf, Debra J. Jordan, and Kathy H. DeGraaf

Protocols for Recreation Therapy Programs
edited by Jill Kelland, along with the Recreation Therapy Staff at Alberta Hospital Edmonton

Quality Management: Applications for Therapeutic Recreation
edited by Bob Riley

A Recovery Workbook: The Road Back From Substance Abuse
by April K. Neal and Michael J. Taleff

Recreation and Leisure: Issues in an Era of Change, Third Edition
edited by Thomas Goodale and Peter A. Witt

Recreation Economic Decisions: Comparing Benefits and Costs (Second Edition)
by John B. Loomis and Richard G. Walsh

Recreation Programming and Activities for Older Adults
by Jerold E. Elliott and Judith A. Sorg-Elliott

Recreation Programs That Work for At-Risk Youth: The Challenge of Shaping the Future
by Peter A. Witt and John L. Crompton

Reference Manual for Writing Rehabilitation Therapy Treatment Plans
> by Penny Hogberg and Mary Johnson

Research in Therapeutic Recreation: Concepts and Methods
> edited by Marjorie J. Malkin and Christine Z. Howe

Simple Expressions: Creative and Therapeutic Arts for the Elderly in Long-Term Care Facilities
> by Vicki Parsons

A Social History of Leisure Since 1600
> by Gary Cross

A Social Psychology of Leisure
> by Roger C. Mannell and Douglas A. Kleiber

Steps to Successful Programming: A Student Handbook to Accompany Programming for Parks, Recreation, and Leisure Services
> by Donald G. DeGraaf, Debra J. Jordan, and Kathy H. DeGraaf

Therapeutic Activity Intervention With the Elderly: Foundations & Practices
> by Barbara A. Hawkins, Marti E. May, and Nancy Brattain Rogers

Therapeutic Recreation: Cases and Exercises
> by Barbara C. Wilhite and M. Jean Keller

Therapeutic Recreation in the Nursing Home
> by Linda Buettner and Shelley L. Martin

Therapeutic Recreation Protocol for Treatment of Substance Addictions
> by Rozanne W. Faulkner

A Training Manual for Americans With Disabilities Act Compliance in Parks and Recreation Settings
> by Carol Stensrud

 Venture Publishing, Inc.
1999 Cato Avenue
State College, PA 16801

Phone: (814) 234-4561; Fax: (814) 234-1651